Keepers of the Game

KEEPERS

CALVIN MARTIN

OF THE GAME

Indian-Animal Relationships
and the Fur Trade

UNIVERSITY OF CALIFORNIA PRESS
Berkeley · Los Angeles · London

University of California Press
Berkeley and Los Angeles, California
University of California Press, Ltd.
London, England
Copyright © 1978 by
The Regents of the University of California
ISBN 0-520-03519-4
Library of Congress Catalog Card Number: 77-78381
Printed in the United States of America

1 2 3 4 5 6 7 8 9

Design: Al Burkhardt
Composition: Freedmen's Organization
Lithography: Publishers Press
Binder: Mountain States Bindery

Text: Compugraphic Paladium
Display: Compugraphic Paladium and
Photo Typositor Palatino
Paper: Westland Publishers opaque, basis 50
Binding: Joanna Arrestox A 34620

FOR JEAN

Contents

Maps

Foreword

A FEW YEARS AGO, I received a manuscript to evaluate for publication, "The European Impact on the Culture of a Northeastern Algonquian Tribe: An Ecological Interpretation." (Subsequently, it was published in the *William and Mary Quarterly* in 1974.) I was completely enthralled by its novel thesis and cogent discussion which showed how pervasive alterations in an eastern Canadian ecosystem could be traced to the functional interplay of what might otherwise have appeared to be unrelated cultural and historical factors. The devastating effects of new diseases from Europe evoked doubts among the local Indians concerning their traditional religious beliefs and practices. In this apostatizing mood, they were ready converts to Christian missionary teaching which undercut all native rituals, including those which had served to maintain a harmonious relationship between the people and other life-forms in their natural environment. Unrestrained by sacred sanctions, the Indians responded to the demands of the fur trade with unremitting exploitation of game, especially beaver, thereby affecting the water system controlled by the beavers' activities to bring about complex and far-reaching ramifications destructive to the total environment.

Who, I wondered, was this Calvin Martin who handled biological and historical data with such skill and originality. Why had I not heard of his work before? It did not occur to me that anyone with so diverse a command of research interests was just embarking on his professional career and the manuscript was an early announcement of his appearance on the scholarly scene. I soon had the pleasure of meeting and getting to know Calvin Martin while he was a pre-doctoral fellow at the Center for the History of the American Indian at the Newberry Library in Chicago. Since he left the Chicago area, I have followed his career with interest and we have maintained a lively correspondence in which I am always amazed at the innovative directions his scholarly curiosity takes him.

In the present book, Calvin Martin pursues his bio-historical studies further with particular reference to the northeastern hunting-and-gathering groups, exploring the seeming paradox presented, on one hand, by well-documented accounts of Indian cosmology which requires careful and reverential use of natural resources and, on the other hand, by equally well-documented evidence of Indians engaging in wanton slaughter of game. Martin turns to the Indian world view and heretofore neglected entries in the documentary record concerning ecological problems to supply missing elements in socioeconomic analyses of the Indian and the fur trade to date. From a fur trader's autopsy of a diseased beaver to Indian etiological concepts that offended animals visit sickness on humankind, Martin provides a persuasive case that far more than mere cupidity for trade goods underlay the Indians' apparent abandonment of their "conservationist" principles.

But were they really conservationists and models for our time? Martin reviews the conflicting opinions on that question and his own conclusions are sure to provoke argument and debate. This, of course, is the mark of signal scholarship, that it can stimulate further research. Whatever new investigations might flow from the fact of Martin's work, he has demonstrated that in attempting to understand the course of human history we must learn to recognize and consider carefully the evidence of environmental imperatives and constraints recorded in the ethnographic and documentary sources.

NANCY OESTREICH LURIE

Acknowledgments

I AM DEEPLY indebted to the following individuals for improving the manuscript in its various stages of emergence: Martha Andresen, Ray Billington, Henry Dobyns, Robert Finlay, Robert Heizer, Wilbur Jacobs, Robert Kahrs, Jeanne Kay, Nancy Lurie, Michael McGiffert, D'Arcy McNickle, Roderick Nash, Alfonso Ortiz, Richard Orsi, Martin Ridge, Jill Schumann, Adrian Tanner, and Wilcomb Washburn. Alain Hénon, my editor, and Chuck Ogrosky, my cartographer, deserve a special note of gratitude.

Funding for the book was provided by a fellowship from the Center for the History of the American Indian, the Newberry Library, Chicago (1973-1974); a summer fellowship from the Henry Huntington Library, San Marino (1976); and a series of Rutgers Research Council grants (1975-1976, 1976-1977, summer 1977). My thanks also go to the director of the Southwest Museum, Los Angeles, for allowing me to use the Museum's fine library.

Finally, I am grateful to the Hudson's Bay Record Society, Professor Adrian Tanner, the Western History Association, and the Smithsonian Institution for allowing me to reprint material they control.

C.M.

Prologue: The Paradox

These imaginary deities become the objects of their invocations
when they are so circumstanced as to require their blessing.
For instance, if an Indian wishes for success on a hunting
excursion, he will direct his offering and prayer to the god
who presides over the deer, the bear, or the beaver, (a
wonderful game-keeper he must be,) that success may attend
him; or, if he desires to catch many fish, or have a prosperous
voyage, he will sacrifice to the god of the waters.[1]

SHORTLY BEFORE his untimely death, the frontier historian
Dale L. Morgan gathered together the random insights of an
ageing master and set them down in an article on "The Fur Trade
and Its Historians." Morgan made it plain that he was unhappy
with the way his colleagues were writing about the North American fur trade. Most of us, he charged, are slavish in our devotion to the early writers, men like Hiram Martin Chittenden,
whose works we should be expanding upon and revising rather
than copying. The hack authors especially irritated him, as he
singled out Stanley Vestal for particular rebuke. An aversion to
research has rendered their unfortunately popular novels grossly
misleading, he lamented. What we need is a literary master the
equal of Bernard DeVoto with the brilliance of a Walter Prescott
Webb to take a fresh, invigorating view of the trade. In short,
Morgan was calling for a rigorous, imaginative, and lively re-
appraisal of the trade.

One dimension which he found especially underdeveloped
was the place of the Indian in this enterprise. "Clearly," he
urged, "the Indian tribes need to be restudied in relation to the
fur trade. Some interesting ideas have been advanced lately
about noneconomic motivations of Indians in their relation to

traders. . . . It would be fascinating to see such studies pursued further."[2] Indeed it would. For all the volumes of literature that have been published on the fur trade, we are still woefully ignorant of the Indian's conception of the trade. What did the trade mean to the Indian partner in this transaction, within his cultural context? How did he interpret the dynamics of the fur trade within his cosmic frame of reference? We scarcely know the answer to either question. There has been a handful of good studies on the subject, the majority of them concerned with Plains or Prairie tribes: Oscar Lewis (1942), E. E. Rich (1960), Preston Holder (1967), Wilcomb E. Washburn (1967), John C. Ewers (1972), Harold Hickerson (1973), and most recently, Arthur J. Ray (1974).[3] But this is only a beginning. There is still a broad field of investigation here which is in need of further elucidation.

Fur trade scholars are in uniform agreement that over the long run, the trade was a disaster for the Indian tribes involved: severe cultural disruption and often physical dislocation were commonplace. Admittedly, the fur trade alone did not bring about these changes. Missionization, the ravages of disease, and frontier encroachment acted in concert with the trade to bring about the Indian's eventual cultural demise. Any serious study of the influence of the fur trade upon the Indian must therefore consider as well these other cultural and social impingements. The question then becomes: Why was European, or white, contact such a ruinous experience for the native—again, over the long term? It is a simple question to ask, yet, as the published record amply shows, the answers to it are many and complex.

Keeping in mind that the fur trade was one among a cluster of interrelated cultural influences, we might refine our question further and ask why the Indian participated in the trade even after he recognized its damaging effects upon him. One thinks, in particular, of the destruction of fur and game resources which was the hallmark of the trade. To put it bluntly, the Indian was everywhere, except in the Rocky Mountain trade, the principal agent in the over-hunting of furbearers. That is undisputed. He

was also, as in the case of the Western Canadian trade throughout the nineteenth century, largely responsible for the intense
exploitation of large herbivores (in this case, bison) whose flesh
was used to provision fur company posts.

What we are confronting is a monumental case of improvi-
dence. It is difficult to imagine how an individual whose subsistence economy was underpinned by a reliance upon fish,
game, wild plant foods, and, in some cases, cultivated plants
could have been so oblivious to wildlife population dynamics
as not to see that his present course of hunting was far too
exploitive. The fur-trading Indian, whether he be a member of
a hunter-gatherer society or a horticultural society, was simply
too skilled a hunter to overlook the ultimate consequences of
wildlife overkill. Early records confirm this skepticism. More
than one fur company agent or missionary recorded in his journal the lament of some heart-sick Indian informant who plainly
recognized that the reckless hunter was digging his own grave.
And yet the raid on furbearers continued, encouraged by Jesuit
missionaries and fur company agents and prosecuted by the
Indian himself.

It is this anomaly and its resolution which form the heart of
the present study. Obviously, it would be impossible to conduct
a detailed analysis of this problem for the entire North American
theater and compress it into a book of reasonable length. I have
chosen, instead, to examine the circumstances of European contact and their effect on what one might call the Indian-land
relationship within one broad zone: Eastern Canada or, in cultural anthropological terms, the Eastern Subarctic and a portion
of the Northeast. Defined geographically, the area covered ex-
tends from roughly Lake Winnipeg to the Canadian Maritimes.
Culturally speaking, we are dealing mainly with Algonkian-
speaking tribes: the Ojibwa of the Upper Great Lakes; the Cree
to the north of them, skirting the southern rim of Hudson Bay
and James Bay; the Montagnais-Naskapi of northern Québec-
Labrador; and the Micmac of Nova Scotia, New Brunswick, and
Prince Edward Island.

In the case studies which follow, special attention has been given to the Micmac, for whom there are unsurpassed seventeenth-century records, and the Ojibwa, for whom there are unsurpassed ethnographic studies. I have found it instructive to supplement the historic and ethnographic reportage on the Ojibwa with comparable information on the Cree and Chipewyan, the latter an Athapaskan group occupying the western shore of Hudson Bay. This has been done only in cases where these societies seem to share common cultural traits.[4] All of these people—Chipewyan, Ojibwa, Cree, Montagnais-Naskapi, and Micmac—were hunter-gatherers, although the aboriginal Ojibwa engaged in some rather casual maize cultivation. Those tribes living north of the St. Lawrence–Ottawa River valleys occupied a boreal forest ecosystem whose characteristic species were spruce, hemlock, fir, aspen, birch, black bear, moose, woodland caribou, and numerous furbearers. It is worth noting that the various proto-Ojibwa groups (Saulteaux, Missisauga, Nipissings, and others) who remained congregated along the northern shore of Georgian Bay and eastern shore of Lake Superior until late in the seventeenth century were actually situated south of the true boreal zone, in the mixed deciduous Southern Great Lakes–St. Lawrence Forest; only later, after 1680 or so when splinter groups began migrating north and west along the shores of Lake Superior, did the northern branch (referred to in the literature as the Northern Ojibwa) move into the Subarctic zone proper.[5]

South of the St. Lawrence, the Micmac lived in a temperate, broadleaf-needleleaf forest biome in company with many of the same faunal species, with the addition of the Virginia (whitetailed) deer and wapiti. The major ecological difference between the Micmac and the majority of these other tribes was the presence of the sea in the former case. Unlike these more interior-oriented tribes, the Micmac came to rely heavily upon marine life in their food quest.[6]

Both in abstract and material culture there was, generally stated, a large degree of cultural uniformity throughout the Eastern Subarctic in late prehistoric–early contact times. Indians throughout this zone shared the same basic technology of bone, wood, antler, stone, and tooth; resorted to stone boiling; for the most part lacked ceramics; relied on the birchbark canoe, the snowshoe, and the toboggan for transportation; participated in the same subsistence activities, as pointed out above; held to roughly the same belief system, with its powerful animistic and shamanistic elements; shared a comparable mythology; and so forth. Socially, they operated as politically autonomous, semi-nomadic bands, hunting in small family groups in the interior throughout the winter months and congregating in riverine or lacustrine villages during the remainder of the year. Virtually all of these Subarctic groups reckoned descent, inheritance, and succession through both the female and male line (bilaterality as distinct from patrilineality or matrilineality) and were virilocal in their residence preferences (meaning that the newly married couple went to live with the husband's natal group), although matrilocality was also practiced aboriginally, at least among the Montagnais.[7,a]

The early historic precursors of the Ojibwa occupied a subboreal zone that was comparatively rich in food resources, especially Virginia deer, moose, caribou, fish, and vegetable products—an abundance of food that allowed these people to live in large, 100–300-person villages throughout much of the year. Each village, it seems, consisted of an entire kin group, which some authorities feel must have been a patriclan. The early seventeenth-century "Ojibwa" thus differed from their Subarctic Cree and Montagnais-Naskapi neighbors in being patrilineal rather than bilateral and semi-sedentary rather than semi-nomadic. Corporate activities were emphasized, as in the celebration of the Feast of the Dead, imported from the Huron, and, later in the eighteenth century, the *Midewiwin*. There appears to have been nothing comparable to these two institutions among contemporary Eastern Subarctic

a. Although the social organization of these Subarctic Indians is of minor importance to the present study, the reader should understand that what I have claimed here with regard to bilaterality, virilocality, and so forth is still very much an open-ended question among specialists. The fact is that the changing pattern of social organization is still in the process of being worked out group by group, but for the time being, anyway, bilaterality and virilocality appear to be true for the majority of the Eastern Subarctic at the time of contact.

groups. Atomization and bilaterality were evidently post-contact transformations among the Ojibwa—reactions to the pressures and opportunities of the fur trade that brought them more in conformity with the Subarctic peoples with whom they now mingled. Those Ojibwa who migrated west along the southern shore of Lake Superior—the so-called Southwestern Ojibwa, or Chippewa—deviated somewhat from this social pattern, for they have retained their predilection for corporate patrilineal descent groups right up into modern times.[8]

The Micmac life-way was probably somewhere in between that described for the proto-Ojibwa and the northern Algonkians. Like their Wabanaki brethren to the south and east, the late prehistoric–early contact Micmac were evidently seasonally migratory, alternating between coastal shellfishing sites in the summer and inland hunting districts in the winter. Moose, wapiti, and beaver were the principal game hunted during the inland phase of the subsistence cycle. An abundance of these and other wildlife and marine life, confirmed by early European visitors and by the size of prehistoric shellfish middens, suggests that food must have been fairly abundant for these people, perhaps more abundant than it was for the Subarctic Montagnais-Naskapi and Cree. It appears, furthermore, that the chief's position was more meaningful in Micmac society than was so in the Eastern Subarctic, which would imply, among other things, that more sedentary communities prevailed here than to the north and west. Beyond these differences there was not much to distinguish the aboriginal Micmac from the other Eastern Canadian tribesmen being considered here.[9]

It is necessary to make these clarifications lest the reader get the erroneous impression that the native societies occupying this huge swath of land were culturally and socially homogeneous. There were, indeed, many congruencies among them, especially in their abstract culture, but these must not be taken for granted. One of the more valuable lessons that ethnologists have taught historians is that they should pay closer attention to the cultural boundaries separating aboriginal societies. The best way to do this, of course, is by consulting the ethnographies of the societies under investigation. Even though the period studied may be much earlier than the present century, when most ethnographies originated, it is still quite acceptable to use these modern sources of evidence alongside the more traditional written records from the period being studied. By using this ethnological-historical— or simply ethnohistorical—technique, we arrive at a much clearer picture of what transpired in seventeenth- and eighteenth-century Eastern Canada—using the present case as an example. As everyone knows, none of these early observers of aboriginal life were trained ethnologists; consequently, much of the surviving contemporary record is obscure on cultural details. Fortunately, however, many of the cultural elements which we find more or less imperfectly documented in early sources have survived, to a limited degree at least, into modern times and have been studied closely by professional ethnologists. By matching the modern equivalent of a cultural trait with its more nebulous historic ancestor, we derive a clearer understanding of what the earlier trait must have been like. Used judiciously, the ethnographic record becomes an invaluable means of clarifying the early history of Indian-white contact. Not only that, it functions as well as a point of reference against which one can judge the objectivity and authenticity of earlier commentators. Such is the ethnohistorical method of research.[10]

One final clarification, or more properly, disclaimer, is in order. Spanning three centuries of American history, the fur trade was a continental enterprise which enlisted the services of Indian societies whose economies were vastly different from that of the Eastern Canadian hunter-gatherers. This would apply, for instance, to the horticultural tribes of the East, including the Huron north of Lake Ontario, and the tribes of the Pacific Northwest who volunteered their services for the sea otter and fur seal trade. Obviously, the native societies examined in the following study should not be construed as being representative of all the native societies which functioned in the trade. In other words, whatever conclusions are arrived at here concerning the Indian's response to European contact as it influenced his behavior toward Nature must not automatically nor indiscriminately be extended to include other tribal societies. One would expect, for example, that horticulturalists such as the Huron or League Iroquois responded to the fur-trading impulse and the pressures of white contact in general quite differently than did hunter-gatherers. This was true, certainly, in gross economic and social terms, where a village-farming existence allowed for greater social cohesiveness and concerted action along with a considerably lessened dependence on the products of the chase for subsistence needs. On the other hand, the same economic and spiritual motives which prompted the hunter-gatherer to wage war on his furbearing brethren and absolved him from responsibility for their welfare perhaps operated more or less forcefully among the horticulturalists—the spiritual rationale probably being less compelling—although this is only conjectural.

Presented with the opportunity to exchange their pelts and skins for European trade goods, Indians, whether horticulturalists or hunter-gatherers, quickly seized the opportunity to effect the transaction. It is conventional, at this point in the discussion, to illustrate this with the story of Jacques Cartier's reception at Chaleur Bay (Québec) in 1534. Cartier was literally mobbed by the local, Algonkian-speaking Indians, seemingly Micmac, who insisted that he trade with them for their furs. The beleaguered captain found it necessary to fire a volley over their heads to dampen their ardor.[11] "Clearly the strangers who controlled the thunder were heavily endowed with manito," writes Alfred Goldsworthy Bailey, "but even the displeasure of the gods could not keep the Micmac [sic] from the source of iron, for iron saved them from days of drudgery and enabled them to vanquish their enemies who were as yet armed only with stone, bone, and wood implements."[12] There, in poetically encapsulated form, is the usual explanation for the Indian's participation in the trade: European hardware and other trade items were immediately perceived by the Stone Age Indian as being far superior in their utility to his primitive technology and general material culture. Without pausing to worry over scruples, so the conventional wisdom goes, the Indian went on the warpath against the now helpless beaver, otter, marten, muskrat, and so forth, since their pelts

were his ticket to the affluence offered by the trade. Which raises
the question: Why didn't the Indian overexploit these furbearers
before the Europeans arrived? We conclude that he did not on
the strength of numerous testimonials attesting to the incredible
numbers of furbearers in early contact times. The usual, text-
book, answer is (*a*) the Indian was handicapped by his rudimentary technology, and (*b*) there was no incentive for it. "If the
Northern Athabaskan and Northern Algonkian Indians husbanded
the land and its wildlife in primeval times," Peter Farb has assured us, "it was only because they lacked both the technology
to kill very many animals and the market for so many furs. But
once White traders entered the picture, supplying the Indians
with efficient guns and an apparently limitless market for furs
beyond the seas, the Indians went on an orgy of destruction."
"The traders economically seduced the Indians by displaying
their wares and in many other ways fostered capitalistic drives."[13]
Harold Hickerson, an eminent scholar of the Ojibwa, sees two
prime reasons for the destruction of furbearers associated with
the fur trade: "the voracity of the traders who had virtually unlimited markets for beaver in Europe and the sea otter in China,
and the absence of a developed concept of conservation on the
part of the Indians. Even if the practice of conservation had been
a conscious tradition (Indians, though not conservationists, if
only due to limited technology, were not wasteful in precontact
times), the application of the practice of conservation would
have taken place too late."[14]

What emerges from these explanations is the notion of a tech-
nologically incompetent, uninspired aborigine who was transformed into a highly efficient agent of wildlife destruction once
he became equipped with a lethal technology and gained access
to the European marketplace. What was his motivation? The
same "bourgeois impulses"[15] which were embedded in the breast
of the white trader, only that in the Indian these capitalistic
drives were latent. "If the Amerind was a truly dedicated ecologist," recently inquired one historian, "why did he so succumb
to the artifacts offered him by Europeans that he stripped his
land of furs and pelts to get them? He did so because he was only

human [i.e., a Western bourgeois]. The white man offered him material goods—iron and woolens and gewgaws and alcohol—which he could not resist. These riches, which is what they were, gave his life an expanded dimension it had never known before. No power on earth could keep him from getting these things by raid or trade, once he had been exposed to them. To ask him to have refrained from making his material life fuller and richer is to ask him for far more than we ever have asked of ourselves. . . . The Amerind was and remains a tremendously human human being [i.e., Western bourgeois]."[16] The Indian's role in the fur trade is thus explained by recourse to Western marketplace theory. Wrote the dean of Canadian fur trade history, Harold A. Innis: "In the language of the economists, the heavy fixed capital of the beaver became a serious handicap with the improved technique of Indian hunting methods, incidental to the borrowing of iron from Europeans. Depreciation through obsolescence of the beaver's defence equipment was so rapid as to involve the immediate and complete destruction of the animal."[17] The Indian's position in the Canadian fur trade has rarely been explained in any "language," i.e., conceptual mode, other than that of the Western bourgeois economist.[b]

b. There is nothing wrong with using Western marketplace terminology to describe Indian behavior in the fur trade, as Innis has done here. My criticism of Innis and others is that they either explicitly or implicitly interpret Indian behavior in the trade within a Western marketplace conceptual framework, what economic anthropologists refer to as the "formalist" frame of reference. Two historians who have avoided this conceptual trap are E. E. Rich, "Trade Habits and Economic Motivation among the Indians of North America," *Canadian Journal of Economics and Political Science* 26 (February 1960):35–53, and Wilcomb E. Washburn, "Symbol, Utility, and Aesthetics in the Indian Fur Trade," in *Aspects of the Fur Trade: Selected Papers of the 1965 North American Fur Trade Conference*, edited by Russell W. Fridley, pp. 50–54 (St. Paul: Minnesota Historical Society, 1967).

Rich explains that the tribes who brokered the trade between the Hudson's Bay Company and interior tribes were unresponsive to artificial incentives for increasing the volume of pelts exchanged. As seasoned traders had pointed out many times, to raise the price of Indian furs would result in the surrender of fewer rather than more beaver skins. The reason for this inelastic supply seems to be that Indians, at least until the early nineteenth century, insisted on viewing the trade as a form of gift exchange. The natives, in sum, would supply themselves with just enough furs to satisfy their limited needs, and there was seemingly nothing the HBC could do to persuade them to go beyond that quota. A limited supply of pelts was therefore exchanged for a predictable

The problem with the conventional economic explanation for the Indian's motivation and participation in the Eastern Canadian fur trade is that it creates an artificial and misleading behavioral model. Economic anthropologists are currently embroiled in a controversy over the applicability of Western economic theory to explain the "economic" functions of pre-industrial societies. On the one hand anthropologists such as Karl Polanyi and his intellectual followers (most notably George Dalton and Marshall Sahlins) argue that pre-industrial peoples are devoid of a systematic, empirical sense of "economics." They provision themselves, to be sure, but they do not do this according to the economic principles of the marketplace mentality. Rather, the production of goods and services is "embedded in political, religious, social and kinship [i.e., noneconomic] institutions."[18] "In the Western meaning of the word," declares Dalton, "there is no 'economy' in primitive society, only socio-economic institutions and processes."[19]

Opposed to this, the "substantivist" school of economic anthropology, is the "formalist" way of thinking, irreverently dubbed the "Business Outlook" by Sahlins.[20] Polanyi distinguished between the two conflicting views in the following manner: "The formal meaning implies a set of rules referring to choice between the alternative uses of insufficient means. The substantive meaning implies neither choice nor insufficiency of means; man's livelihood may or may not involve the necessity of choice and, if choice there be, it need not be induced by the limiting effect of a 'scarcity' of the means."[21] Yet "substantivists" are vague on "precisely what meaning they attribute to the term

number of European "necessaries" (mostly luxuries, to our Western way of thinking). Fret as they may, HBC merchants could never persuade the tribesmen that human wants can and should be insatiable.

Washburn makes a similar point, urging historians to appreciate the fur trade as the Indian conceived of it: as embodying certain principles of gift giving, as a source of major prestige items, and as a forum for social and ceremonial gratification—all of these functions being present along with the more commonly understood economic rationale. See Adrian Tanner, "Bringing Home Animals: Religious Ideology and Mode of Production of the Mistassini Cree Hunters" (Ph.D. diss., University of Toronto, 1976), p. 100, and Cornelius J. Jaenen, "Amerindian Views of French Culture in the Seventeenth Century," *Canadian Historical Review* 55 (September 1974):277.

'economic,'" responds Scott Cook. "They persistently contend that it is a process of materially provisioning society but fail to delineate the specific components of the process. They define economics as an aspect of everything that provisions society but nothing that provisions society is defined as economic. Paradoxically, then, it appears that the economic anthropology advocated by the proponents of the substantivist approach is a study without an empirically ascertainable field of inquiry."[22]

Whatever the merits and demerits of the substantivist and formalist doctrines of economic anthropology, in broad theoretical terms, it is certain that the substantivist approach is the more fruitful way of scrutinizing the Indian's position in the Eastern Canadian fur trade. In an article published in the *Journal of Economic History* several years ago, John McManus attempted "An Economic Analysis of Indian Behavior in the North American Fur Trade" using formalist techniques of analysis, with what he himself conceded to be dismal results. McManus endeavored to gauge the costs of beaver exploitation among the Montagnais-Naskapi of the Labrador Peninsula using classic market theory, but found his methodology foiled by what he referred to as the "Good Samaritan" principle. The moral obligation to allow a needy band member to hunt and trap beaver on another man's territory not only reduced the enforcement costs of private property rights, he discovered, but rendered the calculation of these costs virtually impossible.[23] For McManus, it was a lesson in substantivist economics: the "economy" of these hunter-gatherers was indeed "embedded" in the broader social-cultural sphere. What he had thought to be a baldly materialistic, individualistic enterprise responsive to pressures of supply and demand, pricing, and so forth, turned out to be more than that. Here was a private enterprise whose operation was determined, as well, by a subjective sense of responsibility for the community welfare—by an unpredictable altruistic dimension which made quantification of the system's operations impossible.[24]

It is my contention that the formalist way of thinking, predicated on the insatiability of human needs and the chronic insufficiency of goods, breeds the sort of "economic seduction" rationale, with its corollary of "impotent aboriginal technology," expressed above by Farb and others. Implicit in this point of view is the assumption that the Eastern Canadian hunter-gatherer was already in the proper acquisitive frame of mind to exterminate the hapless furbearers when the Europeans arrived on the scene. All that was needed was an adequate technology, which the Europeans happily furnished, and a steady market for his furs, which was also provided. There are two flaws in this handy equation, however.

The first has to do with the "primitive aboriginal technology" idea, where "primitive" is a synonym for inadequate—the commonly held idea that aboriginal hunting tools and techniques were too rudimentary or quaint to make anything more than the slightest dent in wildlife numbers. In part this position derives from what was until very recently a veritable campaign by social scientists to discredit the hunting and gathering way of life. Hunters were depicted in the literature as being chronically destitute, living hand-to-mouth as they searched endlessly for sustenance. Deprived thus of leisure time, so the theory went, they were strangers to the loftier ideas and pursuits of neolithic man. Theirs was truly a Hobbesian existence: "nasty, brutish, and short." So the armchair theorists thought, until some of them began charting specific hunting-gathering economies through the use of daily diaries and comparing the virtues and shortcomings of the hunting-gathering existence with those of agricultural and industrial societies.[c] Whereupon they found that the hunting-and-gathering

c. See Richard B. Lee, "What Hunters Do for a Living, or, How to Make Out on Scarce Resources," in *Man the Hunter*, edited by Richard B. Lee and Irven DeVore, pp. 30–48 (Chicago: Aldine Publishing Co., 1968). Edward S. Rogers, the Canadian ethnologist, spent an aggregate of about a year with a hunting group of Québec Mistassini (the Matoush group) in the early 1950s and calculated that over the course of the year each male adult averaged roughly fifteen hours of work per week in travel and twenty-eight hours of work per week in hunting, fishing, and trapping. Obviously there were wide fluctuations in the amount of time devoted to these activities from season to season; during the period of spring travel, for instance, an individual might put in forty-eight hours of work per week in transit from the bush camp to the post while spending no time in hunting and very little in fishing and way of life is not so bad, after all. Indeed, much to people's amazement, they discovered that "hunters and gatherers work less than we do [in our industrialized society]; and, rather than a continuous travail, the food quest is intermittent, leisure abundant, and there is a greater amount of sleep in the daytime per capita per year than in any other condition of society."[25]

Hunters, under the new dispensation, have become "the original affluent society."[26] The difference between hunters and neolithic types, or hunters and industrial types, suggests Marshall Sahlins, is that hunters are satisfied with much less material accumulation. "For there are two possible courses to affluence," he theorizes.

Wants may be "easily satisfied" either by producing much or desiring little. The familiar conception, the Galbraithean way, makes assumptions peculiarly appropriate to market economies: that man's wants are great, not to say infinite, whereas his means are limited, although improvable: thus, the gap between means and ends can be narrowed by industrial productivity, at least to the point that "urgent goods" become plentiful. But there is also a Zen road to affluence, departing from premises somewhat different from our own: that human material wants are finite and few, and technical means unchanging but on the whole adequate. Adopting the Zen strategy, a people can enjoy an unparalleled material plenty—with a low standard of living. . . . That, I think, describes the hunters. And it helps explain some of their more curious economic behavior: their "prodigality" for example—the inclination to consume at once all stocks on hand, as if they had it made. Free from market obsessions of scarcity, hunters' economic propensities may be more consistently predicated on abundance than our own.[27]

---

trapping. Yet, even with these seasonal variations, it is clear that life for these people was not one of unremitting exertion. Rogers, *The Quest for Food and Furs: The Mistassini Cree, 1953-1954*, National Museum of Man, Publications in Ethnology No. 5 (Ottawa, 1973), p. 80.

The reader should be warned that the number of hours logged while performing a particular subsistence activity, or activities, does not necessarily reflect the true nature of work among pre-industrial people. As the substantivist group of economic anthropologists argued, so-called economic activities are often embedded in what we in the Western world would classify as non-economic institutions. Quantification of these activities would be impossible, as McManus found. One might make the point, furthermore, that hunter-gatherers often purposely contrive to live precariously close to starvation in order to dramatize their dependence on super-human agencies of support. This seems to be the case among Canadian Subarctic hunters, at least.

Hunters thus have scant ambition to accumulate personal material wealth, not because they have suppressed these desires but because they don't have them to begin with. "We are inclined to think of hunters and gatherers as *poor* because they don't have anything; perhaps better to think of them for that reason as free." Sahlins' advice is that "we should entertain the empirical possibility that hunters are in business for their health, a finite objective, and that bow and arrow are adequate to that end."[28]

Viewed in this light, the self-serving diatribes which Indian spokesmen frequently delivered against the European way of life make more sense. Historians have tended to dismiss these as so much hot air, or "sounding off," when perhaps there was more truth to the simple virtues and freedom from care these orators expounded than we have allowed for.[d] If Sahlins is correct in his explanation of hunter-gatherer behavior, we are hard put to explain the Indian's enthusiastic response to the fur trade if it was not to improve his standard of living through material accumulation. That, at least, is the usual explanation, one whose deficiencies will be discussed in part 3 of this study.

We are left, then, with the distinct possibility that the aboriginal Eastern Canadian hunter-gatherer, the protagonist of the present study, may not have been as economically destitute as we have heretofore been led to believe. It has recently been argued, for instance, that hunter-gatherers the world over have, since the end of the Pleistocene, consciously limited natality. Birth spacing has been common among such people because of the genuine problems of carrying and breast-feeding superfluous infants. Yet the potential for fertility remains, should the community experience a sharp decline or in the event it were to move into a habitat deemed capable of supporting a larger human population. Such conscious, deliberate constraints placed on the birth rate evidently served to limit hunter-gatherer populations to numbers well below the technological limits of exploitation and the

d. I have included just one of these lengthy harangues in the following study; Jesuit priests confided to their journals that the Indians of New France were especially fond of delivering these broadsides.

culturally defined carrying capacity of the land.[29] The impression we are left with, based on studies of modern hunter-gatherers using aboriginal tools, is that these people indeed have had the technological capability to exert greater pressure on their faunal and floral resources than they have chosen to do.

Could the same be true for the Eastern Canadian Indian hunter of the late prehistoric–early historic period? Probably: we know these people were masters at devising ingenious traps of all sorts, for land and aquatic game,[30] while there is abundant testimony to their skill with the bow, itself a most effective weapon for hunting large game. Few people realize that moose and caribou were frequently hunted with lances tipped with bone, antler, or canine tooth. Likewise, most beaver hunting was done with ice chisels and axes, used to break open their lodges in the winter season. Certainly iron, obtained ultimately from Europeans, made a better cutting edge than did these other natural materials, but it would be unreasonable to suggest that iron revolutionized Indian hunting. As for the much vaunted steel trap baited with that irresistible secretion, castoreum (milked from the beaver's musk glands), neither was used extensively in our area until the turn of the nineteenth century, and then only for twenty years or so.

It is difficult to pinpoint exactly when the steel-trap–castoreum method was first employed in the Canadian trade. The fur trader David Thompson implied that it was a technique introduced by southeastern Canadian Indians in the 1790s, although Robin F. Wells has recently turned up evidence which seems to show it was being used by Northeastern Indians well before this date. The reason it became popular at the turn of the century, indeed the preferred method of capturing beaver, is because the European beaver market was in steep decline, a casualty of the French Revolution. Instead of cutting back, southeastern Canadian Indians, at least, trapped even more intensively in a futile effort to maintain their usual income from the sale of pelts.[31] Added to this, of course, was the incentive of competition between the Northwest Company and the Hudson's Bay Company. By the time the two rival firms merged in 1821 and George Simpson was installed as the new governor, beaver were so depleted throughout his domain, especially in the Northern Department, that he ordered an immediate moratorium on the use of steel-traps–castoreum. The Indians were from thenceforth to revert to using ice chisels—less efficient but in the long run more productive hunting tools.[32]

In terms of beaver hunting—beaver being by far and away the most significant mammal in this early fur trade—it is clear that most of it, except for a brief interlude from roughly 1790 to 1821, was prosecuted with the ice chisel and axe. Both of these were aboriginal tools in Eastern Canada and both were frankly improved upon by the substitution of iron for bone, tooth, stone, and antler. Yet the suspicion remains that the Indian, equipped with his traditional tools in protohistoric times, was quite capable of inflicting greater damage on game resources than he apparently did. That is, he was in possession of a hunting technology which probably allowed him to kill up to the limit of what he could use, including food which could be consumed on the spot and food that could be transported elsewhere to be consumed at a later date.

There were several considerations which restrained the hunter-gatherer, at least, in the quantity of game harvested. One of these has already been alluded to: the logistical problem of transporting stored, dried or smoked, provisions. Still, these people could have feasted even more than they did. Another factor limiting the game harvest would have been the great diversity and aggregate abundance of exploitable resources, with the result that hunting and gathering pressures were spread over a broad range of resources rather than unduly concentrated on any particular species. Wildlife abundance was also insured by the hunter's very means of locating game. It is logical that the Indian's sources of information on game movements would be most effective when game were relatively abundant. To put it another way, the probability of achieving satisfaction from divination, conjuring, and scouting was obviously enhanced when there was increasingly more game in the vicinity against which these powers could be directed. These practices were therefore reinforced by having a situation of abundance, while a scarcity of game would render them less effectual. One might guess, then, that scarcity induced by excessive hunting would tend to have been quickly reversed in order that these services might regain their former degree of success. The native hunter was probably not conscious of the conservationist effect of these latter two considerations— the diversity of exploitable resources and the feedback relationship between game abundance and successful methods of detection. It would be more likely that he was considerably more aware of problems of storing and transporting superfluous flesh. For him to harvest anything more than what he could use, either immediately or in the future, would have been not only wasteful but dangerous. And here is the real crux of the issue. The single most important deterrent to excessive hunting, in the Eastern Algonkian's mind at any rate, was the fear of spiritual reprisal for indiscreet slaughter. Prior to European influence, these Indians of the Canadian forest were on amicable terms with the spirits of the game, including the game "bosses," or keepers of the game, and it was the vivid, daily awareness of this courteous relationship which more than anything else precluded overkill.

Herein, then, lies the second flaw in the equation: the Indian hunter's inherent willingness to destroy wildlife on such an unprecedented scale. Maybe contemporary Europeans had few qualms about extinguishing game, but the newly contacted Indian certainly had many—or should have, if his belief system were still operating intact. It would be necessary for the mutually courteous relationship between man and animal to disintegrate before the Indian could make war on his animal brethren. The issue is that there were traditionally powerful, genuinely compelling sanctions against overkilling wildlife. We know they were vestigially operative at the time of white contact because eyewitness observers described them, and they have survived well into modern times in parts of Eastern Canada.[33]

James VanStone, a specialist on the northwestern Athapaskans, is the only scholar I know of to have recognized this curious contradiction. "This shift of emphasis [from the exploitation of the total environment to select furbearing species] and its commercial implications also disturbed the balanced reciprocal relationship between the hunter and his animal spirit helpers, thus undermining a basic aspect of the traditional religious belief system."[34] I will argue in the pages which follow that the "traditional religious belief system" had already been undermined by the time these Indians began participating in the organized fur trade and that the undermining process consisted, in part, of nullifying the traditional sanctions against wildlife overkill. Be that as it may, the fact remains that there was, or should have been, a formidable spiritual obstacle to wildlife overkill when Europeans first penetrated the continent. That it was quite obviously disregarded by the Indian partner in the trade needs some explanation, and I shall try to provide one.

This is not to deny that the Indian, when he did begin trafficking with Europeans or Indian middlemen in a systematic manner, was possessed of acquisitive feelings. No doubt they were there, although not quite in the form that Peter Farb or W. H. Hutchinson have suggested—capitalistic drives reminiscent of Western man. This should become clear in the ensuing pages.

Finally, the issues which are raised in this investigation naturally have enormous implications for the broader, continent-wide issue of Indian land-use subsequent to white influence. For years scholars and amateurs have been claiming for the North American Indian a special fondness for Nature. It was therefore not surprising when the Indian emerged as the spiritual leader of the Ecology Movement of the late 1960s. The Native American, we were told through various sorts of media, was a "natural" conservationist, meaning that his traditional culture—the popular mind insists on thinking of American Indians in monolithic terms—had equipped him with an ecologically sound concept of Nature. Like all popular myths, this one has an element of truth—a germ of truth which is outweighed, and hence vitiated, by its accompanying fallacies and ambiguities. As will become apparent in the Epilogue, where I take up this issue at some length, we have erred in assigning the American Indian a Western-sounding conservationist ethic, just as we have erred in defining his Eastern Canadian ancestor as a petty bourgeois capitalist. If American

Indians were ever conservationist in practice—and there is ample proof to show they were at various times in recorded history—they were not so for the reasons we usually advance: because they had a condescending affection for Mother Earth. Extrapolating from the fur trade evidence discussed here, it will be seen that Angloamericans have once again fallen victim to their ethnocentrism: we have both posed the question about the Indian-land relationship and answered it within a Western frame of reference.

For many readers the story which follows will seem a fantasy, because it is suffused with native oral literature and, especially, spiritual beliefs. However fantastic, this core of belief is the absolutely crucial context of the Indian's familiar environment—the realm in which he operated. He took his behavioral environment completely seriously and conducted himself, even when in the presence of skeptical whites, according to its principles. When white ridicule or religious intolerance made the overt expression of his spiritual beliefs painful, he either took them underground, practicing them clandestinely, or discarded them for the white world view. Even when he chose the latter course, he rarely became estranged from his traditional cosmos altogether. Often white and Indian cosmic elements became fused in some odd combination, and the Indian went on functioning, reconciled to both the white world—which he could not and would not want to shut out altogether—and the Indian world.[35, e] To neglect this "fantasy," then, would be to risk inappropriately fantastic, because Westernized, interpretations of baffling events in this early period of contact history.

Not surprisingly, Subarctic Indians have had their own version of history, a mythology which explains the change in communication between man and Nature. As they would have it,

there have been three successive epochs in the history of the world. In the beginning the animals were the masters, with mankind in a nebulous dream-state on the periphery. This epoch ended with the birth of the "transformer" or culture hero, who rid the world of its primeval monsters and cleared the way for human life. All methods of hunting and

e. I am of course confining my remarks to the Eastern Canadian experience.

fishing, the domestication of the dog and the building of canoes, can be traced back to him; it was through him that man became truly man. After his departure there began the third epoch, which still continues, and in which men and beasts can no longer communicate with each other, and only shamans maintain the link between the human and extra-human spheres. One day the culture hero will return and then the earth will dissolve in flames.[36]

We might appropriately begin with this middle period, when men and animals freely communicated with one another—before that dialogue was effectively terminated by the circumstances of European contact.

Indian Groups

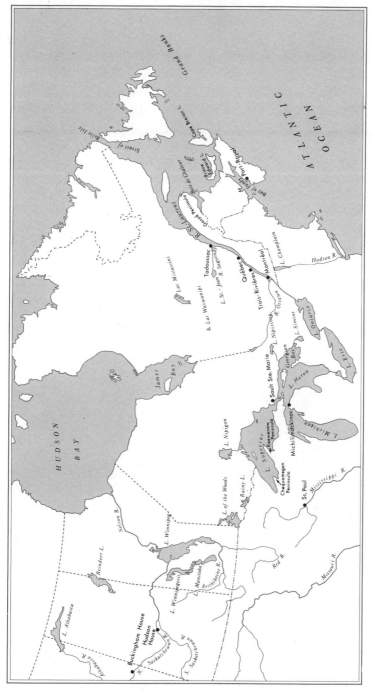

Eastern Subarctic and a Portion of the Northeast Culture Areas

PART ONE

An Ecological Interpretation
of European Contact
with the Micmac*

*This section is an adaptation of my article "The European Impact on the Culture of a Northeastern Algonquian Tribe: An Ecological Interpretation," *William and Mary Quarterly* 31 (January 1974):3–26.

CHAPTER ONE

The Protohistoric Indian-Land Relationship

A s THE DRIVE for furs expanded and gathered momentum in seventeenth-century Eastern Canada, complaints of beaver extermination became correspondingly more frequent and alarming. By 1635, for example, the Huron in the Lake Simcoe area had reduced their stock of beaver to the point where Father Paul Le Jeune, the Jesuit, could flatly declare that they had none.[1] Likewise, a half-century later Baron de Lahontan was present at a council session between the Five Nations Iroquois and the French governor-general, Monsieur La Barre, at which the principal Iroquois spokesman explained that his people had attacked the Illinois and Miami for trespassing on Iroquois territory to hunt beaver, "and contrary to the custom of all the Savages, have carried off whole Stocks, both Male and Female."[2] The severe exploitation of beaver and other furbearing species seems to have been most intense in the vicinity of major trading posts and among the native tribes most intimately associated with the trade (the Micmac, Montagnais, League Iroquois, Huron, Ojibwa, and others),[3] while those tribes which remained beyond the effective limits of European influence and the trade, such as the Bersimis of northeastern Québec, enjoyed an abundance of beaver in their domains.[4]

Long before the establishment of permanent trading posts, it would seem that the Micmac of the extreme eastern tip of Canada were engaged in vigorous trade with European fishermen.[a] The result was that areas important in the early fishing industry, places such as Prince Edward Island, the Gaspé Peninsula, and Cape Breton Island, were cleaned out of moose and furbearers by the mid-seventeenth century.[5] Reviewing this grim situation, Nicolas Denys, a merchant who had lived intimately with the Micmac for forty years, commented that game was less abundant in his time than formerly; as for the beaver, "few in a house are saved; they [the Micmac] would take all. The disposition of the Indians is not to spare the little ones any more than the big ones. They killed all of each kind of animal that there was when they could capture it."[6] In sum, the game which by all accounts had been initially so plentiful was now being systematically exterminated by the Indians themselves.

The hunting, gathering, and fishing Micmac who lived within this Acadian forest, especially along its rivers and by the sea, were omnivores in the trophic (or energy) system of the community. At the first trophic level the Micmac consumed wild potato tubers, wild fruits and berries, acorns and nuts, and the

a. See Wilson D. Wallis and Ruth Sawtell Wallis, *The Micmac Indians of Eastern Canada* (Minneapolis: University of Minnesota Press, 1955), for a thorough ethnographic study of the Micmac. Jacques and Maryvonne Crevel, *Honguedo ou l'Histoire des premiers Gaspesiens* (Québec: Editions Garneau, 1970), give a fairly good general history of the Micmac during the seventeenth century, along with a description of the centuries-old fishing industry. Alfred Goldsworthy Bailey, *The Conflict of European and Eastern Algonkian Cultures, 1504–1700: A Study in Canadian Civilization*, Publications of the New Brunswick Museum, Monographic Series No. 2 (St. John, New Brunswick, 1937), has the best analysis of the effects of European contact on the Micmac and surrounding Algonkians. Cornelius J. Jaenen, "Amerindian Views of French Culture in the Seventeenth Century," *Canadian Historical Review* 55 (September 1974):261–291, and Jaenen, *Friend and Foe: Aspects of French-Amerindian Cultural Contact in the Sixteenth and Seventeenth Centuries* (New York: Columbia University Press, 1976), who relies heavily on Bailey, is useful on early French-Indian relations. See Harold Franklin McGee, Jr., Stephen A. Davis, and Michael Taft, "Three Atlantic Bibliographies," *Occasional Papers in Anthropology*, no. 1 (Autumn 1975), Department of Anthropology, Saint Mary's University, Halifax, Nova Scotia, for a comprehensive bibliography of Micmac history, ethnology, archaeology, and folklore.

like. Trees and shrubs provided in addition a wealth of materials used in the fashioning of tools, utensils, and other equipment. A lack of mortars and pestles, corn husks, and other signs of agriculture in the archaeological record suggests that the pre-historic Micmac were not horticulturalists, this despite a legend which credited them with having raised maize and tobacco "for the space of several years."[7, b] Climatically, the Micmac lived, then and now, within a short summer zone, which would have discouraged maize agriculture, but not absolutely precluded it. They could conceivably have harvested their crop green.[8] Yet, whatever transpired before this time, we are told that by the early seventeenth century the Micmac were acquiring maize, beans, pumpkins, tobacco, and wampum (which they are said to have greatly prized) from New England Algonkians of the Saco River area and possibly regions even further south.[9]

Next to photosynthesizing plants in the energy system of the community were herbivores and carnivores, occupying the second and third trophic levels respectively, with top carnivores situated at the fourth level. The Micmac hunter tapped all three levels of energy-yielding wildlife, aquatic life, and marine life in his seasonal hunting and fishing activities, for these sources of food were "to them like fixed rations assigned to every moon."[10] "Now, for example, in January they have the seal hunting," continued Father Pierre Biard, ". . . for this animal, although it is aquatic, nevertheless spawns upon certain Islands about this time." Biard was writing this from memory, his recollection apparently failing him at this point: North Atlantic coastal seals pup in the spring rather than in mid-winter. Possibly Biard confused June with January in the subsistence cycle.[11] If he were correct, the Micmac were in the habit of interrupting their winter, interior hunting activities and moving back to the coast for the month of January, heading inland once again in February, all of which seems unlikely. Be that as it may, seal fat, whether it

b. Marc Lescarbot, *The History of New France* (1618; first published 1609), translated by W. L. Grant, 3 vols. (Toronto: The Champlain Society, 1907–1914), 3:252–253, claimed that the Micmac definitely grew tobacco, most likely the so-called wild tobacco (*Nicotiana rustica*).

was obtained in mid-winter or spring, was customarily reduced to oil for food and body grease, while the women made clothing from the fur.[12]

Next came "the great hunt for Beavers, otters, moose, bears (which are very good), and for the caribou. . . ."[13] The attorney Marc Lescarbot explained that the Micmac confined their hunting activities to the winter season because there was such a plethora of fish (and we might add shellfish) throughout the rest of the year.[14] Winter was the most unpredictable season for the Micmac, as it was for all of these Eastern Canadian hunter-gatherers, for at no other time of the year were they so dependent on the caprice of the weather—a feast being as likely as a famine. A heavy rain could spoil the beaver and caribou hunt, while the moose hunt suffered from a deep, crustless snow.[15]

Beaver were preferably taken during this season, when their coat was in its prime and they were more readily pursued on the ice.[c] Hunters cooperated by working in teams, demolishing the lodge or cutting the dam with stone axes. Sometimes they brought in dogs to track the fleeing beaver as they sought refuge in air pockets along the edge of the pond. At other times they harpooned the rodent as it came up for air at air holes. In the summer hunt, beaver were shot with the bow or trapped in deadfalls baited with poplar, although the commonest way to take them was to breach the dam and drain the pond. The exposed animals were then slaughtered with bows and spears.[16]

Next to fish and shellfish, moose was the most important item in the Micmac diet, serving as a staple during the otherwise lean

c. See Horace T. Martin, *Castorologia, or the History and Traditions of the Canadian Beaver* (Montreal: William Drysdale and Company, 1892); A. Radclyffe Dugmore, *The Romance of the Beaver: Being the History of the Beaver in the Western Hemisphere* (London: William Heinemann, 1913); and Lewis Henry Morgan, *The American Beaver and His Works* (1868; reprint ed., New York: Burt Franklin, 1970), for treatises on the Canadian beaver. It is significant that the archaeological record from Maine "indicates that the beaver and other sedentary fauna were of considerable importance aboriginally" (Dean R. Snow, "Wabanaki 'Family Hunting Territories,'" *American Anthropologist* 70 [December 1968]:1145), which would suggest this to have been the case among the nearly identical Micmac while revealing that a dependence on beaver antedated European interest in the beast.

winter months when these large ruminants were run down with dogs on the hard-crusted snow. In the summer and spring, we are told that moose were both tracked and stalked and then shot with the bow; in the autumn, during the rutting season, bulls were lured by a clever imitation of the sound of a cow urinating. Another frequently used method was to ensnare the animal with a noose.[17,d]

In the exotic menu of the Micmac Indian, moose ranked first in preference. The entrails, a great delicacy among these people, were carried along with the "most delicious fat" to the campsite by the exultant hunter, who then sent the women to fetch the carcass. It was up to the mistress of the wigwam to determine what was to be done with each portion of the body, every part of which evidently was used. Grease was boiled out of the bones and either drunk pure (with "much gusto," recalled Le Clercq) or stored as loaves of moose-butter;[18] leg and thigh bones were crushed and the marrow consumed; hides were converted into robes, leggings, moccasins, and tent coverings;[19] tools, ornaments, and game pieces were fashioned from antlers, teeth, and toe bones, respectively[20]—in short, the beast was converted into an extraordinary range of necessities and luxuries. Confident of future hunting success, the Micmac typically consumed the moose flesh immediately, preserving the leftovers through a smoking process which, it was claimed, was capable of curing the meat for up to a year.[21] Black bear were likewise captured during the cold months, although such hunting was coincidental and fortuitous. Spring bears found in hibernation were generally shot with the bow.[22]

Eventually, as the lean months of winter passed into the abundance of spring, the fish began to spawn, swimming up rivers and streams in such numbers that "everything swarms with them."[23] In mid-March came the smelt, and at the end of April the herring. Soon there were sturgeon and salmon, and flocks of

d. Frank G. Speck and Ralph W. Dexter, "Utilization of Animals and Plants by the Micmac Indians of New Brunswick," *Journal of the Washington Academy of Sciences* 41 (August 1951):255, have ranked caribou before moose in order of importance but cite no evidence to support their claim.

waterfowl making nests out on the coastal islands—which meant there were eggs soon to be gathered. Mute evidence from seashore middens and early written testimony confirm that the Micmac were heavily dependent on various mollusks, harvesting them in enormous quantities.[24] Fish was another staple for the Micmac, who were thoroughly familiar with the spawning habits of each species harvested. Weirs were erected across streams to trap the fish on their way downstream on a falling tide, while large varieties, such as sturgeon and salmon, were often speared or trapped.[25]

The salmon run marked the beginning of summer in the Micmac calendar, the time of year when the wild geese shed their plumage. Most wildfowl were pursued at their island rookeries; waterfowl, in particular, were generally hunted from the canoe and knocked down as they took to flight; others, such as the Canadian goose which grazed in the meadows, were dispatched with the bow.[26]

As the waterfowl made their exit in the autumn, migrating southward in anticipation of the cold months ahead, the eels began spawning up the many small rivers along the coast. Consequently, from mid-September to October, the Micmac left the ocean to follow the eels—"of which they lay in a supply; they are good and fat," added Biard. October and November were given over to hunting beaver and woodland caribou, we are told, while December brought the tomcod and the turtles bearing their eggs.[27]

Surveying the seasonal cycle of these Indians, Biard was profoundly impressed by Nature's bounty and Micmac resourcefulness. "These then, but in a still greater number, are the revenues and incomes of our Savages; such, their table and living, all prepared and assigned, everything to its proper place and quarter."[28] Although I have omitted mention of many other types of forest, marine, and aquatic life which were also exploited by the Micmac, those listed above were the most significant in the food quest and ecosystem of these maritime Indians.[29]

Placed in the context of this cornucopian situation, the following claim made by Nicolas Denys becomes readily credible:

"Their [the Micmacs'] greatest task was to feed well and to go a hunting. They did not lack animals, which they killed only in proportion as they had need of them." One does not get the impression that the Micmac of protohistoric times, the period to which Denys was alluding, were hampered by their technology in the taking of game. Obviously there must have been seasons of austerity, for whatever reason is immaterial. The point is that in the generality of cases, Micmac technology was quite adequate to keep them well provisioned, even during the winter season. As Denys acknowledged elsewhere: "The hunting by the Indians in old times was easy for them. They killed only in proportion as they had need. . . . When they were tired of eating one sort, they killed some of another. If they did not wish longer to eat meat, they caught some fish. They never made an accumulation of skins of Moose, Beaver, Otter, or others, but only so far as they needed them for personal use. They left the remainder [of the carcass] where the animals had been killed, not taking the trouble to bring them to their camps."[30] Need, then, and not technology, was the overriding factor, and need was determined by the great primal necessities of life as these were understood and regulated by cultural considerations. Hunting was above all else conducted and controlled by spiritual rules.

In order to understand this crucial dimension to the food quest, and hunting in particular, one must first appreciate the world view of the Indian. Up to this point we have been witness to the empirical, objective, physical—or "operational"—environmental model of the observer; what we lack is the "cognized" (emic) model of the Micmac.[31]

Anthropologists generally regard the pre-Columbian North American Indian as having been a sensitive member of his environment, an individual who merged "himself sympathetically into the world of living and even non-living things." The Indian's was a world filled with super-human and magical powers which controlled man's destiny and Nature's course of events.[32] Murray Wax explains:

To those who inhabit it, the magical world is a "society," not a "mechanism," that is, it is composed of "beings" rather than "objects."

Whether human or nonhuman, these beings are associated with and related to one another socially and sociably, that is, in the same ways as human beings to one another. These patterns of association and relationship may be structured in terms of kinship, empathy, sympathy, reciprocity, sexuality, dependency, or any other of the ways that human beings interact with and affect or afflict one another. Plants, animals, rocks, and stars are thus seen not as "objects" governed by laws of nature, but as "fellows" with whom the individual or band may have a more or less advantageous relationship.[33]

American Indian folktales are an especially rich source of information on this subject. Reading them, one is struck by the anthropomorphic nature of animals. "They reside in lodges, gather in council, and act according to the norms and regulations of kinship. In these tales, as in those of many peoples, man and the animals are depicted as engaging in all manner of social and sociable interaction: They visit, smoke, gamble, and dance together; they exchange wisdom; they compete in games and combat; and they even marry and beget offspring."[34]

The essential ingredient in this peculiar relationship between man and animals, and indeed between man and all of Nature, is Power. Power—called *manitou* in Algonkian—is a phenomenon common among pre-industrial people the world over. Roughly defined, it is the spiritual potency associated with an object (such as a knife) or a phenomenon (such as thunder). To the Micmac, as well as to all the rest of these Eastern Canadian hunter-gatherers, manitou was the force which made everything in Nature alive and responsive to man.[35] Only a fool would confront life without it, since it was only through the manipulation and interpretation of manitou that man was able to survive in this world. To cut oneself off from manitou was equivalent to repudiating the vital force in Nature; without manitou Nature would lose its meaning and potency, and man's activities in Nature would become secular and mechanical.

Ethnologists have frequently compared Power to static electricity in its properties, "in the sense that it may be accumulated by proper ritual and then be employed in service or discharged by contact with improper objects." Power, continue the Waxes, "is never regarded as a permanent and unconditional possession, but may be lost by the same kinds of forces and circumstances as it was gained." One handles Power according to the principles of ritual. Ritual thus becomes the means of harnessing, or conducting, Power.[36]

It is important to understand this concept of Power if we are to appreciate fully the Indian hunter's role in the fur trade, something which will receive considerable attention in part 3. Suffice it to say, here, that the world of the Micmac was filled with super-human forces and beings—dwarves, giants, and magicians; animals that could talk to man and had spirits akin to his own; and the magic of mystical and medicinal herbs—a cosmos where even seemingly inanimate objects possessed spirits.[37,e] Micmac subsistence pursuits were inextricably bound up within this spiritual matrix, which, I am proposing, acted as a kind of control mechanism on Micmac land-use, maintaining the natural environment within an optimum range of conditions.

This "control mechanism" was expressed outwardly in the form of seemingly innumerable, and to early French commentators, absurd hunting taboos. Yet these taboos connoted a sense of cautious respect for a conscious fellow-member of the same eco-system who, in the view of the Indian, literally allowed itself to be killed for food and clothing. Beaver, for example, were greatly admired by the Micmac for their industry and "abounding genius"; for them, the beaver had "sense" and formed a "separate nation."[38] Hence, there were various regulations associated with the disposal of their remains: trapped beaver were drawn in public and made into soup, extreme care being taken to prevent the soup from spilling into the fire; beaver bones were carefully preserved, never being given to the dogs—lest they lose their sense of smell for the rodent—nor thrown into the fire—lest misfortune come upon "all the nation"—nor thrown into rivers —"because the Indians fear lest the spirit of the bones . . . would promptly carry the news to the other beavers, which would

e. Stansbury Hagar, "Micmac Magic and Medicine," *Journal of American Folk-Lore* 9 (July-September 1896):170–177, and Frederick Johnson, "Notes on Micmac Shamanism," *Primitive Man* 16 (July and October 1943):54, 56–57, report that such beliefs in the supernatural and spiritual survive even in modern times, although in a suppressed and attenuated form.

desert the country in order to escape the same misfortune." Likewise, menstruating women were forbidden to eat beaver, "for the Indians are convinced, they say, that the beaver, which has sense, would no longer allow itself to be taken by the Indians if it had been eaten by their [spiritually] unclean daughters." The beaver fetus, as well as that of the bear, moose, otter, and porcupine, was reserved for the old men, since it was believed that a youth who ate such food would suffer acute foot pains while hunting.[39]

Similarly with the moose, taboo governed the disposal of its remains—what few there were. The bones of the fawn (and the marten, for that matter) were never thrown to the dogs nor were they burned, "for they [the Micmac] would not be able any longer to capture any of these animals in hunting if the spirits of the martens and of the fawn of the moose were to inform their own kind of the bad treatment they had received among the Indians." Fear of such reprisal also prohibited menstruating women from drinking out of the common kettles or bark dishes.[40] Such regulations imply guarded respect for the animal. The moose and other game animals thus not only furnished food and raiment but were also tied up with the Micmac spirit world.

Along with the above taboos, the Micmac also practiced bear ceremonialism, as it is conventionally called. Esteem for the bear is in fact common throughout the boreal zone of northern Eurasia and North America, exhibiting the following outstanding characteristics: the beast is typically hunted in the early spring, while still in hibernation, and preferably killed with aboriginal weapons; it is addressed, when dead or alive, with honorific titles which serve as euphemisms for its common name; a conciliatory speech is made to the animal, either before or after killing it and sometimes both, by which the hunter sincerely apologizes for the necessity of his act; and the carcass is respectfully treated, those parts not used (especially the skull) being ceremonially disposed of and the flesh consumed while adhering to certain taboos. The stated purpose of all this veneration is to propitiate the spiritual controller, or keeper, of the bears in order that he will continue to furnish game to the hunter.[41]

Among the Micmac in particular, the bear's heart was not eaten by young men lest they become winded while traveling and panic in the face of danger. The bear carcass could be brought into the wigwam only through a special door made specifically for that occasion, either in the left or right side of the lodge. The Micmac reportedly based this ritual on the conviction that women did not "deserve" to enter the wigwam through the same door as the animal. In fact, we are told that childless women actually fled the lodge at the approach of the carcass, and did not return until it had been entirely consumed.[42] Through rituals and taboos such as these the hunter managed to satisfy the lingering soul-spirit of the slain beast.

If taboo was associated with fishing, we have little record of it; the only explicit evidence is a prohibition against the roasting of eels, which, if violated, would prevent the Indians from catching others. From this and from the fact that the Restigouche band of the Micmac wore the figure of a salmon as a totem around their neck, we may surmise that fish, too, shared in the sacred and symbolic world of the Indian.[43]

Control over these supernatural forces and communication with them were the principal function of the shaman, who served in Micmac society as an intermediary between the spirit realm and the physical. The lives and destiny of these people were thus profoundly affected by the ability of the shaman to supplicate, cajole, and otherwise manipulate the supernatural beings and powers. Unfortunately, the seventeenth-century French failed to appreciate the full significance of the shaman's mediating position between the spiritual and the temporal, being much more interested in exposing them as frauds or jugglers in league with Satan. From the seventeenth century to the present these intriguing individuals have been given a uniformly bad review. One still finds the medicine man depicted in the scholarly literature "as a kind of madman," ruefully observes Erwin H. Ackerknecht, himself a physician. "The diagnosis varies from epilepsy to hysteria, from fear neurosis to 'veritable idiocy.'"[44] Using a Rorschach analysis, one researcher recently had his suspicions confirmed that the shaman was an individual with "strong oral and phallic fixations" suffering "from a hysterical personality disorder, with attributes of the imposter."[45] Yet, within their own society, and this is the crux of the issue as Ackerknecht sees it, shamans were generally considered normal, or "autonormal," as he phrases it.[46]

Rather than be concerned with the authenticity of the shaman's performance, we should assess his function in Micmac society. In their opinion, the shaman was a successful soothsayer—a man who worked himself into a dreamlike state and consulted the spirit of his animal-helper to discern the future. He was also a healer, by means of conjuring. We are aware that the Micmac availed themselves of a rather large pharmacopia of roots and herbs and other plant parts, applying these with at least moderate success toward the cure of their physical ailments. When these failed to produce a cure, the sick or injured resorted to the healing arts of the most respected shaman in the district. The illness was frequently diagnosed by the shaman as a failure on the patient's part to perform a prescribed ritual or adhere to a particular taboo; hence an offended supernatural agent had visited the culprit with sickness. At times such as this, the shaman essentially functioned as a psychotherapist, or so it would appear from a Western medical point of view, diagnosing the illness and symbolically (at least) removing its immediate cause from the patient's body.[47,f]

As we reconstruct the Micmac cultural milieu of pre-contact times, using early historic and modern ethnographic sources, the impression we get is that the spiritual realm was the principal conduit, or channel, through which man was linked with his physical and natural surroundings. By operating in a spiritual realm, man found himself able to communicate—to have a dialogue—with Nature around him. Both became intelligible to and communicative with the other through the spiritual medium whose most adept operator was the shaman. It was principally

f. Nicolas Denys, *The Description and Natural History of the Coasts of North America (Acadia)* (1672), translated and edited by William F. Ganong (Toronto: The Champlain Society, 1908), p. 418, felt that most of these ailments were (what we would call today) psychogenic.

through his good offices that the above-mentioned spiritual obligations and restrictions operated to maintain the Micmac ecosystem, as it were, in a well-balanced condition. More specifically, the exploitation of game for subsistence appears to have been regulated by the hunter's attentiveness to the continued welfare of his prey—both living and dead, it is immaterial—as is suggested by the numerous taboos associated with the proper disposal of animal remains. Violation of taboo desecrated the remains of the slain animal and offended its soul-spirit. The offended spirit would then retaliate in any of several ways, depending on the nature of the broken taboo: it could render the guilty hunter's (or the entire band's) means of hunting ineffective; it could encourage its living fellows to abandon the hunter's territory; and it could inflict sickness. In all three instances the end result was the same—the hunt was rendered unsuccessful—and in each it was mediated by the same power—the spirit of the slain animal or its "keeper." Any one of these catastrophes could usually be reversed through the magical arts of the shaman. More to the point, in the Micmac cosmology, as we shall see later on, the overkill of wildlife would have been resented by the animal kingdom as an act comparable to genocide and would have been resisted by means of the sanctions outlined above. The threat of retaliation thus had the probable effect of placing an upper limit on the number of animals slain.

CHAPTER TWO

Early Contact
and the Deterioration of the
Environmental Ethos

THE SUDDEN INJECTION of European civilization into this balanced system initiated a series of reactions which, within a little over a century, resulted in the replacement of the aboriginal ecosystem by another. From at least the beginning of the sixteenth century, and perhaps well before this date, we know that fishing fleets from England (Bristol), France (Normandy and Brittany), and the Basque provinces were visiting the numerous banks off the Atlantic coast of Canada every spring for the cod, returning in the autumn to market their catch in Catholic Europe. Scholars are still very much in the dark as to when all this activity began, there being so little direct evidence for them to go on. One such shred of evidence suggests that Bristol merchants were surreptitiously sailing to Newfoundland in the 1480s. "On July 6, 1481 two balingers (cargo ships) cleared from Bristol for the purpose of 'examining and finding a certain island called the Isle of Brasil,'" notes Carl Sauer, paraphrasing David Beers Quinn. "The ships belonged to a partnership of Bristol merchants. It is known by Bristol records that the ships sailed and returned but not what they found. The chief participant, one Thomas Croft, was given exemption of duty on forty bushels of salt loaded on each ship as not being merchandise but for 'the intent to search and fynde the Isle of Brasile.' This might satisfy the customs record," Sauer shrewdly observes, echoing Quinn, "but why so much salt unless it was to be used as Professor Quinn has surmised, for salting fish at a western fishing ground already known to Bristol? If men of Bristol had discovered the great fishery off Newfoundland, they might not have advertised it in a public record." Quinn elaborates further, explaining that "the difficulties of the Icelandic trade helped to impel Bristol men to find both new markets [for cloth] and new fishing grounds. By 1480 they were turning for markets to the Atlantic islands—Madeira at least, colonized by the Portuguese; and for a fishery they were searching the Atlantic for the Isle of Brasil. If they found the Newfoundland Banks in 1481, as seems quite possible, they had every incentive to keep their discovery to themselves in the hope of keeping out competitors as long as possible."[1,a]

Despite this "conspiracy of silence,"[2] Bernard Hoffman, an ethnologist, concludes "that the Newfoundland fishing fleet acquired considerable proportions at a very early date and many times in excess of the fragmentary indications still surviving in the port archives." "By 1534," he continues, "judging from the indications of ports, harbours, watering places, and islands given upon the *portolanos,* the fisheries extended along the entire Atlantic coastline from southeastern Labrador to southern Nova Scotia."[3] Historians speculate that the fur trade initially developed as an adjunct enterprise to the codfishery—that it was codfishermen who first traded with the coastal Micmac, Beothuk, and Montagnais-Naskapi while drying their catch on land. Ship crews evidently put in at harbors and bays along the coasts of Newfoundland, Labrador, Cape Breton Island, and other likely spots to dry the cod in the sun on stages to which they returned year after year. "Friendly intercourse with the natives must soon have followed," surmises Henry Percival Biggar, "and in time also an exchange of European goods for furs,—the only article of any value that the savages possessed. At first no doubt the barter was carried on in a haphazard way by a few masters or

a. See Bruce J. Bourque, "Aboriginal Settlement and Subsistence on the Maine Coast," *Man in the Northeast,* no. 6 (Fall 1973):3–20, for evidence of an even earlier contact date in the Northeast than this.

sailors desirous of improving the season's returns. As the fishermen and whalers pushed further into the St. Lawrence, and when experience had shown that furs thus to be secured obtained high prices in Europe, this intermittent barter grew into an organized fur trade."[4,b]

The archaeological evidence for the early Atlantic coastal trade seems to confirm Biggar's hypothesis: artifacts turned up from this seemingly initial stage of European trade "are quite different from those of any later stage," claims John Witthoft. "They are not goods made for the Indian trade, nor are they the ordinary domestic objects of Europe; they reflect the ways of the sea. . . . Among parts stripped from ships are bolts, metal rings from rigging, and metal tips from belaying pins. Broad, thin knives appear to have been specialized tools of the fisherman. Spiral brass earrings, worn in the left ears of Indian burials, represent a direct transferrence of the ancient sailor's caste marks; this was the seaman's charm against bad eyesight. Strings of glass beads, especially in blue, probably came from sailors who wore them as a protection against the evil eye." It is interesting to note that these Atlantic coastal tribes at first cannibalized their brass kettles and steel axes, cutting the kettles up into strips to make knives and ornaments and sawing the axes (with sandstone slabs) into smaller pieces from which they made chisels and adzes. The date for this artifact assemblage has been set at approximately 1550; any European trade goods which changed hands before this period have apparently either perished or remain lost.[5]

Far more important, for our purposes, than the subversion

b. Bernard G. Hoffman, *Cabot to Cartier: Sources for a Historical Ethnography of Northeastern North America, 1497-1550* (Toronto: University of Toronto Press, 1961), pp. 198-200, maintains that "wet" fishing, by which cod were salted and packed away while on shipboard, thus diminishing the opportunities for contact with the Indians, was necessitated off the eastern coast of Nova Scotia and southern Newfoundland, since the fisheries here were too far offshore and the fog too common from April to July to allow for adequate sunning. "Dry" fishing, he surmises, must have been limited to the east coast of Newfoundland and Labrador. Yet this is contradicted by Champlain, who stated explicitly that "both dry and green [wet]" fishing were conducted in the vicinity of Gaspé, "Codfish [Mal]" Bay, and Percée. Samuel de Champlain, *Of Savages . . . 1603*, in *The Works of Samuel de Champlain*, edited by Henry Percival Biggar, vol. 1, pp. 81-189, Publications of the Champlain Society (Toronto: University of Toronto Press, 1971), pp. 167-168.

and replacement of Micmac material culture by the European technology, is the almost certain fact that these fishermen were unwittingly infecting the unsuspecting natives with a variety of Old World diseases against which the latter had no immunity. Commenting on this first, or microbial, phase of European conquest, John Witthoft has written:

All of the microscopic parasites of humans, which had been collected together from all parts of the known world into Europe, were brought to these [American] shores, and new diseases stalked faster than man could walk into the interior of the continent. Typhoid, diphtheria, colds, influenza, measles, chicken pox, whooping cough, tuberculosis, yellow fever, scarlet fever, and other strep infections, gonorrhea, pox (syphilis), and smallpox were diseases that had never been in the New World before. They were new among populations which had no immunity to them. . . . Great epidemics and pandemics of these diseases are believed to have destroyed whole communities, depopulated whole regions, and vastly decreased the native population everywhere in the yet unexplored interior of the continent. The early pandemics are believed to have run their course prior to 1600 A.D.[6,c]

At this point it would be well to digress and discuss the matter of American Indian depopulation following European contact, and the logical place to begin is by asking how many Indians were here, in the Americas, in 1492. This is of course an extremely difficult question to answer, in part because the majority of documentary sources which bear on the subject come from early historic records, Indian and European, and pertain only to specific, isolated regions.[d] In the opinion of a number of early twentieth-century demographers, these early contact estimates are simply too high, and they were therefore shaved to bring them

c. See Alfred W. Crosby, Jr., *The Columbian Exchange: Biological and Cultural Consequences of 1492* (Westport, Conn.: Greenwood Press, 1972), pp. 122–164; John E. Lobdell and Douglas Owsley, "The Origin of Syphilis," *Journal of Sex Research* 10 (February 1974):76–79; and Francisco Guerra, "The Problem of Syphilis," in *First Images of America: The Impact of the New World on the Old,* edited by Fredi Chiappelli, vol. 2, pp. 845–851 (Berkeley and Los Angeles: University of California Press, 1976), for the latest thinking on the origins of syphilis, which all three sources feel was indigenous, in one or more forms, to both hemispheres.

d. Historic demographers employ several other methods to calculate early contact or prehistoric populations, in addition to the use of documentary in line with subsequent, lower estimates, often made several generations after initial contact. It is important to distinguish between the high, initial estimates and the invariably lower, subsequent estimates. Many scholars in the early years of this century made no apologies about the fact that they felt more comfortable with the second set of estimates, which seemed to them to be based on more accurate calculations and sounded, quite frankly, more reasonable than the earlier set. Operating on this premise, they simply added up the more conservative population figures for as many regions of a continent for which there were such figures, made a rough estimate of the population in those regions where no figures existed, added the two sets together and reached a total. Whenever they deemed the population estimates at their disposal too extravagant, they arbitrarily trimmed them down to something which sounded more plausible.[7]

Using such a rudimentary, dead reckoning technique, Alfred L. Kroeber in 1939 calculated a hemispheric total of 8,400,000 aborigines at contact. While roughly a decade earlier the Smithsonian Institution had posthumously published James Mooney's population figures, arrived at as well through dead reckoning, placing the aboriginal population of the continental United States, Canada, Greenland, and Alaska at 1,153,000 individuals. Kroeber would subsequently decide that Mooney's figures were inflated and would shrink his million-plus figure to 900,000 aborigines in North America in 1492.[8]

Few scholars cared about the finer points of the argument; most were content to accept a round figure of 1 million Indians for North America and 8 to 12 million for the entire hemisphere. True, there were some demographers who were urging significantly higher figures, but their estimates seemed to be more guesswork than anything else. The majority of scholars subscribed to the Mooney-Kroeber estimates as being the most authoritative.

Then, in 1966, Henry F. Dobyns published his compelling critique of the dead reckoning technique. Using a highly sophisticated calculus of his own devising (the so-called bichronic method),

sources. These are all ably described by William M. Denevan, "Introduction," in *The Native Population of the Americas in 1492*, edited by Denevan, pp. 1–12 (Madison: University of Wisconsin Press, 1976), pp. 8–12.

Dobyns went on to propose a staggering 90 to 112 million natives for the entire New World and approximately a tenth of that figure (9.8 to 12 million) for North America at the time of European landfall.[9] The article understandably attracted a great deal of attention.

Dobyns argued that previous scholars had committed a serious error in their calculations when they overlooked the devastating impact of epidemic diseases on the virgin, New World population. The diseases he had in mind are all believed to have been imported by Europeans and have been enumerated, above, by Witthoft. This blind spot, Dobyns continued, had caused a good many of these early demographers to project a known, post-epidemic population back in time to 1492 on the mistaken assumption that it indeed represented a first contact population. In ignoring or dismissing this critical distinction, demographers (including Mooney and Kroeber) had turned up population figures which grossly underestimated the true aboriginal population. Dobyns graphically illustrated his point in an earlier article on Andean epidemiology.

Discussing the disease environment of the Andean region only "after conquest" begs the question of the total impact of epidemic Old World diseases upon the aboriginal Andean population. For aboriginal disease environment conditions terminated in the Andes several years prior to Spanish conquest. As a result, full accounts of the initial impact of Old World disease agents on a virgin population of susceptible individuals lacking immunities do not exist. Most analysts have apparently confused the concept of "aboriginal times" with "pre-conquest" in the Andean area without realizing that aboriginal times terminated somewhat prior to conquest, at least in biological terms. The Inca Empire conquered by Pizarro's few hundred adventurers probably numbered less than half as many subjects then as it had a decade earlier.[10]

Scholars have long been aware of the traumas which typically follow in the wake of foreign intrusion within a previously virgin territory, as was the case when fifteenth- and sixteenth-century Europeans penetrated the relatively isolated New World. What usually happens is that the indigenous population experiences a marked decline due to the combined effects of introduced disease, warfare with the invading societies, the disruption of food producing activities, and the physical dislocation resulting in part from colonization.[11] In the New World, exotic diseases seem to have eclipsed these other calamities in disastrous effect.

Studies of South and Central America, Mexico, the West Indies, and the American Southwest, and to a lesser extent throughout the rest of the hemisphere, show that there was, especially in coastal and island areas, a depopulation as high as 90 to 95 percent within the first hundred to two hundred years of European contact. Such was the fate, for example, of the central Mexican population, which Woodrow Borah and the late Sherburne Cook have shown was decimated by alien diseases according to the following schedule: from an initial, pre-contact population of 25 to 29 million in 1519, the natives dropped to a mere 16.8 million in 1532, 7.3 million in 1548, 2.65 million in 1568, 1.9 million in 1585, 1.27 million in 1595, and bottomed out at slightly over 1 million in 1605.[12]

A similar pattern prevailed throughout much of the rest of the Spanish New World, where the nadir in the aboriginal population was generally reached by the early to mid-1600s. After that the native population gradually recuperated, often as a hybrid, mixed-blood type seemingly better able to cope with the insidious disease cycles and other social pressures.[13]

Unfortunately, there have been few comparable studies of the temperate, subarctic, and arctic regions of North America.[e] In what is certainly one of the most elegant of these, Sherburne Cook demonstrated that after 100 years of white contact (from 1620 to 1720), one-quarter of an initial New England Indian population figure was eliminated through warfare and four-fifths through exotic diseases. Three Indians were thus dying of some foreign disease in seventeenth-century New England for every one Indian who was succumbing to overt hostilities.[14]

e. After reading the pertinent literature on the early contact Eskimo, Robert Fortuine concluded that "the health of the Eskimos prior to their prolonged contact with western culture was good if not exceptional. The Eskimos showed that they had reached a remarkably effective adjustment to an unkind world and seemed to be thriving, despite some of the usual kinds of ills that all mankind is heir to" ("The Health of the Eskimos, as Portrayed in the Earliest Written Accounts," *Bulletin of the History of Medicine* 45 [March–April 1971]:114). Early European observers noticed that the Eskimos they encountered suffered, at times, from sore eyes, resulting from the combined effects of wind, glare, and smoke; mysterious respiratory ailments; nosebleeds (epistaxis); and in some cases mental disease, mental retardation, and musculoskeletal defects.

It was evidence such as this which convinced Henry Dobyns that the population estimates of his predecessors were in general excessively low and prompted him to attempt a new set of estimates using a rather novel method of calculation: the bichronic method. Put simply, Dobyns determined as closely as he could the depopulation ratio between a known or estimated first contact population and a nadir population for the same region some years (usually about one hundred thirty) thereafter. The areas he analyzed were naturally those from which we have the most complete and trustworthy population figures: central Mexico, coastal Mexico, portions of the Andes, California, Tierra del Fuego, Amazonia, and the Lower Colorado River basin. After uncovering several widely differing depopulation ratios for these regions, he selected a ratio of 20 to 1 as probably being the most sound, although somewhat conservative, figure. This meant that for every Indian alive in, say 1650, in each of these areas, there were 20 Indians thriving at the time of first European impact. Somewhat presumptuously, Dobyns suggested that this depopulation ratio might be applied throughout the remainder of the hemisphere—an assumption not all scholars are willing to allow. Nevertheless, once having made the assumption, it was a relatively easy matter to calculate the nadir population of North America—490,000 Indians in 1930 or so—and factor it by 20 to get a projected 1492 population of 9.8 million. Similarly, from a Mexican population of 1.5 million in 1650 he arrived at a contact population of 30 million. And so on. By taking the sum of each of these regional populations he estimated a grand total of 90,043,000 to 112,553,750 indigenes for the entire Western world at the time of Columbus. Significantly, Cook and Borah's region-by-region studies seem to confirm Dobyns's astronomical figures.[15]

Anyone who reads the early contact literature on the Americas cannot help but be struck by the devastating impact of alien diseases on the aborigines. Scholars might quibble with Dobyns and his supporters over their methodology, and it may be true that we are some years away from wholly reliable estimates of the aboriginal population for the hemisphere and its constituent parts, but the fact remains that early records of European penetration point very clearly to a massive destruction of native populations throughout the Americas in protohistoric times—a destruction by and large triggered by the multitudinous bacteria and viruses which these earliest European visitors unwittingly inflicted on a vulnerable population. The question then becomes: Why were these Native American people so susceptible to catastrophic microbial infection?

Paleopathological studies of prehistoric man in the New World (relying mainly on bones, coprolites, and native materia medica) have turned up evidence or cases of pinta, yaws, syphilis, hepatitis, encephalitis, polio, some limited tuberculosis (not of the pulmonary type), rheumatism, arthritis, some intestinal parasitism, other gastrointestinal illnesses, respiratory infections, and doubtless other ailments. On the whole, however, none of these diseases or functional disorders appears to have been particularly devastating to the overall population. Nor do malnutrition or tooth decay seem to have been significant factors in limiting the aboriginal population. One would guess that most premature deaths in prehistoric times were probably the result of hunting accidents, drowning, burns, suffocation, exposure, animal predation, cannibalism, infanticide, sacrifice, geronticide, suicide, homicide, and warfare.[16]

Scholars explain this remarkable disease-free phenomenon by pointing out that paleolithic man entered the New World via a land bridge (Beringia) connecting Siberia with Alaska, across what is now the Bering Strait. As waves of migrants crossed over from Asia to America during the latter stages of the Pleistocene they were forced to live in and adapt to an arctic tundra and grassland environment where, it is speculated, over a period of several generations they shed many of their Old World diseases —that is, they shed many of those diseases that were left after having lived for an equally indeterminate period of time on the other side of the land bridge in a similar environment. The refrigerator-like climate would seemingly have retarded the growth and dissemination of many of the microbial types we imagine these people might have carried with them. Put another way, the diseases these Paleoindians carried with them were largely screened out by a kind of climatic "germ filter" as they passed through this cold zone on their way south into the interior of the continent.[17] Over the ensuing millennia, prehistoric Indians managed to avoid the sort of microbial infections that were currently sweeping through much of the rest of the world by (a) deliberately or inadvertently avoiding contact with the Old World, except across the Bering Strait, and (b) by domesticating few varieties and numbers of livestock, compared to animal domestication, say, in Europe and the Middle East. An absence of livestock spared a good many American Indians from exposure to livestock diseases to which humans are also susceptible. This advantage was counterbalanced to a certain degree by a vulnerability to wildlife diseases attendant upon a hunting-and-gathering or even horticultural way of life.[18]

Disease, of course, serves the important function of limiting population growth; in its relative absence, populations can expand at a comparatively explosive rate—compared to populations more familiar with contagious, mortal diseases and hence more subject to their influence. Naturally, there are numerous other controls which serve to limit population growth, but the point is that, all things being equal, a population free of the tyranny of disease will far outstrip one subject to the inroads of disease.

Given this state of affairs in prehistoric America, one is not surprised to learn that phenomenally high population densities were achieved in various parts of the hemisphere in pre-Columbian times. In fact, in certain nuclear areas, such as central Mexico, it would appear that populations had surpassed the long-term carrying capacity of the land. People in these over-populated regions were resorting to ingenious methods of plant cultivation (such as irrigation farming, the use of canals, terraces, chinampas, and so forth) in a desperate effort to stretch out diminishing food resources. Signs of severe soil erosion dating from late prehistoric times seem to confirm this conjecture.[19]

Once disease-bearing Europeans arrived, the native population began succumbing in droves. Never having come into contact with these contagions before, Indians lacked the proper immunities to them. That is not to say they lacked the necessary genetic equipment to manufacture appropriate antibodies and so forth, for it would appear that under conducive circumstances they could indeed produce the requisite resistance. The staggering death rate, argues the biological historian Alfred Crosby, Jr., is attributable instead to the manner in which infections were experienced and treated.

Crosby has found evidence to suggest that the major Indian killers (e.g., smallpox and influenza) were most lethal to persons in the age range fifteen to forty years. Infants, he has discovered, were also especially vulnerable, since weaning was typically late in Indian societies and the drying up of a mother's milk spelled doom for the nursing child. Besides the fact that these contagions were most potent among the most productive members of society, there are indications that diseases typically arrived in clusters, and the clusters came in a series punctuated by brief interludes of respite. Consequently, there might be a period when a community was being ravaged by three or four diseases, followed by a few years of remission, followed by another bout with perhaps a different set of microbes. The insidious periodicity of the diseases along with the plurality of diseases goes far toward explaining why native societies were hardly able to develop an adequate immune response—they were rarely given an adequate breathing spell.

When disease did strike, finds Crosby, Indians often reacted in the worst way possible. Terrified, unable to care for themselves, and abandoned by their equally frightened kin, many simply gave up hope. Those who fled effectively carried the disease agents to other communities where the sickness spread just as rapidly as it had in the home community—there was scarcely any concept of quarantine. A common treatment, and often a lethal one, was to take a sweatbath followed by a plunge in a frigid body of water. Many people drowned doing this, when they discovered to their horror that they were too weak to pull themselves out of the river or lake. Those who survived the plunge often found themselves even worse off than before. In many instances, bewildered and distraught victims, determined not to let the grim contagion take its anticipated toll, prematurely destroyed themselves.[20]

This, then, is the context in which we should view the Micmac confrontation with alien disease. Once again, it is problematical when these pathogens first arrived, although it is reasonable to assume they were transmitted by the European fishermen spoken of above. Explorers also no doubt served as sources of infection. In Jacques Cartier's journal, for instance, we find that some sort of epidemic broke out in the neighboring Indian village of Stadacona (present-day Québec) in December of 1535 while Cartier and his party were wintering nearby. Afraid that the disease would soon spread to the French camp, Cartier ordered all communication with the Indians terminated and confined his men to their quarters. His precautions, it seemed—or at least he thought—were futile, since a disease, obviously scurvy, soon worked its way through the French encampment. Cartier assumed it had originated with the local Indians—which it had not, maintains Carl Sauer, who points out that the Indian diet was sufficiently rich in ascorbic acid (vitamin C) to prevent their contracting scurvy. Moreover, scurvy is not a communicable disease. Sauer's point is well taken, especially considering the fact that these very Indians soon showed Cartier how to cure the illness. "The French were not stricken by contagion from the Indians, but the Indians were infected by the French, as was commonly the case when natives first came into close contact with Europeans. In this case the sickness broke out among the Indians in early winter, after they were confined by cold weather to close quarters and new pathogens brought by Europeans found optimal reception and propagation."[21]

Among the so-called Cross-bearing Micmac of the Miramichi River district there was a tradition extant in the late seventeenth century which vividly illustrates the demoralizing effect these protohistoric diseases had on them. As it was related to Father Le Clercq, there was once "a time when their country was afflicted with a very dangerous and deadly malady which had reduced them to an extreme destitution in every respect and had already sent many of them to their graves." While in this dire condition—"overwhelmed with weariness and despair at seeing a desolation so general and the impending ruin of the entire Gaspesian [Micmac] nation"—several of the leading men of the community fell into a deep sleep. "It was, say they, in this sleep filled with bitterness that a man, beautiful as could be, appeared to them with a Cross in his hand. He told them to take heart, to go back to their homes, to make Crosses like that which were shown them, and to present these to the heads of families with the assurance that if they would receive the Crosses with respect they would find these without question the remedy for all their ills." They followed his directions, and were astonished and relieved to find "that the Cross stopped all at once this torrent of sickness and death which was desolating" them. Consequently, the cross became for them a potent spiritual symbol to which they appealed whenever they felt the need for guidance. Yet they apostatized.

Since this Gaspesian nation of the Cross-bearers has been almost wholly destroyed, as much by the war which they have waged with the Iroquois as by the maladies which have infected this land, and which, in three or four visitations, have caused the deaths of a very great number, these Indians have gradually relapsed from this first devotion of their ancestors. So true is it, that even the holiest and most religious practices, by a certain fatality attending human affairs, suffer always much alteration if they are not animated and conserved by the same spirit which gave them birth. In brief, when I went into their country to commence my mission, I found some persons who had preserved only the shadow of the customs of their ancestors.[22, f]

Apparently their rituals had failed to save these Indians when threatened by European diseases and intergroup hostilities; hence their old ritualistic practices were abandoned, no doubt because of their ineffectiveness.

f. The Recollet fathers, and more particularly Father Emanuel Jumeau, were able to stimulate a renaissance of the traditional ritual by encouraging these people to look to the cross once more for their salvation, although, of course, this time it was a Christian cross. We should keep in mind that the cross was an art motif common among non-Christian people and of independent origin from that of the Christian cross. Whether or not the cross mentioned in this particular tradition was of Christian or aboriginal provenience should make little difference, for the story still serves to illustrate the process of apostatization.

Alien disease did more than decimate the native population; it effectively prepared the way for subsequent phases of European contact by breaking native morale and, perhaps even more significantly, by cracking their spiritual edifice.[23] It is my contention that European disease rendered the Indian's (particularly the shaman's) ability to control and otherwise influence the supernatural realm dysfunctional[24]—because his magic and other traditional cures were now ineffective—thereby causing him to apostatize (in effect); this in turn subverted the "retaliation" principle of taboo and opened the way to a corruption of the Indian-land relationship which soon gathered momentum under the influence of the fur trade.

Le Clercq was by no means the only Frenchman who was appalled by the destruction wrought by the new diseases. In pre-contact times, declared Denys with no doubt some exaggeration, "they [the Micmac] were not subject to diseases, and knew nothing of fevers." Yet, since the whites had arrived, "they are astonished and often complain that . . . they are dying fast, and the population is thinning out," recorded Biard. "For they assert that, before this association and intercourse, all their countries were very populous, and they tell how one by one the different coasts, according as they have begun to traffic with us, have been more reduced by disease."[25] The Micmac patriarch, Membertou,

assures us that in his youth he has seen *chimonutz*, that is to say, Savages, as thickly planted there as the hairs upon his head. It is maintained that they have thus diminished since the French have begun to frequent their country; for, since then they do nothing all summer but eat; and the result is that, adopting an entirely different custom and thus breeding new diseases, they pay for their indulgence during the autumn and winter by pleurisy, quinsy [severe tonsillitis] and dysentery, which kills them off. During this year alone [1611] sixty have died at Cape de la Hève, which is the greater part of those who lived there; yet not one of all M. de Potrincourt's little colony [of Frenchmen at Port-Royal] has even been sick, notwithstanding all the privations they have suffered; which has caused the Savages to apprehend that God protects and defends us as his favorite and well-beloved people.[26]

Perhaps the French were endeavoring to poison them, reasoned the natives, or maybe the French surreptitiously gave poison to some of the more unscrupulous Indians, urging them to administer it to their brethren. "Others complain that the merchandise is often counterfeited and adulterated, and that peas, beans, prunes, bread, and other things that are spoiled are sold to them [by the French]; and that it is that which corrupts the body and gives rise to the dysentery and other diseases which always attack them in Autumn. This theory likewise is not offered without citing instances," nervously wrote Biard, "for which they have often been upon the point of breaking with us, and making war upon us. Indeed there would be great need of providing against these detestable murders by some suitable remedy if one could be found."[27, g]

Biard, once again, attributed the increased death rate to the debauched life these Indians were living during the summer months when they trafficked with the French. During the trading season, he charged, they gorged themselves on unhealthy foods—"various kinds of food not suitable to the inactivity of their lives"— which they washed down with quantities of wine and brandy. And this was compounded by another problem: they simply refused to plan ahead, preferring to consume all they had in feasting

g. It was common for Indians in seventeenth-century New France to accuse the French, especially the ubiquitous and mysterious priests, of maliciously spreading disease. See, for example, James P. Ronda, " 'We Are Well As We Are': An Indian Critique of Seventeenth-Century Christian Missions," *William and Mary Quarterly* 34 (January 1977):66–82; and Cornelius J. Jaenen, *Friend and Foe: Aspects of French-Amerindian Cultural Contact in the Sixteenth and Seventeenth Centuries* (New York: Columbia University Press, 1976), pp. 98–104. This explanation, however, was probably not advanced until after these people had been ravaged for some years by the Europeans' diseases. As I will suggest, further on, malevolent animals were quite likely selected as the initial culprits causing the diseases, that is, in the years before the victims experienced sustained contact with European carriers and learned to include them among the probable sources of contagion. By the seventeenth century, Frenchmen were blamed either *along with* wildlife or *instead of* wildlife for disease, or so I would hypothesize.

One should bear in mind that the first wave of epidemics, such as that recounted for Le Clercq by the Cross-bearers, was more than likely not associated with a human source—certainly not a European source. The relatively few Europeans who seeded the coastal areas with their lethal microbes were never beheld by the majority of their victims, since the epidemics they triggered were spread inland by infected natives. Given these circumstances, and the Indian's tendency to associate serious illness with offended wildlife spirits rather than infected humans, it is not unreasonable to assume that animals were the first to be blamed for maliciously spreading disease.

and merriment rather than lay some of it away for future needs. As a result of these calamities and indiscretions, the Micmac population had been reduced to about three thousand souls by the second decade of the seventeenth century, according to information supplied by his native sources. Recovery was slowed by the fact that, in Biard's words, Micmac women were "not very prolific, for at most they do not have children oftener than every two years, and they are not able to nourish their offspring if they have them oftener, as they nurse them for three years if they can."[28] In modern medical jargon, they were practicing birth spacing through prolonged lactation which, along with infanticide, abortion, and abstinence, constitutes one of the most universal and effective methods of population control among hunter-gatherers.[29]

Even as they reeled from the effects of European diseases, the Micmac managed to preserve their enormous vanity, wrote Biard with ill-concealed disdain. He found it incredible that these "savages" would honestly fancy themselves more clever, courageous, wealthy, and in general a better sort of people than the French. " 'For,' they say, 'you [Frenchmen] are always fighting and quarreling among yourselves; we live peaceably. You are envious and are all the time slandering each other; you are thieves and deceivers; you are covetous, and are neither generous nor kind; as for us, if we have a morsel of bread we share it with our neighbor.' " Elsewhere, he accused the Micmac of "self-aggrandizement." "You will see these poor barbarians, notwithstanding their great lack of government, power, letters, art and riches, yet holding their heads so high that they greatly underrate us, regarding themselves as our superiors."[30]

More than a half-century later the Micmac were still defending their life-style before a hostile French audience. Le Clercq recorded a powerful speech delivered by a native spokesman, who began by observing that his people were happier than the French because they were satisfied with what little they had. France must indeed be an impoverished place, he mused; otherwise the French would not subject themselves to such great personal discomfort to enrich themselves on these shores. The dissatisfaction and penury of the French were manifest in their greed for the

" 'old rags and . . . miserable suits of beaver which can no longer be of use to us, and . . . in the fishery for cod which you make in these parts, the wherewithal to comfort your misery and the poverty which oppresses you.' " The Indians, maintained the speaker, were satisfied by the conveniences they found readily at hand, and he contrasted his people's contentment with the work ethic of the French which made them obsessive codfishers. Codfish were so basic to the French diet that when they got bored with it and wished for " 'some good morsels, it is at our expense; and you are obliged to have recourse to the Indians, whom you despise so much, and to beg them to go a-hunting that you may be regaled.' "

Continuing to delineate the pleasures of Indian life vis-à-vis the cares of the French, he reminded the Recollet that his people had lived longer before the arrival of the French, with their bread and wine. But as they gradually adopted the French manner of living so, too, did their longevity decrease. Experience showed that those Indians lived longer who declined French bread, wine, and brandy, choosing instead " 'their natural food of beaver, of moose, of waterfowl, and fish, in accord with the custom of our ancestors and of all the Gaspesian nation.' "

Finally, he summed up his harangue, " 'there is no Indian who does not consider himself infinitely more happy and more powerful than the French.' " For the freedom to live anywhere and be assured of a livelihood, to be his own master with unrestricted hunting and fishing rights, without anxiety, all made the Gaspesian unquestionably more content than the Frenchman.

Le Clercq, who bore the brunt of this diatribe, felt compelled to confess that his informant was correct in his comparison of French and Micmac life. Overlooking their ignorance of Christianity, wrote the Recollet, the Micmac indeed led a peaceful, contented, harmonious existence.[31, h]

h. Although exaggerated in several points of ethnohistorical detail, this speech is revealing in its ringing condemnation of the French character, motives, and institutions. The possibility of its being fictive, or at least partly embroidered by the recorder, is real. Other European commentators (e.g., Lahontan in his famous interview with the sachem Adario) are known to have put high-flown orations in the mouths of imaginary Indian spokesmen in order to vent their

There could be no shunting aside of the Christian mysteries, however, despite whatever virtues the heathen life could boast. That sweet message would bring civilization and salvation to the "savage." To Biard, the mission was clear: "For, if our Souriquois [Micmac] are few, they may become numerous; if they are savages, it is to domesticate and civilize them that we have come here; if they are rude, that is no reason that we should be idle; if they have until now profited little, it is no wonder, for it would be too much to expect fruit from this grafting, and to demand reason and maturity from a child. In conclusion, we hope in time to make them susceptible of receiving the doctrines of the faith and of the christian and catholic religion, and later, to penetrate further into the regions beyond. . . ."[32] The message was simple and straightforward: the blackrobes would enlighten the Indians by ridiculing their animism and related taboos, discrediting their shamans, and urging them to accept the Christian gospel. But to their chagrin the Micmac proved stubborn in their ancient ways, no matter how unsuited to changing circumstances.[33]

Since the advent of European diseases and the consequent disillusionment with native spiritual beliefs and customs, some Indians appear to have repudiated their traditional world view on their own initiative, while others clung desperately to what had become a moribund body of ritual. One would expect that the Christian message was more readily accepted by the former, while the latter group, which included the shamans and those too old to change, would have fought bitterly against the missionary teaching.[34] But they resisted in vain for, with time, old people died and those shamans whose magic was less potent than that of the missionaries were discredited.[35, i] What eventually

personal disenchantment with Old World society. But in this case the views recorded by Le Clercq are confirmed in essence by Biard (see, e.g., Reuben Gold Thwaites, ed., *The Jesuit Relations and Allied Documents: Travels and Explorations of the Jesuit Missionaries in New France, 1610–1791*, 73 vols. [Cleveland: The Burrows Brothers Company, 1896–1901], 2:79; 3:83, 85, 135, 123, hereafter cited as *Jesuit Relations*), lending credence to their authenticity.

i. See Father Chrestien Le Clercq, *New Relation of Gaspesia, with the Customs and Religion of the Gaspesian Indians* (1691), translated and edited by William F. Ganong (Toronto: The Champlain Society, 1910), pp. 220–221, where he speaks of converting a noted shaman to Christianity. André Vachon, emerged from this clash of belief systems was an amalgam of both. Speaking of the Eastern Algonkian area in general, Alfred Bailey notes that

by a process of blending, some of the Christian deities and sacred personages were identified or confused with Algonkian supernatural beings. Possibly sometimes the local beings were supplanted or thrust into the background. Thus, Jesus, a powerful deity of the Europeans was at first identified with the sun or the spirit that dwelt within it. Gluskap [the Micmac culture hero] played the part of Noah or of the instigator of the flood while at the same time retaining some of his own characteristics. At other times he was the rival or the forerunner of Christ. The guardian spirits and other supernatural beings were akin in function to the Christian saints. In more than one case a malicious trickster no doubt degenerated into the person of Satan. Dreams were extremely vivid forms of religious experience which at first hindered but eventually aided conversion after they had assumed a Christian character.[36, j]

It is important to recognize that the missionary was successful only to the degree that his power exceeded that of the shaman. The nonliterate Indian was awed, for example, by the magic of handwriting as a means of communication.[37] Even more significant was the fact that Christianity was the religion of the white man, who, with his impressive technology and greater success

"L'Eau-de-vie dans la société indienne," in the Canadian Historical Association . . . *Report* of the Annual Meeting (1960):22–32, has observed that the priest replaced the shaman and sorcerer in Indian society by virtue of his superior power. By discrediting his Indian counterpart and rival, the priest became the shaman-sorcerer (i.e., a source of both good and evil power). See Alfred Goldsworthy Bailey, *The Conflict of European and Eastern Algonkian Cultures, 1504–1700: A Study in Canadian Civilization*, Publications of the New Brunswick Museum, Monographic Series No. 2 (St. John, New Brunswick, 1937), p. 145; and Robert Conkling, "Legitimacy and Conversion in Social Change: The Case of French Missionaries and the Northeastern Algonkian," *Ethnohistory* 21 (Winter 1974):1–24.

j. See Gertrude P. Kurath, "Blackrobe and Shaman: The Christianization of Michigan Algonquians," *Papers of the Michigan Academy of Science, Arts and Letters* 44, 1958 meeting (1959):209–215, for a superb discussion of the Jesuit program among the Central Algonkians. Madeleine and Jacques Rousseau, "Le Dualisme religieux des peuplades de la forêt boréale," in *Proceedings and Selected Papers of the 29th International Congress of Americanists: Acculturation in the Americas*, edited by Sol Tax, vol. 2, pp. 118–126 (Chicago: University of Chicago Press, 1952), speak of a dualistic religion among modern-day Québec Algonkians, where Christian and aboriginal beliefs are both adhered to in the same individual—the two systems all the while remaining distinct.

at manipulating life to his advantage, was believed to have recourse to a greater Power (manitou) than the Indian. In the native
intellect, an object was efficacious according to the degree of
Power it housed; the more functional a tool, the more Power it
obviously possessed. For example, the Micmac believed that there
was a spirit of his canoe, of his snowshoes, of his bow, and so
forth. For this reason a man's material goods were either buried
with him or burned, in order that their spirits might accompany
his to the spirit world, where he would need them. Just as he had
hunted game in this physical-spiritual world, so his spirit would
again hunt the game spirits with the spirits of his weapons in the
land of the dead.[38] Denys, in a charming episode, underscored
the fact that even European trading goods were considered animated when he related how the copper kettle was known to have
lost its spirit (or died) when it no longer rang when tapped.[39]

In a very real sense, European technology of the sixteenth and
seventeenth centuries was largely incompatible with the spiritual
beliefs of the Eastern Canadian Indians, despite the observation
made above that the Micmac readily invested trading goods with
spiritual power akin to that possessed by their own implements.
As Denys pointed out, the trade goods which the Micmac so
eagerly accepted were accompanied by Christian religious teaching and French custom, both of which gave definition to these
alien objects. By accepting the European material culture, the
natives were thus impelled to accept the European abstract culture, especially the European religion. The result was that their
own spiritual beliefs were subverted as they abandoned their
implements for those of the white man. Native spiritual beliefs
lost not only their practical effectiveness, in part owing to the
replacement of the traditional magical and animistic view of nature by the monotheistic and exploitive European view, but they
were no longer necessary as a source of definition and theoretical
support for the new Europe-derived material culture. Western
technology, in a word, made more "sense" if it was accompanied
by Western religion: Christianity.[k]

k. See Ralph Linton, *The Study of Man: An Introduction* (New York: D.
Appleton-Century Company, 1936), chapter 23; Homer G. Barnett, "Culture

For these reasons Christianity, which to the Micmac was the ritual harnessing all of this Power, became a potent force among them. And yet the priests who worked among the Indians frequently complained of their relapsing into heathenism, largely because the Micmac came to associate Christianity and civilization in general with their numerous misfortunes, together with the fact that they never clearly understood the Christian message but always saw it in terms of their own cosmology.[40,1]

Just as all religious systems reflect their cultural milieux, so did seventeenth-century Christianity. Polygamy was condemned by the French missionaries as immoral, the consultation of shamans was discouraged, the custom of interring material goods was criticized, eat-all feasts were denounced as gluttonous and improvident, and the Indians were successfully "disabused" of many of their so-called superstitions (i.e., taboos). "They had in old times many beliefs [taboos] of this kind, which they have no more at the present time, and of which we have disabused them," confirmed Denys.[41] The French clergy and laity, in short, attacked the Micmac culture with a marvelous fervor and some success.[m] Although they could not have appreciated it, they were aided in this endeavor by an obsolescent system of taboo and spiritual awareness; Christianity merely delivered the coup de grace.

The result of this Christian onslaught on a decaying Micmac cosmology was of course the despiritualization of the material

Processes," *American Anthropologist*, n.s. 42 (January-March 1940):21–48; Barnett, "Invention and Cultural Change," *American Anthropologist* 44 (January-March 1942):14–30; and Melville J. Herskovits, *Man and His Works: The Science of Cultural Anthropology* (New York: Alfred A. Knopf, 1948), chapter 32, on the borrowing and rejection of alien cultural elements. See Selwyn Dewdney, *The Sacred Scrolls of the Southern Ojibway* (Toronto: University of Toronto Press for the Glenbow-Alberta Institute, 1975), p. 159.

l. See *Jesuit Relations*, 2:89, where baptism was misunderstood by the Micmac (of Port-Royal, at least) "as a sort of sacred pledge of friendship and alliance with the French."

m. Le Clercq, *New Relation of Gaspesia*, p. 225, reported, for instance, that since the introduction of Christianity, and especially baptism, the "Devil" had not afflicted the Indians to the degree that he did formerly. See also Le Clercq, *New Relation of Gaspesia*, pp. 229–233, where there are cases recorded of native men and women who seemed to feel a divine call and ordination, representing themselves as Christian priests among their fellows.

world.[42] Commenting on this secularization process, Denys (who was a spectator to this transformation in the mid-seventeenth century) remarked that it was accomplished with "much difficulty"; for some of the Indians it was achieved by religious means, while others were influenced by the French customs, but nearly all were affected "by the need for the things which come from us, the use of which has become to them an indispensable necessity. They have abandoned all their own utensils, whether because of the trouble they had as well to make as to use them, or because of the facility of obtaining from us, in exchange for skins which cost them almost nothing, the things which seemed to them invaluable, not so much for their novelty as for the convenience they derived therefrom."[43, n]

Under such early contact circumstances, the Micmac's role within his ecosystem changed radically. No longer was he the sensitive fellow-member of a symbolic world; under pressure from disease, European trade, and Christianity, he had apostatized—he had repudiated his role within the ecosystem. Former attitudes were replaced by a kind of mongrel outlook which combined some native traditions and beliefs with a European rationale and motivation. My concern here is less to document this transformation than to assess its impact on the Indian-land relationship. In these terms, then, what effect did the trade have on the Micmac ecosystem?

The most obvious change was the unrestrained slaughter of certain game. Lured by European commodities, equipped with European technology, urged by European traders,[o] deprived of

n. In return for skins of beaver, otter, marten, and moose, and of other furbearers, the Indians received a variety of fairly cheap commodities, principally tobacco, liquor, powder and shot (in later years), biscuit, peas, beans, flour, assorted clothing, wampum, copper kettles, and hunting tools. Marc Lescarbot, *The History of New France* (1618; first published 1609), translated by W. L. Grant, 3 vols. (Toronto: The Champlain Society, 1907–1914), 2:281–282, 323–324; 3:158, 168, 250; *Jesuit Relations*, 3:75–77; Le Clercq, *New Relation of Gaspesia*, pp. 93–94, 109; Sieur de Dièreville, *Relation of the Voyage to Port Royal in Acadia of New France* (1708), translated by Mrs. Clarence Webster and edited by John Clarence Webster (Toronto: The Champlain Society, 1933), pp. 132–133, 139–141.

o. See *Jesuit Relations*, 1:175–177; and Nicolas Denys, *The Description and Natural History of the Coasts of North America (Acadia)* (1672), translated

a sense of responsibility and accountability for the land, and no longer inhibited by taboo, the Micmac began to overkill systematically those wildlife which had now become so profitable and even indispensable to his new way of life. The pathos of this transformation of attitude and behavior is illustrated by an incident recorded by Le Clercq. The Indians, who still believed that the beaver had "sense" and formed a "separate nation," maintained that they "would cease to make war upon these animals if these would speak, howsoever little, in order that they might learn whether the Beavers are among their friends or their enemies."[44] Dièreville, the surgeon-botanist, conveyed a kindred sentiment in some wretched verse on the art of beaver hunting.

> They [the natives] take precautions in regard to all
> The varied needs of life. The Indian Race,
> Well qualified to judge the point, because
> Of its familiarity with all their arts,
> Believe that they [beaver] have been endowed
> With an abounding genius, and hold too
> It is pure malice that they do not talk.[45]

Unfortunately for the beaver, they never communicated their feelings. The natural world of the Indian was becoming inarticulate.

It is interesting that Dièreville, who observed the Micmac culture at the beginning of the eighteenth century, was the only witness to record the native superstition which compelled them to tear out the eyes of "Fish, Birds and Beasts." Such an act evidently served to blind the lingering spirit of the animal to the irreverent treatment accorded its carcass. To have left the eyes intact would have risked having the spirit witness the outrage, whereupon it would surely inform the surviving members of its kind of the act and these, in their turn, would resist capture.[46] The failure of earlier commentators to mention this particular superstition suggests that it was of fairly recent origin, a manifestation of the general spiritual decay and overexploitation of game which were characteristic of the Micmac way of life by

and edited by William F. Ganong (Toronto: The Champlain Society, 1908), p. 439, for confirmation of the French lust for furs.

the turn of the century. To the Micmac mind, haunted by memories of a former time, the practice may have been intended to hide his guilt and insure his continued success.[p]

Along with this depletion of wildlife went a reduction of dependency on the resources of the local ecosystem. The use of improved hunting equipment, such as fishing line and hooks, axes, knives, muskets, and iron-tipped arrows, spears, and harpoons,[47] exerted heavier pressure on the resources of the area, while the availability of French foodstuffs shifted the position of the Micmac in the trophic system, decreasing his dependency somewhat on local food sources as it placed him partly outside of the system. To be sure, a decreasing native population relieved this pressure to a degree, but, according to evidence cited above, not enough to prevent the abuse of the land.

Other, less obvious results of the fur trade were the increased incidence of feuding and the modification of the Micmac settlement patterns to meet the demands of the trade.[48] Liquor, in particular brandy, quickly became a favorite item of trade—one for which the Indians "would go a long way."[49, q] And its effects were devastating. Both Jean Saint-Vallier (François Laval's successor as bishop of Québec) and Biard blamed liquor as a prime

p. Father Robert J. Sullivan, S. J., was informed by his Koyukon (Athapaskan) hosts in the 1930s that hunters would destroy a slain bear's eyes for fear of reprisal from the offended animal's spirit.

The Ten'a [Koyukon] believe that the *yega* [spirit] of the bear is very powerful, so precautions are taken even after the animal has been killed. The first thing a man does after he catches a bear is cut off the fore-paws; he is afraid that the bear *yega* would somehow enable the bear to follow him and inflict harm on him, if he neglected to do this. Then he must burst the eyes or punch them out, so the bear cannot see him to injure him in any way. In this connection an account was given me of an incident which took place a few years ago. A native and his son were returning one night from hunting. On their way back they discovered a bear hole, and although they managed to kill the bear, they were unable to pull it out of the hole—and hence couldn't burst the eyes immediately. A year later that man's son was blind, and the people said this happened because they failed to burst the bear's eyes.

Robert J. Sullivan, *The Ten'a Food Quest*, Catholic University of America, Anthropological Series No. 11 (Washington, D.C.: Catholic University of America Press, 1942), p. 86.

q. If we are to believe Craig MacAndrew and Robert B. Edgerton, *Drunken Comportment: A Social Explanation* (Chicago: Aldine Publishing Company, 1969), p. 111, the Kwĕdĕch (Laurentian Iroquois) encountered by Jacques Cartier along the shore of Gaspé Harbor in 1534 were the first historically documented North American tribe to receive European liquor.

cause for the soaring death rate of the natives. Bedlam usually resulted when the Indians got hold of a quantity of liquor, as the inebriates tore into each other in spectacular drunken brawls. At such times the French tried to stay away, but often they too became involved as rampaging Indians would spill over into the French community, pillaging and burning whatever lay in their path. Surprisingly, in spite of all this mayhem, the natives refused to accept any blame for their drunken behavior. They were conveniently possessed by the spirit of the bottle, they protested, and it was he who was responsible for any destruction or loss of life which ensued.[50, r]

European contact should thus be viewed as a "trigger factor," that is, something which was not present in the Micmac ecosystem before and which initiated a concatenation of reactions leading to the replacement of the aboriginal ecosystem by another.[51] European disease, Christianity, and the fur trade with

r. Out of a rather large body of mostly journal literature on contemporary and historic North American Indian drinking habits, alcoholism, and rehabilitation programs, the following studies are recommended for their more broadly theoretical approach to the psychological and cultural dimensions of Indian drinking: Vachon, "L'Eau-de-vie dans la société indienne"; MacAndrew and Edgerton, *Drunken Comportment*; Nancy Oestreich Lurie, "The World's Oldest On-Going Protest Demonstration: North American Indian Drinking Patterns," *Pacific Historical Review* 40 (August 1971):311–332; Donald Horton, "The Functions of Alcohol in Primitive Societies: A Cross-Cultural Study," *Quarterly Journal of Studies on Alcohol* 4 (September 1943):199–320; R. F. Bales, "Cultural Differences in Rates of Alcoholism," *Quarterly Journal of Studies on Alcohol* 6 (March 1946):480–499; Irvin L. Child, Margaret K. Bacon, and Herbert Barry, III, Supplement Number Three, *Quarterly Journal of Studies on Alcohol* (April); Edward P. Dozier, "Problem Drinking among American Indians: The Role of Sociocultural Deprivation," *Quarterly Journal of Studies on Alcohol* 27 (March 1966):72–87. Not all of these analyses deal with American Indian drinking directly or solely—Horton, Bales, and the Child group consider drinking among pre-industrial people in general.

Anyone bothering to read the pertinent literature is immediately struck by the shallowness of a good deal of it and the limited temporal and regional relevance of much that is left. Explanations of Indian motivation range from an urge to recall the "good old days" and the effort to achieve spiritual ecstasy (Vachon), to drinking as a "time out" period (MacAndrew and Edgerton), to drinking as a kind of protest demonstration against oppressive whites (Lurie), to drinking as a means of reducing anxieties resulting from the individual's culturally and socially subordinate status (Dozier, Bales, Horton), to the use of alcohol as a vehicle for satisfying culturally thwarted dependency cravings (Child, Bacon, and Barry). We obviously need some kind of synthesis of this disparate material.

its accompanying technology—the three often intermeshed—
were responsible for the corruption of the Indian-land relationship in which the native had merged himself sympathetically
with his environment. By a lockstep process European disease
rendered the Indian's control over the supernatural realm inoperative, and the disillusioned Micmac apostatized, debilitating
taboo and preparing the way for the destruction of wildlife
which was soon to occur under the stimulation of the trade. For
those who believed in it, Christianity furnished a new, dualistic
world view, lending spiritual support to the fur trade by elevat-
ing man above Nature and making the hunt profane. Meanwhile, participation in the trade drove the Indian even further
into a position of uncompromising callousness toward Nature,
as he progressively shifted his allegiance from the spirits of his
handicrafts to the secular commodities of Western Europe. The
function of the Indian within his ecosystem now changed from
conservator to despoiler: certain game animals were heavily exploited while others were virtually exterminated. Unfortunately
for the Indian and the land, this grim tale was to be repeated
many times over along the moving Indian-white frontier. Life
for the Micmac had indeed become more convenient, but convenience cost dearly in much material and abstract culture loss
or modification.

PART TWO

The Ojibwa Cosmos and the
Early Fur Trade

CHAPTER THREE

Pimadaziwin: The Good Life

FROM ITS CASUAL beginnings on the shores of the Maritimes, the Canadian fur trade soon spread westward. It was only natural that the trade would find one of its most lucrative and enduring markets in the interior, in that great swath of land bounded by the Great Lakes, Lake Winnipeg, and Hudson Bay. Here were innumerable lakes and ponds—pockets gouged out of of the resilient Canadian Shield by millennia of glacial movement—interconnected by a network of streams. This was lake country, the home of the beaver, muskrat, otter, fisher, marten, and mink.

In the creation myth of the indigenous Indians, these and other beasts were once related to mankind. Chipewyan legend had it that woman was the first human being. In her nocturnal dreams she imagined herself sleeping with a handsome youth, who was in reality her pet dog transformed. One day a giant appeared in the land. With mighty strokes he shaped the rough-hewn landscape into lakes and rivers and mountains—all the landforms we know today. Then he stooped down and caught up the dog, "and tore it to pieces; the guts he threw into the lakes and rivers, commanding them to become the different kinds of fish; the flesh he dispersed over the land, commanding it to become different kinds of beasts and land-animals; the skin he also tore into small pieces, and threw it into the air, commanding it to become all kinds of birds; after which he gave the woman and her offspring full power to kill, eat, and never spare, for that he had commanded them to multiply for her use in abundance."[1,a]

After the creation, in Cree and Ojibwa legend, the culture hero, *Wisekedjak*, was enjoined by the Great Spirit (*Kitchi Manitou*) to teach man and beast how to live properly together. Ignoring his solemn commission, he instead taught pleasure and incited quarrels, and the ground soon became stained with the blood of man and animals. Repeatedly the Great Spirit warned him to end this mutual slaughter, but *Wisekedjak* ignored the admonition. Finally, exasperated to the limit, the Great Spirit destroyed all creation in a flood. Only a beaver, an otter, and a muskrat survived, as they took refuge with the now distraught *Wisekedjak*. When the waters eventually subsided, man and all other life-forms were remade, but *Wisekedjak*, the "Flatterer," was stripped of his great authority. From then on he was to be a deceiver only: a trickster-transformer.[2]

In those olden days, legend had it, men were mightier than they were now. The beaver were people, as were the bear, lynx, and fox; they lived among man and spoke with him.[3] That was the dawn of creation, an event still vivid in the collective imagination of the Ojibwa, Cree, and Chipewyan at European landfall. Tales of culture hero and trickster-transformer; phallic, cannibal, animal tales; tales of adventure and of passion all originated in those days of heroes and powerful magic.

Early seventeenth-century Jesuits and coureurs de bois who came among the Upper Great Lakes hunting-and-gathering bands could scarcely appreciate this supernaturalistic world view.[b]

a. The "never spare" injunction is not typical of Indian origin myths or other racial recollections, which usually stress wildlife preservation. The present anomaly is probably explained as an attempt by Hearne's Chipewyan traveling companions to rationalize their wasteful slaughter of game before the critical Englishman.

b. I use the word "supernaturalistic" as a convenience for the reader. To the Indian the spirit world was not distinguished from the natural world; for him there was nothing supernatural.

Yet their writings, even with their cramped ethnocentrism, are vital in reconstructing Ojibwa abstract culture. Supplementing these early sources are the records of late observers, including literate Indians and modern ethnographers, which, used in conjunction with Cree and Chipewyan sources, serve to expand our consciousness and understanding of the Ojibwa cosmic view and cultural setting. For all three groups—Cree, Chipewyan, and Ojibwa—shared in large measure the same belief and value system.[4]

Nature, as conceived by the traditional Ojibwa, was a congeries of societies: every animal, fish, and plant species functioned in a society that was parallel in all respects to mankind's. Wildlife and plant-life had homes and families, just as man did. Each species had its leaders, reminiscent of the Micmac cosmology, known in recent years as "bosses"—an apt expression borrowed from the modern lumber camp. In the old days they were more quaintly termed "masters" or "keepers" of the game, and each local band of a particular species was said to have its own boss. Indians are reluctant to talk about these things today, for fear of ridicule; nevertheless, these beings were (and in some areas continue to be) very real to them. Animal, bird, and fish bosses are typically white and larger than the rest of their species. To see one of them is a rare privilege indeed.[5,c]

The game keepers were minor manitous in an Ojibwa universe that is said to have "teemed" with such beings. "Those of the forest clothed themselves with moss," recalled the young Ojibwa chief George Copway; "during a shower of rain, thousands of them are sheltered in a flower. . . . The Ojibway, as he reclines beneath the shade of his forest trees, imagines these gods to be about him. He detects their tiny voices in the insect's hum. With

c. See George Copway, *The Traditional History and Characteristic Sketches of the Ojibway Nation* (London: Charles Gilpin, 1850), pp. 137–139; and Copway, *The life, history, and travels, of Kah-Ge-Ga-Gah-Bowh (George Copway), a young Indian chief of the Ojebwa nation, a convert to the Christian faith, and a missionary to his people for twelve years; with a sketch of the present state of the Ojebwa nation, in regard to Christianity and their future prospects* . . . (Albany: Weed and Parsons, 1847), p. 55, where an Indian inveighs against those whites who, by their ridicule, have shamed the Indian into silence about his traditional beliefs.

half closed eyes he beholds them sporting by thousands on a sunray. In the evening they are seen and heard."[6] Manitous like these saturated the Indian's world. There were many others, some of them remote but still felt.

Kitchi Manitou, the Great Spirit, was the creator and sustainer of all things. A benevolent being equated with the sun by the early Jesuit fathers, he was too physically distant and omnipotent to influence affairs directly. So his will was executed by a descending hierarchy of subordinate manitous, each of whom had a unique function and abode. Evoking an image familiar in American politics, Ruth Landes writes that "among the manitos the mighty ones, like the great birds and beasts, were solitary Characters (a respectful appellation for them) who met in smoke-filled councils to discuss cosmic affairs."[7] Just as everything had a purpose, so everything had its manitou, or spirit, whose power and influence depended on its significance to the Indian. Spectacles of Nature—waterfalls, rivers and lakes, large or peculiarly formed rocks, aged trees—had especially strong manitous. So, too, did the elements, which in the Indian mind were personified: northwind, thunder, lightning, cold, and so forth. All things animate and inanimate had spirit, and hence being.[8]

Man and Nature were conceived of as tripartite beings: each had body, soul, and shadow. The soul was the seat of being, the life principle. Should it ever become lost (in sleep or unconsciousness) or stolen (by a malevolent conjuror), the individual would be accounted dead, even though his life signs might show him alive and healthy. Shadow, the third part, was the "eye" of the soul, since through it the soul was informed.[9]

The aboriginal Ojibwa was thoroughly immersed in this great and complex system which he strove to manipulate to his advantage. Man's niche or, more appropriately, his purpose in the natural order was to live the Good Life: *pimadaziwin*, in Ojibwa. "The central goal of life for the Ojibwa," wrote the ethnologist A. Irving Hallowell, "is expressed by the term *pimadaziwin*, life in the fullest sense, life in the sense of longevity, health and freedom from misfortune."[10] In the words of Matonabbee, Samuel Hearne's Chipewyan guide, "These people have . . . 'nothing to do but consult their own interest, inclinations, and passions; and to pass through this world with as much ease and contentment as possible.'"[11] This was what each individual normally expected for himself; if it was not forthcoming, *someone* was to blame. Events could legitimately be personalized because they were either personalities (or beings) in their own right—as were legends and myths—or they were perpetrated by human or "other-than-human" persons.[12] Hence, if the Good Life was to be realized man was obliged to address himself to this composite society of life in a way that would be least likely to give offense. Success for the Ojibwa therefore depended upon his paying scrupulous attention to innumerable details of comportment.

Lest such a life seem unduly precarious, it should be emphasized that the Indian implicitly believed he had a right to success: as long as he conformed to the rules of the system he could fear nothing. This was the ideal, at any rate. In reality, the rules were constantly broken, and this often unconsciously. *Pimadaziwin* could be restored by hiring a conjuror to reveal the source of the problem, if it were not already known, followed either by public confession of the designated transgression (in recent years, anyway) or by some other appropriate remedy. In modern times, at least, a disease sanction against socially disapproved acts—inhospitality, stinginess, ridicule, the selection of a marriage partner not of the cross-cousin category, sexual deviancy, and so on—has operated as a highly effective means of maintaining normative behavior: proscribed behavior results in punishment (as disease), which is relieved through public confession, which in turn reinforces the canons of normative behavior and accentuates the disease sanction concept.[13]

As we extend these ideas further, we come to realize that the key to understanding the Indian's role within Nature lies within the notion of mutual obligation: man and Nature both had to adhere to a prescribed behavior toward one another. If the Indian had any concept of a balance of Nature, this was it. Catastrophe resulted when either one or both parties broke the contract by some extraordinary act which caused injury to the other. For, in contrast to the exalted position of man in Judeo-Christian tradition, Ojibwa cosmology conferred upon the Indian a rather humble stature. What innate intellectual or physical abilities did mankind have that would rank him above the rest of creation, reasoned the Indian? Surely he was not as sagacious as the beaver, who could build a lodge, fell trees, make burrows, and dam a watercourse with such ingenuity. Nor did he have the remarkable instincts of many other species.[14] Man, instead, had been given the awesome right to harvest Nature: he was, by definition, the hunter and gatherer, dependent upon wildlife and plant-life for his subsistence.[15] All his livelihood—his tools, weapons, clothing, shelter, food, etc.—was collected from these other life-forms. He knew that he must never abuse them by taking more than he needed for the present,[16] nor insult them through ridicule or blasphemy,[17] nor torture them in any fashion.[18] For their part animals, fish, birds, and plants were to yield themselves up to man for his needs. This relationship of the hunter to the hunted, and its perversion following white contact, will be explored in greater detail later on, in a subsequent chapter. Suffice it to say for now that the Ojibwa hunter was acutely aware of the boundaries of propriety which he was not to transgress. If he did he ran the risk of revenge from outraged game spirits. Conversely, wildlife were not to subject man to duress, since he in turn might retaliate with his arsenal of sanctions.

The Indian child reared in this kind of behavioral environment was taught that nothing was profane. Every activity, whether it be hostile, sociable, subsistence, or whatever, had spiritual overtones; all of his relations and functions were above all else spiritual. The socialization process drilled this into the youth until it became his guiding principle. On the practical level, this meant that the Indian would approach every situation fortified with spiritual power. Life was, by definition, a spiritual enterprise.[19]

Consequently, in Ojibwa society, the newborn male was conferred a name suggestive of success, generally in the hunt, since by its meaning a name conveyed magical power. The puberty fast marked the next rite of passage—the critical transition from childhood to adulthood. On this most solemn occasion the youth entreated the spirit beings of the universe for guidance throughout the rest of his life.

One summer in a wood, he was to examine his ambitions and prostrate himself through ritual fasting, thirsting, sleeplessness, fierce concentration on the goal of "seeing and hearing" a well-disposed manito, weeping and blackening his face with charcoal from the fireplace and rubbing ashes on his hair. He recalled all he had heard about "power," in his ears were the pleas of grandparents and parents to "make something" of himself, "to fill [his] emptiness." To the manitos he declared his pitiableness, his utter dependence on spiritual aid, the desperateness of life. Through the miasma of hysterical fear there came to the fortunate seeker—dry-mouthed, empty-bellied, and light-headed—a kindly spirit voice that assured, "My grandson, here is something with which to amuse yourself. . . ."[20]

The manitou instructed the lad to gather certain articles and place them in a pouch, a medicine bag, which from thenceforth would hold the charms needed for success. Possessed of his tutelary spirit and medicine the youth was finally prepared to meet the world on its own terms.[21]

The puberty fast, explained Hallowell, signified the change in a boy's dependence on human to super-human beings. A new set of obligations accompanied the transformation.

He must respect his blessings and use them carefully. In effect, the basic principle involved might be stated as the obligation to preserve the equilibrium of nature. Nature's bounty depends on his using his powers skillfully, being self-reliant, ready to endure hardship, even starvation. He may be aggressive, predatory, in relation to the flora and fauna of his habitat, for his was a food-gathering and hunting economy. But he must only take what he actually needed to provide food, clothing and warmth for himself and his family. He must not be destructive or greedy, and he must never torture any animal. If he acts otherwise the animals will be withdrawn from him by the superhuman entities who directed them to him. In the end he will destroy himself since neither the material nor spiritual sources of life will be any longer available to him.[22]

Together with fasting, dreams constituted another means of direct communication with the spirit world. Through them spirit beings intruded upon man's consciousness, instructing him what he must do upon awaking, or forewarning of danger, or possibly giving insight to a perplexing problem. The dreamer seemed to sense which dreams were frivolous and which were not, and in these latter he placed absolute faith. Whenever dreams and fasts and divination (often scapulimancy—divining with a scapula) failed to inform, there was always the conjuror to turn to. By means of his greater powers of spiritual coercion the supplicant might succeed in obtaining satisfaction. Fasting, dreaming, and conjuring thus provided a conduit for dialogue between the spirit world and man.

Super-human aid was likewise crucial in Ojibwa subsistence pursuits, as will become more evident further on. Friendly spirit helpers—a man's own and those of sympathetic game bosses— whose services were augmented by potent magical charms and a good bit of cunning, were the prerequisites to hunting success. Paradoxically, there was nothing in this to suggest foul play, for man and beast had agreed that each of these was a legitimate technique, or in Harvey Feit's apt terminology, "recipe," in the chase.[23]

Clearly the Micmac had a great deal in common with their Eastern Subarctic brethren: both groups shared a profoundly animistic view of the universe. As was the case with the Micmac, these interior tribes endowed mechanical tools with both spirit and body, the understanding being that the spirit was the animating force, rendering a tool effective or useless.[24] Samuel Hearne was deeply perplexed by this conviction on the part of his Chipewyan companions. He derided as a "superstition" that which prompted them to tie "birds bills and feet" and the "toes and jaws of . . . otters and jackashes" to newly made fishing nets. "Unless some or all of these be fastened to the net, they will not attempt to put it into the water, as they firmly believe it will not catch a single fish." The first fish caught in such a net was to be ritualistically broiled as a first-fruits offering. "A strict observance of these rules is supposed to be of the utmost importance in promoting the future success of the new net; and a neglect of them would not render it worth a farthing." Added he in a note, "They frequently sell new nets, which have not been successful." Rivalry between nets was another problem to watch out for, he discovered, for if they were positioned too close to one another, "one net would be jealous of its neighbour, and by that means not one of them would catch a single fish."[25]

Fishing with hook and line was hedged about by "equally absurd" superstitions.

For when they bait a hook, a composition of four, five, or six articles, by way of charm, is concealed under the bait, which is always sewed round the hook. In fact, the only bait used by those people is in their opinion a composition of charms, inclosed within a bit of fish skin, so as in some measure to resemble a small fish. The things used by way of charm, are bits of beavers tails and fat, otter's vents and teeth, muskrat's guts and tails, loon's vents, squirrel's testicles, the cruddled milk taken out of the stomach of sucking fawns and calves, human hair, and numberless other articles equally absurd. Every master of a family, and indeed almost every other person, particularly the men, have a small bundle of such trash, which they always carry with them, both in Summer and Winter; and without some of those articles to put under their bait, few of them could be prevailed upon to put a hook into the water, being fully persuaded that they may as well sit in the tent, as attempt to angle without such assistance. . . . The same rule is observed on broiling the first fruits of a new hook that is used for a new net; an old hook that has already been successful in catching large fish is esteemed of more value, than a handful of new ones which have never been tried.[26]

Hunting magic, both imitative and contagious, was thus the order of the day. The northern Indians operated on the principle that game could be tricked, cajoled, and coerced into their hands. The first of these schemes, deception, was a favorite ploy. Animal shadows, so the theory went, were constantly on the alert for the hunter—actually the hunter's shadow. In fact, Diamond Jenness was informed by Parry Island Ojibwa that one of the principal reasons for their changing hunting territories was because their shadows would become too familiar to the animal shadows. It was well known that animals hid themselves from hunters whom they recognized. Based on the premise that animals are psychologically identical to man, particular rules of conduct were necessary for the hunter to deceive successfully the game shadows. Jenness explained: "A primary rule in hunting is not to concentrate all your attention on the game you are seeking. Look at the trees around you and consider whether they are suitable for making fishspears or can be turned to other uses. Examine the plants at your feet and consider whether they will make beneficial medicines." Animals are readily duped by man, so he was told. "The shadow of the deer (or moose) will be thrown off its guard, will believe that you are not engaged in hunting, and will fail to carry back a warning" to its congeners. Charcoal was often smeared on the face to disguise the hunter's visage " 'and throw the animals off their guard.' "[27]

Starving times called for another form of deception. Whites were frequently confounded by the Indians' ability to endure severe, protracted hunger with a completely detached air. Rather than betray their anxiety they usually went to the other extreme and assumed a joyful demeanor. The motive behind this peculiar, seemingly contradictory, behavior was, again, deception. For, "if nothing was taken in the hunt, it was a sign of death . . . ; animals saw the Indian's spirit in mourning and fled away." So the maverick fur trader Alexander Henry, the Elder, recalled that whenever food was scarce during his captivity, "the custom was to black our faces with grease and charcoal, and exhibit through resignation a temper as cheerful as if in the midst of plenty." And Samuel Hearne recorded in his memoirs that his spirits were frequently buoyed by his comrades' "merry and jocose" air when the party was in fact starving.[28]

Setting out on the winter hunt the Ojibwa hunter commonly sought the goodwill of the manitous by offering them a dog in sacrifice. By this means game spirits and their bosses were put in a good humor and became well-disposed to capture.[29] Seeking even further advantage, the hunter and his family invoked the lingering shadows of departed relatives and friends, requesting their support in the hazardous months ahead. In this latter ceremony, it might be pointed out, there inhered a compelling reason for permanent family hunting territories. Ancestral spirits, valuable for the aid they offered, could be found only on these lineal territories; to hunt elsewhere would be to cut oneself off from their care.[30] The dog sacrifice and the ancestral invocation were used to make the hunt propitious; they gave the hunter the confidence he needed that all was in order. Perhaps, as an additional source of aid, he might dream the whereabouts of the game that was concealed to all but the spiritual eye within the fastness of his vast range.

Success rested on more than these, however. Charms were still needed to make hunting gear infallible, and the hunter must of course be adept at deception. If the weather was inclement, it too could be made cooperative by magical means. The buzzer, a hollowed bit of wood with string attached, was swung about the head to bring the northwind. Or, if a soft, slushy snow hindered the capture of large game, a snowman was fashioned to entice cold weather and give the snow a firm crust.[31] When game was still not forthcoming, in spite of all these inducements, the desperate hunter applied directly to *Nanabozo*, the Great Hare, the hunter's special manitou, in what became known as the "medicine hunt."[32]

The ceremony, wrote the nineteenth-century ethnographer Joseph N. Nicollet, "is celebrated in times of distress . . . when the land has been exhausted, and when families lie dying of hunger. The native who can no longer bear the spectacle of misery surrounding him, whose vain efforts of the hunting grounds result only in his own exhaustion, and who is at the end of his rope decides to implore the manitos to be charitable unto him."[33] Only if he were a *mide*, a member of the curing society, or *Midewiwin*, could the man perform the ritual himself. Otherwise he would enlist the services of one to conduct the ceremony for him.

The supplicant retired alone to his lodge where, seated in the dark, he carefully sketched out the stylized form of the animal species he craved. *Nanabozo*, an essential participant, was represented in a carved figurine. Placing both of these before him, in tangible representation of the hunter and the hunted, he prayed most earnestly for the manitou to save his starving family by leading him to the elusive game. Then he paused, calmly waiting for the expected vision with eyes closed in deep concentration. Eventually, in his imagination, he detected the animals cautiously approaching his lodge. They were giving themselves up to him. Exuberant, the supplicant rushed out to inform the band of his vision, the men proceeding to the spot where they knew the game graciously awaited them.[34]

Once the game had been captured a whole new set of rituals and taboos came into play. For nothing was more offensive to the game bosses and the shadows of the slain than to have the carcass desecrated—bones gnawed by dogs, flesh eaten by menstruating women, and other insults. Rituals of disposal and consumption found their most elaborate form of expression in the celebrated bear cult, already described. The elder Alexander Henry recalled the scene that followed his shooting of a hibernating female. "The bear being dead, all my assistants approached, and all, but more particularly my old [adopted Ojibwa] mother . . . , took her head in their hands, stroking and kissing it several times; begging a thousand pardons for taking away her life; calling her their relation and grandmother; and requesting her not to lay the fault upon them, since it was truly an Englishman that had put her to death."[35] Their effusive condolences did not prevent his Ojibwa relatives from butchering the carcass with dispatch, however. The severed head was adorned with ornaments and set on a scaffold within the lodge, with a plug of tobacco placed near the snout.

The following morning a ceremonial feast of atonement was held. When the lodge had been swept and all had been placed in order, "Wawatam blew tobacco smoke into the nostrils of the bear, telling me to do the same, and thus appease the anger of the bear on account of my having killed her." Henry balked, protesting that he was not afraid of the animal's displeasure, but his host prevailed upon him to comply with custom. "At length the feast being ready, Wawatam commenced a speech resembling in many things his address to the manes [spirits] of his relations and departed companions; but having this peculiarity, that he here deplored the necessity under which men labored thus to destroy their *friends*. He represented, however, that the misfortune was unavoidable, since without doing so, they could by no means subsist."[36] With this, the assembled company proceeded to consume the bulk of the carcass—truly a gastronomic feat of perseverence.

The "eat-all" feast, so christened by incredulous white observers who dismissed it as an improvident orgy, was in reality a ceremony of communion with the spirit of the slain beast. Jenness wrote that the shadow of the slain bear "accompanies the carcass to become a guest in the hunter's wigwam."[37] Under the watchful, anxious eye of the unseen shadow the various parts of the beast's anatomy were devoured in set fashion. All of this scruple was necessary "if they [the communicants] are to expect the god of the earth to grant to the village his favor and abundance of his blessings," wrote a somewhat confused, although essentially accurate, Nicolas Perrot. "It is not without making great efforts that they come to the end [of the feast]. . . . There are some of them who die from such excesses, and others who are scarcely able to recover from them." When all had been consumed the celebrants were congratulated by the rest of the village. "They reply to all those civilities by saying that it is only the proper thing for brave men to do their duty on such an occasion."[38, d]

For some obscure reason, bear meat was the only food that required immediate and total consumption. But even this rule was not always observed, as in the Henry case (above) when some meat from the slain sow was preserved. More typically, however, the edible portions of the animal were devoured forthwith. Henry elsewhere related a curious incident involving a Frenchman who found himself unable to finish his assigned portion on one of these occasions. Being of a resourceful nature, he concealed the surplus under his shirt and made his way to the door. All of a sudden he was set upon by the dogs, who had scented the concealed flesh, which they now tore from him and began devouring—to his acute embarrassment. "The Indians were greatly astonished; but presently observed that the Great Spirit had led the dogs by inspiration to act in order to frustrate the profane attempt to steal away this portion of the offering. As matters stood the course they took was to put the meat into the fire and there consume it."[39]

The underlying purpose of this and related ritual and taboo

d. Adrian Tanner, in his work among contemporary Mistassini Cree, has offered some insights on the ideology of the feast which may have some bearing on the seventeenth- and eighteenth-century Ojibwa eat-all feast described here. "Food served at a feast is in a sacred condition," he writes, "and must be consumed by the participants or given to the spirits, either by putting it in the fire," and so forth. Elsewhere he explains that the surplus must be concealed in order not to incur the wrath of the game spirits. This is done either by overeating and concealing the surplus in one's stomach or by wrapping up and carrying out the excess. It appears, furthermore, that the animal being consumed is understood to symbolize sexual union, and hence reproduction, between the males and females of the commensal family. Adrian Tanner, "Bringing Home Animals: Religious Ideology and Mode of Production of the Mistassini Cree Hunters" (Ph.D. diss., University of Toronto, 1976), pp. 296, 313–314, 324.

was of course the desire to propitiate the soul-spirit, or shadow, of the slain animal. Were the hunter foolishly to ignore these ceremonials the offended shade would report the outrage to the other members of its species, who in retaliation would withdraw from that locality or inflict disease. Above all, the bones of the animal or fish carcass were to be scrupulously protected from harm. Generally they were deposited, intact, in their natural element—aquatic, marine, or terrestrial. For the Ojibwa and their neighbors were convinced that the souls and spirits of slain animals and fish returned, in due course, to re-inhabit and re-clothe the bones thus preserved. Indeed, the Indian applied this principle to explain the fluctuations in game numbers that are readily apparent in this part of the country. "Sometimes many souls come up from below to be reborn, sometimes only a few; then there are correspondingly many or few animals upon this earth. The bosses of each species regulate their numbers. . . . So a district may teem with hares one winter and contain hardly any the next, because their boss has ordered them to move into another district or has sent their souls back to their home below."[40] This strange belief in the reincarnation of wildlife spirits was also remarked upon by Father Allouez, in his *Relation* of 1666–1667. The Ottawa residing at Chequamegon, he reported, "believe . . . that the souls of the Departed [fish] govern the fishes in the Lake [Superior]; and thus, from the earliest times, they have held the immortality, and even the metempsychosis, of the souls of dead fishes, believing that they pass into other fishes' bodies. Therefore they never throw their bones into the fire, for fear that they may offend these souls, so that they will cease to come into their nets."[41, e]

e. One is liable to get the impression from reading Ruth Underhill, "Religion among American Indians," *Annals of the American Academy of Political and Social Science* 33 (May 1957):130, and other ethnographic sources (e.g., Frederica de Laguna, "The Atna of the Copper River, Alaska: The World of Men and Animals," *Folk* [Dansk Etnografisk Tidsskrift] 11/12 [1969/70]:22; and Robert J. Sullivan, *The Ten'a Food Quest*, Catholic University of America, Anthropological Series No. 11 [Washington, D.C.: Catholic University of America Press, 1942], pp. 94–96, 107–108, 110), that trapped animals, especially aquatic mammals, could be continuously regenerated merely by throwing their bones back into the water, the implication being that the northern Indian

Infractions against this subsistence code resulted in starvation, as has been outlined above, or disease. Taken together, these were the two greatest crises that pre-Columbian Ojibwa society faced. Out of anxiety over the former there evolved a psychosis

hunter could resort to this procedure indefinitely and so capture unlimited quantities of furbearers without risk of offending the game spirits. This is not so.

A prominent theme which recurs time and again in the ethnographic literature on Canadian Indian hunting is that game must not be hunted to excess. There is a very clear injunction against wasting game, in the sense of hunting or trapping too many game. Harvey Feit found that Waswanipi "hunters feel themselves under an obligation to limit kills to those animals they know are harvestable without initiating a decline in the population." Or elsewhere, "It is part of the responsibility of the hunter not to kill more than he is given, not to 'play' with animals by killing them for fun or self-aggrandizement" (Harvey Feit, "Twilight of the Cree Hunting Nation," *Natural History* [August-September 1973], pp. 56, 54–56, 72; Feit, "The Ethno-Ecology of the Waswanipi Cree; or How Hunters Can Manage Their Resources," in *Cultural Ecology: Readings on the Canadian Indians and Eskimos*, edited by Bruce Cox, pp. 115–125 [Toronto: McClelland and Stewart, 1973], pp. 117, 121; A. Irving Hallowell, *Culture and Experience* [Philadelphia: University of Pennsylvania Press, 1955], p. 361). Robert Sullivan, S.J., remarked that "the indiscriminate slaughter of caribou after the introduction of firearms" among the Koyukon was "clearly in direct violation of the general belief that the Supreme Being punishes waste . . ." (*Ten'a Food Quest*, pp. 75–76). Thus, returning the bones to the water may indeed have guaranteed their regeneration, although this was not construed by the Indian as a license to kill these animals in unlimited numbers.

Yet some might argue that the anxiety Feit witnessed among his Waswanipi Cree informants over the excessive slaughter of game is a recent development, a case of spiritual obligations and considerations conforming to a white-induced conservationism (the family hunting territory system). One could then modify the preceding argument somewhat and make the case that, *aboriginally*, these people had only to throw the bones of beaver and other commercially valuable aquatic mammals back in the water to produce them in unlimited numbers for slaughter and trade. I would dispute this, on the grounds that (*a*) such a crass conviction flies in the face of the hunter's *normally* cautious and solicitous relationship with game animals which, moreover, appears definitely to be aboriginal, antedating fur company programs aimed at encouraging efficient game management; and (*b*) it is further belied by the spirit of hostility and vengeance which enveloped the early fur trade in this area—native hunters would not have displayed negative emotions toward the beaver they were harvesting, as I will continue to show they did, if all they had to do was return the bones to the water to be guaranteed a new crop.

I realize these objections do not constitute an unassailable case in my favor, and that one could continue to challenge the issue. Yet I feel, from reading a large body of ethnographic and historic literature on the subject, that Feit's informants held to an aboriginal hunting ethic—that to kill too many game was to risk the ire of the game bosses—which was suspended for the majority of the fur trade era and subsequently revived as game conservation once more became practicable with the inauguration of the family hunting territory system. See the Epilogue, p. 176, for further discussion of this point.

of the *wittiko*, a mythical cannibalistic giant with an insatiable appetite for human flesh. In the harsh environment of the north woods, extreme hunger experienced by emotionally insecure individuals often drove them to distraction, to an insanity which rendered them incorrigible cannibals, in behavior much like the mythical cannibal-giant. The only cure, often insisted upon by the *wittiko* itself, was death.[42, f]

But our concern, here, is primarily with the latter problem: disease, and native theories of disease etiology. In his published doctoral dissertation on "Chippewa Preoccupation with Health: Change in a Traditional Attitude Resulting From Modern Health Problems," Robert Ritzenthaler observed that the Ojibwa have had a long history of excessive concern with health, an interest which he felt may well have anticipated white contact.[43]

Without a doubt the most visible expression of that concern has been the famed Midewiwin, a kind of community health organization equipped with a wide range of ritual paraphernalia and the principal repository of tribal folk-history. Admission to the "Grand Medicine Society" was an arduous process, beginning with extensive (and often expensive) instruction by one of the mide priests, whereupon the candidate was qualified to enter but one of the four stages of knowledge and medical proficiency.[44]

The cult has languished in recent years, however; there seem to be few individuals, men or women, knowledgeable enough in its mysteries—or willing enough—to transmit them to understudies. Likewise, there appear to be few individuals interested in learning them. The Society enjoyed its greatest popularity in the eighteenth and nineteenth centuries, and the early decades of this century, especially among the southern Ojibwa groups who, with their predilection for a village way of life, were more inclined to subscribe to a corporate religion. The Northern Ojibwa, scattered throughout Ontario and Manitoba and pursuing a more particularistic way of life, have preferred visionary shamanism over the Midewiwin.

f. See Cornelius J. Jaenen, *Friend and Foe: Aspects of French-Amerindian Cultural Contact in the Sixteenth and Seventeenth Centuries* (New York: Columbia University Press, 1976), for *wittiko* cases reported from the seventeenth century.

It now seems clear, thanks largely to the efforts of Harold Hickerson, that the Midewiwin was a post-contact, nativistic cult. Hickerson, who has combed the *Jesuit Relations* and other appropriate seventeenth-century sources, found no signs of it prior to the early eighteenth century. Its antecedents appeared to him to have been embedded in shamanistic practices which may have been influenced and transformed by the roughly contemporaneous medical societies existing within surrounding tribes, such as the early seventeenth-century Huron.[45] One should bear in mind that this is only conjectural, however.

In a series of incisive essays, Hickerson has maintained that the Society served as a crucial integrating device in the newly emerging, unified southern villages at the turn of the eighteenth century. Prior to this, in the second and third quarters of the seventeenth century, while the progenitors of the Ojibwa were living as semi-autonomous clans occupying discrete territories along the northern shores of Lakes Huron and Superior, there was apparently no social-political need for anything like the Midewiwin. The Feast of the Dead served their integrative needs admirably. Periodically, Hickerson has found, these related clans would congregate at some site, such as Sault Ste. Marie—usually a site that straddled an important fur trade route—to celebrate the Feast. Through its various functions—the cementing of existing alliances and the solemnizing of new ones through the intermingling of the bones, the bestowal of chiefly titles on survivors, and the acquisition of prestige through the ostentatious and lavish distribution of wealth—the ceremony served as an effective forum for conducting diplomacy among the related clans.

Yet the Feast had been rendered obsolete by the turn of the century, as the French assumed control over diplomatic initiatives (both intertribal and Indian-white), and as the clans or lineages began edging westward, northward, and southward along the shores of Lake Superior in pursuit of greater hunting and trading advantages. The northern branch of the tribe shunned the village life of their southern relatives, who now began coalescing in large, multiclan communities at strategic trading sites. The first such major southern village was formed at Chequamegon, at the tip of the peninsula of the same name, on the south shore of Lake Superior. And it is here that the Midewiwin first emerged as a highly effective institution binding the disparate clans together into an unprecedented village unity. Whereas before, at Sault Ste. Marie for example, the village had been a loose confederation of allied kin groups, the new multiclan village (e.g., Chequamegon, with its satellite village at Keewenaw) was a tight, unitary society comprised of increasingly insignificant kin segments. Previously, the Feast of the Dead had served to maintain the unity of allies; now the Midewiwin functioned to maintain solidarity within a single society, the village, which was rapidly becoming a discrete segment of a tribe: the Chippewa.[46] "The Midewiwin, then, may be described as the ceremonial of a representative body of men (and women) drawn from all the cohering kin-segments of the village organism. Implicit is the fact that the members of the priesthood belonged to any and all gentes and functioned in the village interest. The wealth distributed in initiation fees and in the feasts passed among village members and not outside the village. Perhaps most important, the Midewiwin through its priesthood provided the village with a tribal tradition through the symbolism of the megis [the money cowrie, *Cypraea moneta*, which the Ojibwa must have procured from Europeans] and other mythical devices."[47,g]

During the course of its development, the practitioners of the Midewiwin took it upon themselves to record on birchbark scrolls the late prehistoric–early historic westward migration of their ancestors. Candidates seeking admission into the cult were instructed from these and other charts, which appear to have been copied and re-copied numerous times over the centuries, with some apparent modifications introduced along the way. The so-called Origin and Migration scrolls are of particular interest to us, here, since in the majority of cases they show the late prehistoric or protohistoric Ojibwa situated on the Atlantic coast of Canada. Over a period of some years they allegedly

g. See Selwyn Dewdney, *The Sacred Scrolls of the Southern Ojibway* (Toronto: University of Toronto Press for the Glenbow-Alberta Institute, 1975), pp. 71–72, on the source of the megis.

migrated west, following the St. Lawrence Valley, to the Great Lakes, where they were first encountered by Europeans.[48]

William Warren, one of the first historians of his people, related that he was once spectator to a mide initiation ceremony where the following "migration" speech was given by the presiding priest, Tugwauganay, his maternal great-uncle. "The language and phrases were so obscure to a common listener," prefaced Warren,

that it would be impossible to give a literal translation of the whole speech. The following passage, however, forcibly struck my attention.

"While our forefathers were living on the great salt water toward the rising sun, the great Megis (sea-shell) showed itself above the surface of the great water, and the rays of the sun for a long period were reflected from its glossy back. It gave warmth and light to the An-ish-in-aub-ag (red race). All at once it sank into the deep, and for a time our ancestors were not blessed with its light. It rose to the surface and appeared again on the great river which drains the waters of the Great Lakes, and again for a long time it gave life to our forefathers, and reflected back the rays of the sun. Again it disappeared from sight and it rose not, till it appeared to the eyes of the An-ish-in-aub-ag on the shores of the first great lake [Ontario]. Again it sank from sight, and death daily visited the wigwams of our forefathers, till it showed its back, and reflected the rays of the sun once more at Bow-e-ting (Sault Ste. Marie). Here it remained for a long time, but once more, and for the last time, it disappeared, and the An-ish-in-aub-ag was left in darkness and misery, till it floated and once more showed its bright back at Mo-ning-wun-a-kaun-ing (La Pointe Island [i.e., Chequamegon]), where it has ever since reflected back the rays of the sun, and blessed our ancestors with life, light, and wisdom. Its rays reach the remotest village of the wide spread Ojibways."

Warren was understandably puzzled by the speech. Could it have any basis in fact, he wondered? Determined to find out, he visited the old man in his lodge one evening and asked him to re-tell the story, this time stripped of its allegorical element.

After filling his pipe and smoking of the tobacco I had presented, he proceeded to give me the desired information as follows: —

"My grandson," said he, "the megis I spoke of, means the Me-da-we religion. Our forefathers, many string of lives ago, lived on the shores of the Great Salt Water in the east. Here it was, that while congregated in a great town, and while they were suffering the ravages of sickness and death, the Great Spirit, at the intercession of Man-ab-o-sho [*Nana-bozo*, the Ojibwa culture hero], the great common uncle of the An-ish-in-aub-ag, granted them this rite wherewith life is restored and prolonged. Our forefathers moved from the shores of the great water, and proceeded westward. The Me-da-we lodge was pulled down and it was not again erected, till our forefathers again took a stand on the shores of the great river near where Mo-ne-aung (Montreal) now stands.

"In the course of time this town was again deserted, and our fore-fathers still proceeding westward, lit not their fires till they reached the shores of Lake Huron, where again the rites of the Me-da-we were practised.

"Again these rites were forgotten, and the Me-da-we lodge was not built till the Ojibways found themselves congregated at Bow-e-ting (outlet of Lake Superior), where it remained for many winters. Still the Ojibways moved westward, and for the last time the Me-da-we lodge was erected on the Island of La Pointe, and here, long before the pale face appeared among them, it was practised in its purest and most original form. . . . This, my grandson, is the meaning of the words you did not understand; they have been repeated to us by our fathers for many generations."[49]

Scholars, including linguists, archaeologists, and ethnologists, are skeptical of the idea that the ancestral Ojibwa might have originated somewhere far to the east, on the Atlantic coast.[50] They are still arguing among themselves over whether the proto-Ojibwa occupied the entire northern shore of Lake Superior at first contact or whether they were restricted to the subboreal zone east of Michipicoten Bay.[51] As far as I know, no one has yet attempted to set the eastern boundary of the late prehistoric Ojibwa, an assignment which would be fraught with difficulties: there is the problem of the intervening Laurentian Iroquois, who apparently controlled Tugwauganay's east-west migration route for at least part of the sixteenth century; added to which there are linguistic discontinuities between Atlantic coastal Algon-kians and the historic Upper Great Lakes Ojibwa.

And yet Roland Dixon felt he detected a substantial similarity between Micmac and Southwestern Ojibwa mythology. Con-cluded he: "The Cree, Saulteaux, and Menomini form a closely related group, with which the Mississagua shows much in com-mon. The [Southwestern] Ojibwa stands somewhat apart, being

connected with the group, and particularly with the Cree, largely by its culture-hero elements, and showing a strong similarity
to the Eastern group of the Micmac, Abnaki, and Maleseet in
so far as regards the non-culture-hero elements. It also has more
affiliations with the Iroquoian tribes than any other in the whole
Western group. . . . The Eastern tribes make up a pretty coher-
ent group, for the most part unrelated to the Western, in which,
however, the Micmac stands out markedly, by reason of its
strong similarities to Western, particularly Ojibwa, elements."
From here he went on to postulate that "traditionally the Ojibwa
had moved west, from a position much farther to the east, and
north of the St. Lawrence; this would bring them closer to the
Micmac geographically, with whom, and not with the Abnaki,
their agreements are found."[52] He reiterated his theory in a subsequent article on "The Early Migrations of the Indians of New
England and the Maritime Provinces": The Micmac may have at
one time occupied a great sweep of territory from the Upper St.
Lawrence to its mouth. "In their earlier habitat the Micmac were
in contact with the Ojibwa, who at that time lived much further
east than in historic times, this association accounting for the
close mythological similarities between the two tribes."[53] The
advancing (Laurentian) Iroquois presumably pushed the Micmac
east to their historic location, and in the process wedged themselves between the heretofore comingling "Ojibwa" and Micmac. Archaeological data are too inconclusive at this point to
throw much light on the issue, which undoubtedly sounds rather
fanciful to most specialists.

Someone subscribing to the Dixon theory might construe Tugwauganay's statement, that his people were hammered by epidemic disease while living "on the shores of the Great Salt Water,"
as an oblique reference to a protohistoric contact situation, when
the ancestral Ojibwa contracted alien diseases from the same
European fishermen who were trafficking with the coastal Micmac. Such an interpretation would allow one to reconcile the
tale of Warren's maternal ancestors "suffering the ravages of
sickness and death" while located on the Atlantic coast and the
visitation of the "great Megis," which transmitted to them "this

rite wherewith life is restored and prolonged," with the oddly similar tale of woe recounted by the Cross-bearing Micmac. The Micmac version had it that there was once "a time when their country was afflicted with a very dangerous and deadly malady" from which they were delivered by the timely intervention of "a man, beautiful as could be, [who] appeared to them with a Cross in his hand" and admonished them to fashion and venerate a like symbol, as it would drive away the pestilence.[54, h] Significantly, in both instances, Micmac and Ojibwa, the people apostatized. The mide priest, Tugwauganay, claimed that devotion to the cult was rekindled several times before it was finally "practised in its purest and most original form" at Chequamegon (La Pointe), where Hickerson and Selwyn Dewdney are agreed it originated.[55] Despite these parallels, the case for an Atlantic coastal origin must be rejected as being too speculative at this stage of inquiry.

There are several things that we might salvage from this evidence, however. One is the distinct possibility that the Midewiwin existed in some form prior to its full differentiation at Chequamegon—that it had waxed and waned in a more rudimentary form for several generations prior to the turn of the eighteenth century. Another is that the Ojibwa may well have been hounded by disease throughout the course of some sort of westward migration—if not from the Atlantic coast, as Tugwauganay and other mide priests would have us believe, then from some indeterminate point further west, possibly even as far west as Sault St. Marie. Finally, it appears certain that the Midewiwin developed, in part anyway, as an institutionalized reaction to that tragic situation.

h. There are peculiar similarities between the agent of relief in both the Micmac and Ojibwa accounts. In Tugwauganay's version of the Origin myth the agent was a megis shell sent at the instigation of *Nanabozo*, who had interceded on the Indian's behalf before the Great Spirit. In other versions, he is identified as a bear, in others an otter, and in still others as the sun manitou. Yet others claim that a man was sent over from western Europe as the special messenger of the Manitou Council, bearing with him the gospel of the Midewiwin (Dewdney, *Sacred Scrolls*, pp. 32–36, 41–46, 54–56, 158–159, 170–176; Laura Makarius, "The Crime of Manabozo," *American Anthropologist* 75 [June 1973]:663–675). One can only wonder at the connection between this enigmatic figure, of such fluid identity, and the Micmac "beautiful" man carrying the cross.

By the time Frenchmen began noticing them in the mid-seventeenth century, in their habitat southeast of Lake Superior, the Ojibwa were already reeling from what were obviously European-derived diseases. No one can say for certain when these diseases first arrived; the only evidence we have to go on is folkloristic testimony, which seems to put the inaugural date well before the actual physical appearance of whites. I, at least, am inclined to agree with this interpretation, since it fits a pattern established for many other parts of the New World and since local circumstantial evidence appears to corroborate it. In sum, I would postulate that the proto-Ojibwa contracted Old World disease well before they laid eyes on their first Frenchman (probably Etienne Brulé, who penetrated the area in 1621–1623); that these diseases began thinning their ranks while they were in the process of moving west to the north shore of Lake Huron; and that a rudimentary form of the Midewiwin had evolved to cope with new disease environment conditions which were firmly established by the time Europeans began documenting them in the mid-seventeenth century.

Shifting from the Origin and Migration scrolls to the so-called Master scrolls and ritual charts, which depicted the various spirit powers associated with the cult and showed the candidate how they were to be approached, one finds a striking association of animals with disease. W. J. Hoffman, in his classic account of the Midewiwin as he observed it in 1889 on the White Earth reservation, Minnesota, wrote of the various evil manitous—serpents, bears, a panther and lynx—which "occupied and surrounded" the first three degree lodges. When the candidate eventually reached the fourth and final structure of initiation, he had to brace himself to meet a most sinister panel of disease-mongering manitous: the panther, the turtle, the "big" wolverine, the fox, the wolf, the malevolent bear, the lynx, the serpents—these in company with yet more wildlife figures. These had "now assembled about this fourth degree of the Midē'wigân to make a final effort against the admission and advancement of the candidate." "They are the ones who endeavor to counteract or destroy the good wrought by the rites of the Midē'wiwin, and only by the aid of the good man'idōs can they be driven from the Midē'wigân so as to permit a candidate to enter and receive the benefits of the degree."[56] Subsequent researchers would make the same sort of observation: malevolent, disease-dealing spirit agents were symbolized as various animals on the scrolls.[57] The cosmic struggle against disease thus reduced to one pitting the "good man'idōs" of uncertain taxonomy against a host of evil animal spirits. I shall say more about this curious identification of wildlife with disease, further on.

Pursuing the disease theme even further, one finds that virtually all major illnesses were ascribed to some supernatural agent in traditional Ojibwa society. The categories of such disease varied: soul loss, sorcery, breach of taboo, disease-object intrusion, and spirit intrusion.[58] Briefly explained, soul loss or incapacitation usually meant that the victim had been raided by a malevolent conjuror who, typically, had snatched the soul away while the victim slept. Another symptom of the same misfortune was evident in the case of an intractable illness; for here again, in spite of the patient's apparent life signs, he was considered already dead—his soul had vanished. Recovery in either case was achieved by engaging a conjuror who had notoriously potent magic, hopefully more powerful than that of the thief.[59]

The second category, sorcery, involved black magic once more. Sorcery, incidentally, is probably the most common reason given by contemporary Ojibwa for "Indian" sickness. One Indian is convinced that another, who bears him a grudge for some insult, "has been employing his art in conjuring to make him unhappy or unsuccessful"; or, to put it more quaintly, someone has "thrown bad medecines [*sic*]" his way.[60] Once again, the victim would hire a conjuror to identify the source and, if possible, turn the tables on his tormentor. The commissioned shaman, or mide, then consulted his manitou or manitous (in the shaking tent rite) regarding the appropriate cure, after which he "implores, begs, beseeches, commands, and directs the spirits to deliver the patient from" the disease's grip. Rummaging through his medicine bag, he locates a suitable cure—a certain herb—which he administers orally.[61]

Passing over breach of taboo, which has already been explained, we find that disease-object intrusion was a favorite diagnosis of the so-called sucking doctors (a type of conjuror), furnishing them the opportunity to demonstrate their remarkable skills of legerdemain. Some wicked sorcerer had imbedded an infectious object (a sliver of wood, or bone, some hair, or just about anything) in the victim's body, which could only be extracted by pressing the mouth (or a tube) to the affected part and sucking it out.[62] Samuel Hearne was impolitely amused as he witnessed Cree shamans assiduously using a variant of this technique: they clapped their lips to the anus of the patient and blew vigorously. As far as he could tell, the sole effect was defecation in the face of the blower punctuated by blasts of flatus.[63] Spirit intrusion, the final category, was similar to disease-object intrusion, except that the victim in this instance was tormented by an evil spirit requiring exorcism.

Taken together, the foregoing ideology of disease, belief in hunting magic and ritual, and super-human world view animated the Ojibwa hunter-gatherer on the eve of European landfall. "Their native belief system, in short," wrote Hallowell on the Saulteaux Ojibwa, "defines the psychological or behavioral environment in which they live, and no purely objective account of their geographical locale, its topography, its fauna and flora would be sufficient to account completely for their behavior in relation to this physical environment."[64] Herein lies the meaning of the Indian's response to the fur trade and the contact experience in general.

CHAPTER FOUR

Contact and Nature's Conspiracy

JUST WHEN the loose collection of bands known as the Ojibwa first felt the European influence is problematical. We would guess that their initiation was through middlemen, easterly tribes who carried the news, the contagions, the paraphernalia, and the fur-trading impulse west to the Upper Great Lakes.[a]

a. Father François du Peron wrote in a letter of April 1639, describing the Huron, that these people were trading with the French and surrounding tribes, including the Saulteaux Ojibwa. *Jesuit Relations,* 15:155.

The standard general works on the Ojibwa are Ruth Landes, *Ojibwa Sociology* (New York: Columbia University Press, 1937); Landes, "The Ojibwa of Canada," in *Cooperation and Competition among Primitive Peoples,* edited by Margaret Mead, pp. 87–126 (New York: McGraw-Hill, 1937); R. W. Dunning, *Social and Economic Change among the Northern Ojibwa* (Toronto: University of Toronto Press, 1959); Harold Hickerson, *The Southwestern Chippewa: An Ethnohistorical Study,* American Anthropological Association Memoir 92, vol. 64, no. 3, part 2 (June 1962); Hickerson, *The Chippewa and Their Neighbors: A Study in Ethnohistory* (New York: Holt, Rinehart and Winston, 1970); Hickerson, "The Chippewa of the Upper Great Lakes: A Study in Sociopolitical Change," in *North American Indians in Historical Perspective,* edited by Eleanor Burke Leacock and Nancy Oestreich Lurie, pp. 169–199 (New York: Random House, 1971); and Charles A. Bishop, *The Northern Ojibwa and the Fur Trade: An Historical and Ecological Study* (Toronto: Holt, Rinehart and Winston of Canada, 1974). Specialized topics which bear on the present subject are found in Diamond Jenness, *The Ojibwa Indians of Parry Island, Their Social and Religious Life,* Canada, Department of Mines, *National Museum of Canada, Bulletin No. 78,* Anthropological Series No. 17 (Ottawa, 1935); A. Irving

Situated deep in the interior of the new continent, this *terra incognita*, the emergent Ojibwa were hunter-gatherers, meaning that they farmed very little or not at all. There is some evidence, as was mentioned in the Prologue, that certain bands, such as the Missisauga, Nipissings, and Saulteaux—bands which resided for a portion of the year along the shores of the Upper Great Lakes—cultivated maize.[1] Because of a short growing season, the crop was harvested green. For the most part, however, the Ojibwa relied on wild plants, fish, Virginia deer, moose, caribou, furbearers, and waterfowl for their subsistence.[2]

Along the edges of swampy lakes and creeks they harvested wild rice in autumn, great quantities being husked and laid up "for the consumption of the year," to be boiled when the time came with fat, fish, maple sugar, or meat of all sorts.[3] Late in the season, with the wild rice secure, the individual (extended) families broke camp and quit the shore, moving inland in the company of several other related families to hunt and trap a communal territory throughout the winter months (November through March).[4,b] This was the season for gathering furs and hides for clothing and numerous other domestic uses. As for the tools and techniques of the chase, they were, generally speaking, identical to those utilized by the Micmac. There is a suspicion that the Ojibwa were more inclined to preserve food than were their Micmac brethren—meat typically being cut into strips and smoked over a low fire, rendering it lighter of load and preserving it for future use—but the evidence for this is inconclusive.[5] These constituted the lonely months, when starvation stalked the land in the figure of the dreaded *wittiko*.

Hallowell, *Culture and Experience* (Philadelphia: University of Pennsylvania Press, 1955); and Landes, *Ojibwa Religion and the Midéwiwin* (Madison: University of Wisconsin Press, 1968). See Helen Hornbeck Tanner, *The Ojibwas: A Critical Bibliography* (Bloomington: Indiana University Press for the Newberry Library, 1976), for a useful guide to the great corpus of literature on these people.

b. The origins and nature of the Algonkian family hunting territory system have been debated for years by ethnologists. See Charles A. Bishop, "The Emergence of Hunting Territories among the Northern Ojibwa," *Ethnology* 9 (January 1970):1–15; Bishop, *Northern Ojibwa*, pp. 206–220, 284, 287, 289–296, 308; and Calvin Martin, "The Four Lives of a Micmac Copper Pot," *Ethnohistory* 22 (Spring 1975):111–133.

The spring breakup brought the scattered hunting bands together once again in the festival of maple sugaring. Old acquaint-
ances were renewed, new ones struck up, gossip freely passed
around—and conjuring indulged in. The women did the actual
tapping and boiling; it being up to the men to secure the food
and collect the wood.[6] After the feasts and frivolity the bands
moved on to summer quarters. Here, in patriclan villages, there
might be a hundred to three hundred individuals camped on a
body of water that was sure to yield them plenty of fish. Hooks
and nets (including seines) brought in the smaller varieties, while
the larger sturgeon and whitefish were speared.[7] The Saulteaux,
who took their name from the rapids at Sault Ste. Marie, on the
St. Mary's River, were famous for their adroitness at this latter
technique. Carefully guiding the canoe down the maelstrom, the
sternman steadied the craft while his companion, standing, im-
paled the whitefish as they battled the current upstream.[8] It was
by all accounts a marvelously choreographed spectacle.

As the days got shorter and the air brisk, family members
went out to pick the wild berries (blueberries, in particular),
many of which were preserved.[9] After the berrying season came
the wild rice season, once more, as the subsistence cycle moved
full circle.

We get our first sustained view of the Ojibwa in the *Jesuit
Relations*, where fathers Jogues (immortalized by Francis Parkman) and Raimbault are described as having been the first of
their order to have visited a segment of the tribe, in 1641, at
what was to become, through the subsequent efforts of Father
Allouez, the mission of Sault Ste. Marie. Jogues and Raimbault
were succeeded in 1660 by Father Menard, who wintered the
year on Keweenaw Bay, Lake Superior, and disappeared, mys-
teriously, the next. Father Claude Allouez succeeded the ill-fated
Menard, reaching Chequamegon in 1665, where he erected the
mission of La Pointe (later to be called St. Esprit) in the midst of
refugee Ottawas (close kinsmen to the Ojibwa) and Hurons
(actually Tobacco Indians) driven west by the marauding League
Iroquois. "For thirty years did Alouez travel from tribe to tribe,

through the forests and over the prairies of the vast wilderness which a century later came to be organized into the Northwest Territory, and established missions. . . ."[10] Writing to his superior in Québec, this remarkably energetic man outlined his mission at Chequamegon. "Here we have erected a little Chapel of bark, where my entire occupation is to receive the Algonkin and Huron Christians, and instruct them; baptize and catechize the children; admit the Infidels, who hasten hither from all directions, attracted by curiosity; speak to them in public and in private; disabuse them of their superstitions, combat their idolatry, make them see the truths of our Faith; and suffer no one to leave my presence without implanting in his soul some seeds of the Gospel."[11] Like his predecessor Pierre Biard, the reverend Father Allouez was a man with a powerful vision.

The one persistent theme of these Jesuit authors was the devastation, especially of a spiritual nature, wrought by disease among the mission tribes. From their letters it would appear that the fathers occupied themselves mainly with praying for and ministering to the sick, baptizing those whom they could. At first, the Indians were suspicious of baptism, fearful that it caused death, but they were soon convinced otherwise. In the words of Allouez, "A circumstance greatly facilitating the Baptism of these Children is the belief, now very common, that those sacred waters not only do not cause death, as was formerly held, but even give health to the sick and restore the dying to life."[12] Thus it was with these tender words that Cree parents comforted their feverish children at the Sault, " 'Do not cry,' they said to them when the children moaned in their sickness; 'Do not cry, Baptism is going to cure you.' "[13] Many were miraculously cured, or so the fathers claimed in their journals, frequently triggering the patient's conversion and, less often, a community revival. "No sooner had he [Father Gabriel Druilletes] landed here [Sault Ste. Marie] than a grievous disease broke out among the greater part of our Savages; yet, instead of checking the course of the Gospel, it, on the contrary, brought it into great repute by many wonderful cures. This made such an impression on these peoples' minds that, by the grace of our Lord, they declared themselves openly for the faith; and all the elders have publicly promised to embrace it when they are sufficiently instructed."[14]

A countertheme to the ministrations of the fathers was the bitter opposition of the shamans. In predictable fashion the shamans found themselves discredited before their people for their inability to effect a cure by traditional means. Whereupon the priest was summoned—he was usually waiting in the wings anyway, eager to seize just such an opportunity. Oftentimes, it seems, by invoking his Christian resources, he shamed his rival by working a cure. The loss of face was naturally resented by the shamans, some of whom in their anger breathed threats against the blackrobes. Others who had experienced the efficacious power of Christianity renounced their "jugglery" to become devoted followers of Christ.[15]

Yet, from remarks scattered here and there in the *Relations,* we gather that these and other mission Indians were not constant in their new-found faith; many of them apparently relapsed into heathenism after a short period of time, reminiscent of the Micmac experience.[16] Allouez judged the Ottawas at Chequamegon to be a people with "very little inclination to receive the faith, since they are extremely addicted to Idolatry, superstitions, legends, polygamy, unstable marriages, and every sort of licentiousness, which makes them renounce all natural shame." "They freely acknowledge that what I teach them is very reasonable," he complained, "but license prevails over reason, and, unless grace is very strong, all our teachings are of slight effect."[17] Nearly fifty years later, Father Gabriel Marest found the Saulteaux at Michilimackinac to be of the same disposition. "Religion does not take so deep root in them as we could wish; and there are only a few souls who, from time to time, give themselves truly to God, and console the Missionary for all his labors."[18]

The Ojibwa and other tribes among whom the blackrobes moved were tenacious of their ancient beliefs not because they were savages, as the Jesuits accused, but rather because their world view and ritual had been functional up until then. Naturally, therefore, they were reluctant to jettison it altogether. It is an obvious point, yet nonetheless worthy of emphasis. Any success at proselytization must be interpreted within the larger context of the epidemic diseases. Indians were dying off in droves, and at least some of them saw in Christianity a panacea. So long as Christianity offered relief from their physical anguish the Ojibwa and others were willing converts; the more virulent the epidemic the more successful the conversion. With cure or a lull between epidemics, apostatization was rampant. Nothing was more frustrating to the resident Jesuits than this cycle of disease-Christianity-interlude-apostatization. Blind to this process and rationale, the fathers could not discern that there was nothing inherently virtuous about the Gospel to these people; instead, they charged the Indians with having a capricious nature.

Christian conversion must be understood, then, as an adjunct to disease. The two greatest killers were probably smallpox and plague, smallpox becoming endemic to the area by the mid-seventeenth century. Over the years these were joined by rickets, tuberculosis, syphilis, typhus, cholera, scarlet fever, and others —diseases which would sweep through a vulnerable native population in insidious clusters, decimating and demoralizing the victims. Consider the course of one of these contagions: smallpox. We know from documentary evidence that by 1641 the entire St. Lawrence–Great Lakes region had been ravaged, probably repeatedly, by a smallpox epidemic which had started among the Montagnais seven years earlier. One might interject that Jesuits, their *engagés*, the coureurs de bois, and explorers were carriers of the virus, as were Indian intermediaries and such contaminated trade goods as blankets and clothing. Smallpox may have struck again in 1662–1663, or thereabouts, as it spread throughout New France. The intervening years between this outbreak and another known to have occurred in 1738 may very well have witnessed several other visitations. It was back, again, in 1752 and 1781–1782. The younger Alexander Henry, nephew to the other Henry, furnished a crude estimate of the death toll of this latter epidemic as it moved through the heavily populated site of present-day Winnipeg. "Many hundreds of men, women, and children were buried there," he bitterly recalled in his journal.[19, c] It evidently took another hundred years for the disease finally to be brought under control.[20]

So prevalent was disease that a band of enterprising Nipissings almost succeeded in discouraging a party of fur-laden Indians from descending to Montréal by warning that "the pest" was stalking the French colony. A skeptical Frenchman, who happened to be traveling with the latter group, recognized it as a bluff to frighten his companions into dumping their furs and turning back. It was certainly odd, he declared facetiously, that "ignorant" Nipissings could have survived the sickness unscathed when the surrounding French were succumbing. "The Nepicirinien replied to him. 'Our spirits have preserved us.' 'Your spirits,' the Frenchman answered, 'are incapable of that, and are no better able to do you any good. It is the God of the French who has done everything for you, and who supplies your needs, although you do not deserve it.' "[21] The truth is that he was right. The manitous of the Indians had lost their protective powers—and the Indians knew it.

Neither the obstructionism of wily Nipissings or other intervening tribes nor the depredations of the Iroquois could prevent the furs from pouring into the warehouses at Montréal, Three Rivers (Trois-Rivières), and Québec.[22] When hostilities between the French colony and the Five Nations Iroquois became so intense as to close off the river routes, the western tribes impatiently stockpiled the pelts, waiting for the chance to run the blockade.

Furs, after all, were the business of New France. As expressed by Father Nau, with scarce exaggeration, "Monsieur The Count

c. "When Hudson Bay was discovered," wrote David Thompson, "and the first trading settlement made, the Natives [i.e., the Cree] were far more numerous than at present. . . . In the year 1782, the small pox from Canada extended to them, and more than one half of them died; since which although they have no enemies, their country very healthy, yet their numbers increase very slowly" (Thompson, *Narrative, 1784–1812*, edited with an introduction and notes by Richard Glover [Toronto: The Champlain Society, 1962], pp. 92, 236–237). Samuel Hearne, *A Journey from Prince of Wales's Fort in Hudson's Bay to the Northern Ocean, 1769, 1770, 1771, 1772* (1795), edited with an introduction by Richard Glover (Toronto: Macmillan Company of Canada, 1958), pp. 115–116, estimated that nine-tenths of the Chipewyan had died of smallpox recently contracted from the Cree.

de Maurepas is right when he says that The officials in canada are looking not for The western sea but for The sea of beaver."[23] These same officials were careful to impress that fact on the Jesuit missionaries who, however reluctantly, appear in general to have promoted the trade. "We try as much as we can," Father Nouvel reassured Count Frontenac in the spring of 1673, "conformably to what Monsieur the Governor and Monsieur the Intendant have written to us about it, to incline them [the Saulteaux] to continue their intercourse with the french."[24, d] Nicolas Perrot carried the message to the Potawatomi, close kin of the Saulteaux, when he visited their country sometime between 1660 and 1700. His hosts, who evidently had never laid eyes on a European before, insisted he must be " 'one of the chief spirits' " because he used iron. Capitalizing on their naiveté, Perrot politely inquired whether they might like to trade with the French, "as the beaver was valued by his people"—something of an understatement.[25]

Nouvel's obsequious letter of compliance may well have been prompted by a new threat that was causing the governor some anxiety. Three years earlier the restored Stuart monarch, Charles II, had chartered the Hudson's Bay Company, magnanimously granting it a monopoly of the trade throughout the Bay's vast watershed. For the next hundred and fifty years, until the merger of the Northwest Company with the Hudson's Bay Company in 1821, the interior would be mercilessly raided for its furs, the scene of a fur-trading war whose principal casualties were the beaver and the Indian. To his discredit the Indian capitalized on the rivalry, in somewhat the same fashion that the League Iroquois had earlier played the imperial powers of England and France off one another. No one company or native hunter could count on other Indians for support in maintaining a sustained

d. Bruce Trigger, "The Jesuits and the Fur Trade," *Ethnohistory* 12 (Winter 1965):30–53, maintains that the Jesuits, in Huronia at least, were not agents of the fur trade. Although they were obliged to barter in furs, these being the standard medium of exchange, they did not have a stake in or an obligation to the fur business. I suspect that the blackrobes compromised their isolationist and protectionist position as the century progressed and they increasingly alienated their New French audience.

yield policy of harvest, the best advice in such a cutthroat atmosphere therefore being to "trap out and get out," which is precisely what most Indians did; over-hunting became the only viable alternative.[26, e]

Beaver were already scarce along the southwestern shore of Lake Superior by the time the Hudson's Bay Company began doing business.[27] Indeed, wildlife destruction now occupied the primary energies of the Saulteaux, declared Perrot. They "have degenerated from the valor of their ancestors, and devote themselves solely to the destruction of wild animals."[28] "A few years ago beaver were plenty on the upper part of these forks," confirmed Alexander Henry, the Younger, referring to the confluence of the Rat with the Red River, "but now they are nearly destroyed."[29] Beaver were likewise depleted in the Nipigon country by the end of the eighteenth century. Confided the Nor'wester, Duncan Cameron, to his business partners in Montréal, "I am, however, sorry to remark that this part of the country is now very much impoverished since; beaver is getting scarce, but I have nevertheless managed to keep up the average of returns by shifting from place to place every year and increasing the number of posts, which, of course, augmented the expenses and made the trade dearer, but that cannot be helped at present, and we must conform to circumstances and hope to see a reform soon."[30] The "circumstances" he alluded to were these: the Indians were less zealous trappers and hunters than they had been formerly, and intense competition for their furs between the Northwest Company and the Hudson's Bay Company had made them careless about repaying credits. Added to that, the operating costs of the trade had skyrocketed, fueled in large part by unscrupulous traders who were overpaying the natives for their

e. Daniel Harmon, *A Journal of Voyages and Travels in the Interior of North America, . . . During a Residence of Nineteen Years, in Different Parts of the Country . . . ,* transcribed by Daniel Haskell (Andover: Flagg and Gould, 1820), p. 432, listed the following furbearing species, in descending order of importance, as being the most sought after by the Northwest Company in the early decades of the nineteenth century: beaver, otter, muskrat, marten, bear, fox, lynx, fisher, mink, wolf, and buffalo. In an accompanying list he showed the relative weights of furs, again in descending order, annually exported by the Company: beaver, marten, muskrat, bear, otter, wolf, buffalo, lynx, "etc."

catch. This, of course, encouraged the Indians to clamor for more. Meanwhile, the beaver were becoming ever more scarce —driving up costs even higher. The fur trade had simply extended itself to its farthest geographical limit, wearily concluded Cameron. The rapidly diminishing game resources within this now-confined area could yield only correspondingly diminishing returns, should the Company prolong the enterprise. Further exacerbating the problem was the Hudson's Bay Company's confounded premium system, whereby HBC factors were awarded a bonus for each skin they secured. Here was the ultimate folly: commercial suicide.[31]

Things were really not as bleak as Cameron made them out to be; the Nipigon country was not abandoned nor did the Northwest Company go bankrupt. Cameron himself, although perhaps unwittingly, contributed to the overall instability by capriciously assigning hunting territories to indebted Indians.[32] It is not difficult to imagine how the hunter, devoid of spiritual ties to a new and arbitrary hunting territory, chosen merely because of its expediency to the trade, would have few qualms about cleaning out its furbearers. On a much broader geographical scale, roving bands of Indian pelt-hunters were abandoning exhausted territories within their tribal areas to raid those of their neighbors, where there were still furs to be found. Samuel Hearne thus felt the Hudson's Bay Company served to gain when Chipewyan hunters made peace with their Cree neighbors, whose territories they promptly began scouring for furs.[33] And Daniel Harmon found Iroquois as far west as the Mackenzie Subarctic, indiscriminately slaughtering beaver on Carrier territory.[34] Similarly, the "Chippewas [Ojibwa] have lately come from the southward where their own countries are exhausted of the Beaver and the Deer [caribou]" to hunt on Cree territory, complained Thompson. Formerly, he continued, the "great western forest"—the area between Lake Winnipeg and the Rocky Mountains—"had very many Beaver." Had it not been for the ruthless competition of fur companies these western Indians would have had an abundance of beaver, he maintained, certainly enough to satisfy their needs. But Canadian traders, i.e., Nor'westers, had imported "a great number of Iroquois, Nepissings and Algonquins who with their steel traps had destroyed the Beaver on their own lands in Canada and New Brunswick."[35,f]

Not only were the beaver and other furbearers vanishing, but so were the moose and caribou, mainstays of the Northern Ojibwa diet. The result was predictable: whereas hunger had previously been sporadic in Ojibwa society, by the early nineteenth century it had become a way of life.[36] The Ojibwa captive John Tanner, having narrowly escaped death by starvation, reflected on the terrifying experience: "This is but a fair specimen of the life which many of the Ojibbeways of the north lead during the winter. Their barren and inhospitable country affords them scantily the means of subsistence, that it is only with the utmost exertion and activity, that life can be sustained; and it not unfrequently happens that the strongest men, and the best hunters, perish of absolute hunger."[37] Before the victim succumbed to "absolute hunger," an inadequate diet rendered him extremely vulnerable to infectious disease.[38] The hunter and his family became caught in a vicious circle of debilitating disease curtailing hunting, which in turn impoverished the diet, which in turn invited infection, and so forth. Malnutrition and illness thus developed a synergistic relationship. Sometimes relief came in the form of rations dispensed by humane traders, yet these were scarcely enough to carry a family through the hungry winter months or even through a short-term famine. Those unfortunates who were caught in such desperate straits resorted to eating their dogs, first, and then their moccasins. When these proved insufficient to tide them over, they tried eating the inner bark (i.e., cambium) of firs, or boiling a loathsome mush known as *tripe de roche* (an edible lichen), or even consuming caribou dung—anything to stay alive.[39,g]

f. In an editorial note, Richard Glover has dated this influx at about 1798.

g. Bishop, *Northern Ojibwa*, has plotted the course of Northern Ojibwa decline in exquisite detail.

It is clear, he feels, that things were going well for the majority of them during the middle and later decades of the eighteenth century and indeed for a few years after the turn of the new century: trade goods were plentiful as the HBC and Northwest Company competed vigorously for the products of the chase. There seemed to be plenty of furs to go around, and Indians prospered as

In spite of such tragedies and austerities, the trade ground on. Casting about for some sort of meaning to all of this, David Thompson concluded that it was inevitable, and that was all there was to it. "Previous to the discovery of Canada . . . this Continent from the Atlantic to the Pacific Ocean, may be said

---

they moved from post to post, applying for and getting easy credit. These were the years of reckless hunting of both furbearers and large game (moose and caribou), the latter providing the bulk of the Indian's diet. It appears that hunting for furs was largely secondary to hunting for food during these flush years. It also appears that the Ojibwa were scarcely dependent upon European trade goods. Meanwhile, social organization was changing in response to new environmental conditions and the pressures of the fur trade: clan segments were giving way to bilateral kin groups of several dozen members (i.e., composite bands of twenty-five to thirty individuals). Bishop emphasizes repeatedly that the Ojibwa lived very well before the turn of the nineteenth century; starvation was probably extremely rare, and the Ojibwa enjoyed a significant population increase.

The decades of over-hunting began to register in 1805/1810 or so. Both furbearers and cervines (moose and caribou) were becoming alarmingly scarce by the first one or two decades of the century. Native hunters were now forced to turn to alternate sources of food, in particular hare and fish. What few moose and caribou remained were soon killed off, as were most of the surviving beaver. Hunting for food now occupied an increasingly larger proportion of their time just when they found themselves increasingly dependent upon the trading post for relief. Store-bought food, European clothing, and other supplies suddenly became critical to survival, and yet they became more and more difficult to obtain as fewer pelts were surrendered in exchange. Not surprisingly, the credit sytem was much abused during these years of austerity.

Things only got worse with the HBC–Northwest Company merger in 1821. Seeking to economize, the newly amalgamated firm closed unprofitable posts, making it more difficult for dependent Indians to move around in order to secure the hare, fish, and furs which were now so vital to their continued existence. The few beaver that remained were rendered even more inaccessible by the inauguration of a beaver conservation program which included the resting of certain hunting areas and the Company's refusal to accept summer beaver. Almost perversely, the HBC raised the price of trade goods right at the point when they were indispensable to the Indian's livelihood. And to cap it all off, the credit system was replaced by the unpopular ready-barter system, placing the higher priced goods even further out of reach.

All of this served to make the Indian less mobile and consequently more dependent on the post for food, clothing, blankets, twine (for nets), leather (for footwear and clothing), guns, and ammunition. Food shortages were endemic from the early decades of the nineteenth century until the turn of the twentieth, when the moose and caribou returned to the area. Indeed, Ojibwa hunters found that their physical survival was often intimately tied to hare cycles—such was the degree of their destitution. It was during this period that the staking of beaver lodges became commonplace and furs were reckoned to be the property of the individual who had secured them. This, together with the atomization of the hunting group into small family units, marked the beginning of land tenure in severalty for the Northern Ojibwa.

to have been in the possession of two distinct races of Beings, Man and the Beaver."[40] The two were locked in mortal combat, with the Indian the perennial underdog. Man's primitive tools were pitifully inadequate to penetrate the fortress-like lodge, reasoned Thompson. So the Indian stood by and watched, helplessly, as beaver multiplied and became a nuisance, and then a menace, assuming possession of every waterway that lent itself to their purposes.

Every River where the current was moderate and sufficiently deep, the banks at the water edge were occupied by their houses. To every small Lake, and all the Ponds they builded Dams, and enlarged and deepened them to the height of the dams. Even to ground occasionally overflowed, by heavy rains, they also made dams, and made them permanent Ponds. . . . Thus all the low lands were in possession of the Beaver, and all the hollows of the higher grounds. . . . the dry land with the dominions of Man contracted, every where he was hemmed in by water without the power of preventing it.[41]

And still they increased, and the Indian sullenly retreated before the plague.

Thompson, a sober man, was not indulging himself in a mere flight of fancy; Cree legend confirmed and very likely informed this passage. He was a keen observer of Indian ways, taking a special interest in their spiritual complex. Whatever information he gleaned on Cree beliefs, he assured the reader, was painstakingly obtained from those old enough to recall the aboriginal sentiments. He thus scrupulously avoided recording anything that he suspected might have been contaminated by white influences. "My knowledge," he declared, "has been gained when living and travelling with them and in times of distress and danger in their prayers to invisible powers. . . ."[42] We would seem justified, then, in considering him a serious and credible source.

It is from Thompson and Alexander Henry, the Elder, whose veracity as an adopted Ojibwa is likewise unimpeachable, that we learn of the Indian's underlying spiritual motive for exterminating the game in the name of the fur trade. The revelation came to Thompson, although we are by no means certain he appreciated its full import, in the course of a conversation with two aged Cree in the vicinity of Lake Winnipeg. The discussion having drifted to the subject of beaver, his hosts began to reminisce for the benefit of their English guest.

They said, by ancient tradition of which they did not know the origen [sic] the Beavers had been an ancient People, and then lived on the dry land; they were always Beavers, not Men, they were wise and powerful, and neither Man, nor any animal made war on them.

They were well clothed as at present, and as they made no use of fire, and did not want it. How long they lived this way we cannot tell, but we must suppose they did not live well, for the Great Spirit became angry with them, and ordered Weesaukejauk to drive them all into the water and there let them live, still to be wise, but without power; to be food and clothing for man, and the prey of other animals, against all of which his defence shall be his dams, his house and his burrows. . . .

The old Indian paused, became silent, and then in a low tone [they, the two Cree] talked with each other; after which he continued his discourse. I have told you that we believed in years long passed away, the Great Spirit was angry with the Beaver, and ordered Weesaukejauk (the Flatterer) to drive them all from the dry land into the water; and they became and continued very numerous; *but the Great Spirit has been, and now is, very angry with them and they are now all to be destroyed* [emphasis added].[43]

Henry corroborated and elaborated upon this bizarre tale of divine wrath. Sometime in the past the Great Hare, *Nanabozo*, "took from the animals the use of speech. This act of severity was performed in consequence of a conspiracy into which they had entered against the human race. At the head of the conspiracy was the bear; and the great increase which had taken place among the animals rendered their numbers formidable." *Kitchi Manitou*, explained Henry in another context, had deprived the beaver of speech "lest they should grow superior in understanding to mankind."[44]

Fitting these legends together, we find that the Indian's initial impulse to destroy wildlife may not have been a desire to harvest their furs for trade. That came later. However improbable it may seem to our Western way of thinking, the explanation seems to lie in the fact that on the eve of European contact man and beast were at war. The Indian, true to the behavioral environment in which he operated, was convinced that the bear and the beaver (doubtless in league with other species) had conspired against man to destroy him. The case against the beaver has already been made in part: mankind was intimidated by the continual encroachment of this animal upon his domain—dry land. As for the bear, the ringleader of the plot, he had turned his superior physical and spiritual strength against the weaker Indian. Thompson conveyed this hostility in a speech made by a Cree hunter to a bear about to be slain. "The eldest man now makes a speech to it; reproaching the Bear and all it's [sic] race with being the old enemies of man, killing the children and women, when it was large and strong, but now, since the Manito has made him, small and weak to what he was before, he has all the will, though not the power to be as bad as ever, that he is treacherous and cannot be trusted, that although he has sense he makes bad use of it, and must therefore be killed."[45] He might just as well have inserted the phrase "European technology" for the word "Manito," since the Indian gained the upper hand in the struggle, armed with rifles, with steel traps, steel axes, steel knives; and with steel-tipped spears and chisels. "Thus armed the houses of the Beavers were pierced through, the Dams cut through, and the water of the Ponds lowered, or wholly run off, and the houses of the Beaver and their Burrows laid dry, by which means they became an easy prey to the Hunter."[h] "Every animal fell before the Indian; the Bear was no longer dreaded, and the Beaver became a desirable animal for food and clothing, and the furr [sic] a valuable article of trade."[46]

Summarizing the cosmological sequence of events as reconstructed from legend: *Nanabozo*, the special guardian of the Indian race, had confounded the conspiracy of the beasts by striking them dumb. Yet they still pressed in upon man, who trembled before the powerful game bosses as they kept filling the land with their kind. Things changed with the advent of

h. The reader will recall that I chided Harold Innis, on p. 10, for expressing a nearly identical sentiment. Innis seemed to accept as a foregone conclusion that the beaver would be excessively exploited once the Indian began pursuing it with European-improved weapons. What he failed to understand is that destruction of the beaver was prompted by an antecedent hostility, an antipathy which found in the new technology its most convenient means of expression.

European technology, which put the Indian on the offensive. Through the spirits (manitous) of his new weapons the hunter waged a brief, holy war of extermination.[47,i] For a few years, perhaps decades, the Indian hunter gloried in his omnipotence. Nature, which had once rejected his supplications and frightened him, now lay prostrate at his feet.

i. Throughout his journal Hearne made reference to the senseless slaughter of game, for which the Indians could offer no satisfactory explanation. I would submit that it was due to a superiority they now felt over an animal kingdom which had once frightened and defied them.

PART THREE

The Paradox Resolved

CHAPTER FIVE

The Hunter's Relationship with the Hunted

Up to this point in the narrative the conclusions drawn have been fairly conservative. Most people would agree, I imagine, with the general notion that widespread secularization, or despiritualization (a term I prefer), occurred throughout Eastern Canada following white contact. Yet the connection between this process and the Indian's exuberant exploitation of furbearers and other game remains obscure. At several points in the previous chapters I have briefly touched on the Indian ideology of hunting—the hunter's relationship with the hunted, and vice versa. Once this peculiar relationship became corrupted, a point I have made before, nothing remained to impede the overkilling of game for purposes of trade. The task, now, is to show more explicitly how this corruption came about, and the place to begin is in the mind of the traditional native hunter.

Perhaps the most stunning way to phrase the Eastern Canadian Indian conception of hunting is to say that it was nothing short of a "holy occupation." "To the Montagnais-Naskapi—hunters on the barest subsistence level—the animals of the forest, the tundra, and the waters of the interior and coast, exist in a specific relation. They have become the objects of engrossing magico-religious activity, for to them hunting is a holy occupation." "This simple statement," declares Frank G. Speck with powerful conviction, "explains the whole economic and social doctrinal program of the natives."[1] Although Speck was referring in this case to the Montagnais-Naskapi of Québec and Labrador, his ideas apply with equal validity to the rest of our area.[a]

Elsewhere, he elaborated on this provocative concept.

a. See Adrian Tanner's extraordinarily perceptive doctoral dissertation, "Bringing Home Animals: Religious Ideology and Mode of Production of the Mistassini Cree Hunters" (Ph.D. diss., University of Toronto, 1976), which is scheduled for publication.

While spending a winter season with the Nichicun band of Mistassini, Tanner became deeply impressed with the cyclical nature of the hunting experience and the peculiar social relationship hunters had with their game. He spends pages describing the religious, symbolic arrangement of domestic space vis-à-vis outdoor space. Hunters go forth from the lodge, the soiled human realm, to the bush, the clean, spirit realm, and secure game whose presence they had long before detected and whose spirit they had already pacified. After the kill it is imperative, for the group's psychic survival and future success, that the animal remains be properly disposed of: certain inedible parts are disposed of in a ritual-like manner, the carcass is displayed and treated in a way pleasing to the game spirit, and so forth. The intriguing thing is that these various customs dealing with the disposal of the animal all make symbolic reference to social relations within the hunting group. In a real sense the carcass, or the animal, mediates relations within the group between sexes and different age groups. Tanner's point is that hunting for these people is suffused with religious symbolism—hunters feel they "own" the game, not the land; hunters make friends with the game; cautious hunters treat the game with "respect"; etc.—a symbolism underpinned by a sense of kinship, or social relations, with the game. The social relations with the game are then transferred to members of the hunting group: just as the game is laid out in the lodge along sexual and social axes, and its flesh when consumed sustains them, so the sexual and social relations within the group are reaffirmed and sustained by the act of "bringing home animals." See also Frederica de Laguna, "The Atna of the Copper River, Alaska: The World of Men and Animals," *Folk* (Dansk Etnografisk Tidsskrift) 11/12 (1969/70):17–26; Robin Ridington, "Beaver Dreaming and Singing," in *Pilot Not Commander: Essays in Memory of Diamond Jenness*, edited by Pat and Jim Lotz, pp. 115–128, *Anthropologica*, Special Issue, n.s. 13, nos. 1 and 2 (1971); Edward S. Rogers, *The Quest for Food and Furs: The Mistassini Cree, 1953-1954*, National Museum of Man, Publications in Ethnology No. 5 (Ottawa, 1973); David Merrill Smith, *Inkonze: Magico-Religious Beliefs of Contact-Traditional Chipewyan Trading at Fort Resolution, NWT, Canada*, National Museum of Man, Ethnology Division, Paper No. 6, Mercury Series, Ottawa (June 1973); Robert J. Sullivan, *The Ten'a Food Quest*, Catholic University of America, Anthropological Series No. 11 (Washington, D.C.: Catholic University of America Press, 1942).

The animals . . . pursue an existence corresponding to that of man as regards emotions and purpose in life. The difference between man and animals, they believe, lies chiefly in outward form. In the beginning of the world, before humans were formed, all animals existed grouped under "tribes" of their kinds who could talk like men, and were even covered with the same protection. When addressing animals in a spiritual way in his songs, or using the drum, the conjuror uses the expression . . . "you and I wear the same covering and have the same mind and spiritual strength." This statement was explained as meaning not that men had fur, not that animals wore garments, but that their equality was spiritual and embraced or eclipsed the physical.[2]

Hallowell has depicted the nonliterate hunter's attitude toward his quarry in much the same manner. We in Western society have never fully appreciated native hunting methods because of our mechanistic bias: the hunter's success depends upon the physical capability of his weapons and his skill in using them. "We ignore," however,

the subjective aspect of the food and pelt quest which, I think, bulks larger in the consciousness of the individual hunter than the knowledge and skill which so forcibly impress us at first glance. That is to say, the primitive hunter finds himself in a radically different position with regard to the game he pursues than can be inferred from our own habits of thought. To him the animal world often represents creatures with magical or superhuman potencies, and the problem of securing them for their hide, meat or fur involves the satisfaction of powers or beings of a supernatural order. Consequently, strategy and mechanical skill are only part of the problem. Success or failure in the hunt is more likely to be interpreted in magico-religious terms than in those of a mechanical order.[3]

Conceding that "the aboriginal bow and arrow, spear and snare, and the modern gun and rifle are naturally indispensable in hunting," Speck has insisted that "the spiritual preparation, the willingness of the beasts to submit to the weapons, and the permission of their deific 'owner' are of utmost importance."[4]

Here is a novel idea indeed: animals, in the Indian cosmology, consciously surrendered themselves to the needy hunter. "Game animals were gifts of the Creator and of lesser supernaturals to the hunter, provided the hunter did his work properly and well and conducted his affairs in a precisely correct fashion. This involved matters of conservation, ritual, and taboo," writes John Witthoft for the Pennsylvania Susquehannock and surrounding Northeastern tribes. It is a notion completely foreign to the Western way of hunting. "The white man regarded game animals as meat from which to supply his needs, as mere objects to be taken. The Indian," on the other hand, "considered the animal as an intelligent, conscious fellow member of the same spiritual kingdom. His own destiny was linked with that of the animals by the Creator, and he felt that both he and his victims understood the roles which they played in the hunt—the animal, in other words, was resigned to its fate."[5] Such a concept of "ordained killing" appears universal throughout the Northeast and Eastern Subarctic. "The animals know beforehand when they are to be slain, when their spirits have been overcome by the hunter's personal power or magic. They exact also a certain respect, which is shown to them in different ways, though generally by the proper treatment of their remains after they have been killed for their flesh or skins. If this respect is not accorded to them," warns Speck, "the animals refuse to be killed, or their souls may not be reborn."[6] More recently, Adrian Tanner found that "a central attitude in the conduct of hunting is that game animals are persons and that they must be respected. The rules of respect after the killing involve essentially taking care of all elements of the carcass, and not allowing anything to be thoughtlessly discarded." "According to Cree ideology," Tanner has elaborated, "hunting rests on a kind of social relationship between men and animals. Throughout the cycle of hunting rites men emphasize their respect by means of symbolic expressions of their subordination to animals. . . . After the killing, a gradual shift takes place in this ideology. The corpse of the animal begins to be treated less as a person, and more like a sacred substance. The meat is eaten, but the sacred part still remains in the inedible parts, and these must then be disposed of according to strict rules. At the feast, these rules of disposal are also applied to the

food itself, so that eating sacred food becomes a symbol for communication with the mystical power of animals."[7,b]

All of this might sound absurd to Western ears, not accustomed
to hearing rodents and other wildlife described as sentient beings.
It makes no difference whether we or our European ancestors
put much stock in such convictions; the point is that the newly
contacted Indian perceived his furry quarry thus, and it is in this
context that we must seek to explain his behavior as a fur trader.
Echoing what his seventeenth- and eighteenth-century French
and English predecessors wrote, Speck was informed that "the
beaver . . . embodies extraordinarily high spiritual endowments.
It can transform itself into other animal forms, that of geese and
other birds being specifically mentioned. The beaver can disappear by penetrating the ground, by rising aloft into the air, or by
diving into the depths of lake or stream and remaining any length
of time desired. In short, 'he can escape or hide himself if he
wishes to, so that he can never be taken.'" "Again we are told
it is only with the amiable consent of the beaver himself that the
animal can be killed, and this consent is in some curious way
dependent upon the volition of the giant beaver [i.e., beaver
keeper, or boss]."[8]

Speck's informants revealed a similar feeling about the bear.
"The inner self or spiritual element of the bear is one of great
power and influence among the spirits of animals. It has control
over them much as the physical bear is their superior in respect
to strength and sagacity. His soul-spirit knows especially when
the hunters are on his trail, and so he does what he thinks best
to do in order to save himself or else he allows himself to be
overtaken and killed."[9] "Hunting by divination in general, and
bear hunting in particular," Tanner discovered, "is characterized
by the outcome being known in advance, or known with some
degree of certainty once the animal has been located. Along with

b. Father John Cooper, "Field Notes on Northern Algonkian Magic," *Proceedings of the Twenty-Third International Congress of Americanists*, New
York, September 1928 (1930):514–515, was overwhelmed by a "bewildering
variety" of such hunting taboos and rituals, claiming that "a detailed account of
field-notes collected would run into many pages."

this relative predictability, the animal has a size and ferocity with which to attack the hunter, but since such an attack seldom, in fact, happens, the killing of a bear epitomizes another Cree ideal of the hunt: the animal is believed to lose the 'natural' inclination to hide, to flee or to attack, and instead to 'offer' itself to be killed. In a sense, bear hunting epitomizes the ideals on which the religious aspect of all hunting is based."[10, c] Working among the Cree in the vicinity of James Bay, Alanson Skinner was told that "bears are supposed . . . to understand everything said to them." Indeed,

the [Cree] Indians believe that all animals are speaking and thinking beings, in many ways not one whit less intelligent than human beings. The reason that they are less successful in life is that they are unfortunate, "their medicine [Power] is not as strong." The reason that the Indian is able to prey upon them is that he is more fortunate, not more intelligent. In some cases, however, certain animals have a greater supernatural ability than the Indian. This is particularly true of the bear who is considered more intelligent and to have greater medicine powers in many ways than mankind. He walks upon his hind legs like a man, and displays manlike characteristics. In fact, some tribes regard the bear as an unfortunate man.[11]

Speck uncovered comparable sentiments among the Montagnais-Naskapi for caribou and fish; in each case wildlife were regulated not by man and hunting pressures but by the keeper of the fish and game—or so the Indian thought.[12]

Practically speaking, we might inquire how this process of voluntary surrender and capture worked and what its results were in terms of actual numbers killed. The traditional Indian hunter of the Eastern Canadian forest had evolved an elaborate system of communication and spiritual control over wildlife, a system which we judge, from references contained in the early documentary sources described above, to have been thriving at the time of first European contact. For many of these hunter-gatherers the basic oracle of life was one's soul-spirit, or Great Man, as the Naskapi put it. "This is the term by which the soul

c. See Tanner, "Bringing Home Animals," p. 286, for evidence of beaver being the symbolic equivalent of the bear.

in its active state is referred to, and, as we shall see, the active state of the soul is one which means guidance through life and which provides the means of overcoming the spirits of animals in the life-long search for food."[13] Chief Joseph Kurtness, of the Lake St. John Naskapi, explained to Speck that "the Great Man reveals itself in dreams. Every individual has one, and in consequence has dreams." We flatter our Great Man by probing our dreams, and in turn we are rewarded by an even more productive communication with him. "The next obligation," Speck was told, "is for the individual to follow instructions given him in dreams, and to memorialize them in representations of art." Those who neglected their dreams lost touch with their Great Man, "and cessation of revelations as to when and where to go for game, how to proceed, and how to satisfy it when it is slain, would result in the loss of a powerful and far-seeing guide, the individual's 'Providence'—and a doom of failure and starvation. Thus autistic thought and behavior become dominant factors in life." Observant Naskapi thus came to rely implicitly on the promptings of this inner voice, since their success in all spheres of activity was achieved, they felt, through his direction.[14] Whatever one's Great Man dictated had to be executed, irregardless of its consequences; to ignore or refuse his commands was bound to incur his wrath. "A good Naskapi, for instance, a righteous, self-considering man, could not be a total abstainer from intoxicants, nor from the excessive inhalation of tobacco, nor from gluttony when he feels an inclination toward these excesses. For his Great Man prompts these desires. Even though they upset the physical well-being for a time, their mental stimulation, the ecstatic state, is a sign of his senses that his Great Man is being stimulated according to wish and will afford him full necessary protection." One of the most common methods of nurturing the soul-spirit was by smoking, the resultant dizziness being considered proof of inner stimulation.[15]

A man's soul-spirit furnished the vital link between himself and his animal quarry, since only through its utterances or behavior could he comprehend the whims of the game upon which he was so utterly dependent. One of the curious and at the same time perfectly reasonable consequences of this man-game rapprochement was that hunters characteristically developed extraordinarily close ties with wildlife. Indeed, Adrian Tanner has found that among the Mistassini Cree, who adhere to a family hunting territory system of land tenure, hunters "own" the game, not the land: "Cree ideology proposes . . . that property relations with respect to land are a matter of a mystical relationship with animals, and . . . a matter of inheritance."[16] The Ojibwa interviewed by Ruth Landes in western Ontario and northwestern Minnesota in the 1930s appear to have had a roughly similar notion: "the hunting lodge . . . 'belonged,' in Ojibwa parlance, to the wife, who occupied it with the young children. The woods and the hunt 'belonged' to the man, who left the wigwam almost daily for his quarry."[17] Tanner found a charming element of affection in this proprietorship over the game. "The hunter who has, over many years, killed an extraordinary number of a particular species is felt to have a friendship relationship with that animal. Such an animal may be spoken of as the man's 'pet,' and the relationship is often marked by the hunter collecting and sometimes decorating an inedible part of the animal." Upon the man's death and burial, his "pet" species went into mourning and avoided the interment ceremony. This proved to be an especially anxious moment for the man's survivors, because the species was liable to leave the area unless the friendship were continued with another man. In order to preclude such an abandonment, the ageing hunter would designate his heir and pass on not only his right to the land but, more importantly, his spiritual relationship with the resident fauna. Spiritual continuity with the game —the crux of the historic family hunting territory system and, presumably before that, the loosely defined hunting area—was thus maintained from generation to generation (not necessarily biologically related, adds Tanner).[18]

When it came right down to the actual business of dispatching the game the hunter invoked all the spiritual resources at his command, first to subdue the animal's spirit, and then, anticlimactically, its body. It was the preliminary spirit hunt, as we might call it, which really mattered; by the time the hunter got around to actually bagging the animal it was as good as dead, as far as he was concerned. The most complete evidence we have for this sort of thinking comes, not surprisingly, from modern ethnographic sources. Yet we are safe in assuming the aboriginal, first contact ancestors of these people adhered to similar practices and beliefs, since we find abundant testimony to them in the early historic records. The fact that they were taken down in a somewhat incoherent fashion by these early chroniclers does not diminish the fact that they existed. Basically, what we are talking about is the dreaming, divination, singing, drumming, sweating, and other forms of hunting magic which were engaged in prior to the final assault on the victim.

In the "hunt dream," performed the night or several nights before the physical hunt, a man's soul-spirit reveals the whereabouts of certain game. Dreaming thus becomes a much-desired state of mind. "Anything that will induce dreaming is a religious advantage: fasting, dancing, singing, drumming, rattling, and sweat bath, seclusion, meditation, eating certain foods, as well as drinking animal grease, various kinds of medicine, both alcoholic drinks and drugs, when such things . . . can be gotten."[19] Speck has recorded the caribou lure song chanted on these occasions by an old Naskapi, Jérôme Antoine: " 'Because he who comes [referring to the caribou seen approaching in the dream] looks so fine!' " Evidently the song, endlessly repeated and accompanied by drumming, would force the singer into concentrating on the game he had in mind, until he became totally mesmerized.[20] Sweatbaths were also useful in this regard, as they too stimulated dreams, prepared the hunter for entry into the "clean," spirit realm of the bush, and weakened "the resistance of the animal."[21]

The real test came in interpreting the message of the dream. And here is where hunting divination, usually scapulimancy, came into play. Father Le Jeune gave a perfectly accurate description of this process in his *Relation* of 1634 when he wrote that "they [the Montagnais] put upon the fire a certain flat bone of the Porcupine; then look at its color attentively, to see if they will hunt these animals with success."[22] Modern-day Naskapi informants told Speck that " 'we generally use the caribou shoulder blade for caribou hunting divination, the shoulder blade or hip bone of beaver for beaver divination, fish-jaw augury for fishing, and so on.' "[23] Speck explained how the process was supposed to work.

In the rite of consultation this tablet-like bone is subjected to heat, and the burnings, in the form of blackened spots, cracks and breaks, are then interpreted by the cunning and ingeniousness of the practitioner. Imagination suggests the likeness of the marks produced by the heat, to rivers, lakes, mountains, trails, camps and various animals— the latter either single or in groups. The direction of the burnt marks and their respective locations are also significant. Persons are also believed to be represented by the spots or outlines. Abstract ideas may be represented: life, death, success, failure, plenty, famine, sickness, chicanery, time periods, warnings, encouragement; and general good or bad luck are likewise indicated by the cabalistic figures.

The bones were made to "talk," as it were, through what Speck called the "force of fire."[24]

Scholars, today, in general conclude that divination aids a hunting group by facilitating the decision-making process when there is little information on local game—that it insures group cohesion, while simultaneously it randomly reorients the hunting strategy, increasing the chances of success and lessening the probability of overexploitation.[25] Adrian Tanner, a specialist on the Mistassini Cree of northern Québec, disputes this view. After a winter spent hunting with a group of Mistassini, Tanner concluded that scapulimancy functions less as a decision-making device in a context of general ignorance than as a ritual confirming what is already known about the hunt. He was especially impressed by the fact that Mistassini hunters accumulate a vast wealth of information on all available game within their hunting territories over the course of the winter hunting season; they are remarkably careful observers of animal signs and movements.

When the decision is made to proceed against a certain species, he found, it is made with deliberation, with a thorough knowledge of the animal ecology of the region. Even the arrival of the animal poses no surprise, for typically the hunters have been charting its progress within a territory for some time before they decide to pursue it. "After sufficient knowledge is gained it will be decided that the time has come for a change of diet," he has noted, "and for a break in the [beaver] trapping routine. The hunters may then know a good deal about their prey, and they also select a time when the animals can be approached and killed easily. Both general knowledge of the habits of the animals, and the specific observations about the area being hunted, are used in locating the animals quickly, and preventing their escape. . . . It is during the period when this knowledge is being accumulated that divinatory signs will appear." "In what I have just said," concluded Tanner, "I have tried to give the impression that most hunting is conducted within a system of data gathering and judgement, and that divination tends to crop up at a time when the hunters do not lack the means to decide where to go hunting. Since on the face of it divination is used to discover where to go hunting, it might be argued that divination is done in order to decide among an abundance of equally attractive places to hunt."[26] Based as it is on first-hand, extensive observation, Tanner's analysis carries a good deal of weight. Moreover, as we shall presently see, Harvey Feit will make much the same sort of claim for "abundance" among the Waswanipi Cree southeast of James Bay.

Hunting magic, both imitative and contagious magic, was used to augment these various sources of information. Tanner has related that among the Mistassini the northwest quadrant symbolizes the cold and north wind, personified as *ciwetincu:* (variously spelled *chuetenshu*): the grandfather of the northwest who is hostile to man. Hunters, afraid of offending the northwest being, are careful not to leave traces of blood on the snow after a kill, or else *ciwetincu:* is liable to send snow and cover the tracks of the game. Also, hunters who face the northwest too long will get frostbite—they have been kissed by the northwest, so to speak. Despite his antagonism for man, the northwest being can also be useful, especially in the fall and spring when cold and snow are vital for the chase. At times such as these the Mistassini hunter dramatically insults the northwest grandfather by defaming an animal which can withstand the cold (i.e., an animal associated with *ciwetincu:*) or by destroying something thought to belong to him.[27] With the same end in mind, Lake of the Woods and Rainy Lake Ojibwa were given to throwing a rabbit skin over the fire, allowing it to scorch, in order to arouse the northwest grandfather. Likewise, Father Cooper encountered Subarctic hunters who would catch and pluck several feathers from the Canada jay before setting it free, under the conviction that this brought cold weather.[28]

Not all types of magic were designed to tease, however; some, the imitative kind, were aimed at rudimentary duplication. This was the point of building a snowman, for instance, or swinging a buzzer or bullroarer about the head—any one of these strategies would bring cold weather by imitating the north wind or its effects.[29, d] Pictorial representation became yet another effective means of imitative magic, since it was felt that the symbolic form "is equivalent to the creature or object itself. Hence, we may say, to put it roughly, that there is an analogy in far northern Algonkian philosophy between symbol or picture and control-power, in bringing the objects portrayed under the dominance of the individual human spirit for the accomplishment of its needs."[30, e] Henry R. Schoolcraft, Indian agent to the Ojibwa in the mid-nineteenth century, claimed much the same thing about his native wards. "Images of the animals sought for, are carved in wood, or drawn by the Metas [mide] on tabular pieces of wood, by applying the mystic medicine to which, the animals are supposed to be drawn into the hunter's path."[31]

The spiritual preliminaries over with, the hunter was now ready to move confidently against his victim. "In concise terms, when gifted with the sight of game waiting to be killed somewhere within the hunting territories as the result of conquest by

d. Cooper has conceded the possibility that the buzzer and bullroarer may show European influence.

e. See Tanner, "Bringing Home Animals," pp. 150, 252–253, 256–257, on the advantages of decorating clothing and hunting gear.

the hunter's soul-spirit, and adjusted between him and his quarry through the medium of dreams, the devout native appears on the scene to fulfill the destiny of the animal. He does not—or perhaps more properly should not—dash impetuously into the midst of them, but bides his time patiently to take cool and quiet advantage by killing them when they have taken to the water, or by posting himself at a point where they will pass within range of his weapon."[32]

We might illustrate this with an example taken from the Waswanipi Cree. These people typically seek out moose in January, a month of heavy snow, for they know that moose are likely to congregate in the hardwood hills, where the snow is not as deep as it is elsewhere. Here they yard, making paths through the snow—paths which the hunter easily discovers. The Waswanipi maintain that some days are better than others for this sort of hunting: days with a slight breeze (to obscure any sounds made by the approaching hunter), days that are cold (so the snow will be powdery)—but not so cold that twigs snap—these are the most opportune moose-hunting days. Once it has detected the hunter the moose will run, but the Indians know that within an hour or two it will be so completely exhausted that it will simply come to a halt, allowing the snowshoed hunter to dispatch it. By far the best time to hunt moose, they claim, is late March–early April, when a slight crust forms on the deep snow. The fleeing moose lacerate their legs on the crust, which they of course sink through, whereas the hunter remains on top, giving him greater mobility than the beast. It is claimed that moose in this condition will often not even bother to flee or resist death.[33]

Feit's evidence, collected over a two-year period of study, belies the common assumption that large mammal hunting is "unpredictable, unreliable, and inefficient because the animals themselves are widely dispersed and highly mobile. Cree hunters," he finds, "do not share this assessment; they speak of big game hunting as a reliable, efficient, and productive means of subsistence." "The Waswanipi hunters stress . . . that killing a moose is easy. I was consistently told that when they are hunting moose, they are happy when they see tracks because they know they will soon be eating moose. . . . When I questioned them as to what they did when they could not locate any moose, I was told that this never happened." And again, the "Waswanipi themselves . . . say that, when they want a moose they get a moose, and when asked what happens if they don't get a moose on a given day, they say they try again later, and they will get a moose."[34]

The reason for the Waswanipis' phenomenal hunting success is that they hunt efficiently. Explains Feit:

Waswanipi then have a very substantial knowledge of the environment in which they live and this knowledge makes plausible their claims for the reliability, efficiency and affluence of their subsistence system; their expertise also suggests that it is possible to choose when to use resources. For each animal species the Waswanipi harvest, they attempt, like for the moose, to utilize it at times when chances of success are highest and the efficiency of capture is maximized. The Waswanipi account of their annual cycle is a model for integrating the various harvesting activities so that each resource is used at periods of maximum vulnerability and efficiency, and ideally so that at least two resources are available at each period throughout the hunting season.[35, f]

---

f. Adrian Tanner has described similar attitudes and behavior among the Mistassini Cree, who take the "planned approach to hunting and trapping" ("Bringing Home Animals," pp. 82, 61–62). He cautions, however, that food shortages continue to occur, at times, as when the plant and animal ecology of the area have been disturbed in such a way as to make hunting precarious. Yet even then there are often other sorts of game, usually smaller forms, which can be utilized for support.

Recent ethnographers and early European-American observers of Canadian Indians have made much of the starvation/famine issue among these people, just as I have in the preceding pages. Yet I would submit that there were occasions when food shortages were purposely induced in order to underscore and dramatize humankind's dependence on wildlife and Nature for meaning in life. We read in Sullivan, *Ten'a Food Quest*, for example, that the Koyukon, an Athapaskan people situated along the Yukon River, would throw lavish communal feasts in the late summer, mid-winter, and late spring, and that after each (especially the latter two) their larders would be left nearly bare. Sullivan noted that families often experienced real hardship after the midwinter ceremony, while certain of the younger members confided that, in their opinion, it was folly to consume so much food during the late spring feast. Nonetheless, the feasts went on, since that was the Koyukon "way." One gets the distinct impression that these people might not have run short on food if they had dispensed with their feasts. The sense one gets is that they deliberately created a food crisis—or purposely lived on the brink of starvation—in order to savor their unique commitment to spiritual sources of support.

Efficiency thus confers success, and success brings with it the potential for overkill. In such a situation, where the

> most critical problem is . . . not the locating and killing of game . . . but rather limiting kills that their prodigious skills make possible . . . , the Waswanipi recognize that the hunters must balance their kills. While the animals a hunter kills are gifts from *Chuetenshu*, one of the obligations a hunter must fulfill is to determine which of the animals he encounters is being given to him. This decision depends on integrating information from a variety of sources—signs of the animals, weather conditions, the behavior of the animals, dreams and visions, and the hunter's past success. . . . The most general informational frame within which this data is placed is the hunter's own previous hunting success.
>
> The belief is that if a hunter should kill more animals than he was given in any year, then *Chuetenshu* and the animals will be angry and will give the hunter fewer animals the next year. The success of past hunting and its implications for current hunting are communicated to the hunter by the animal signs he sees. Hunters constantly note signs of the frequency of game and compare their evaluations of the trends in the animal populations. These trends are the most important indicator for a hunter of what he will be given in the present season, and through them most hunters formulate a definite expectation.
>
> At the beginning of each hunting season most Cree dream or are told by *Chuetenshu* how much big game they will be given. This information is constantly checked and revised as the season progresses. The result is that the hunters feel themselves under an obligation to limit kills to those animals they know are harvestable without initiating a decline in the population.[36]

Today, most Waswanipi practice some sort of short-term rotational scheme, letting all or a portion of their territory lie fallow for a period of time in order to allow the game population to recoup and to enhance the efficiency of their hunting. Even under such a system, "hunters constantly evaluate the state of the animal populations on the land they hunt, and any drop in the success of the hunt, the number of animals sighted or the number of animal signs seen, is taken as an indication of overhunting or of other transgressions by the hunter. The state of the animal populations on a given territory is constantly known and Waswanipi always can discuss the trend in the population on their territories, and compare the populations to what they were last year, ten years ago, or when they first started hunting."[37]

How much of all the foregoing is aboriginal? It is certainly a legitimate question, and we would be remiss were we to avoid it. What is startling about Feit's disclosures is that Waswanipi hunting "recipes" are fundamentally aboriginal. The addition of European hardware to this hunting complex might have facilitated the actual, final dispatch of the animal, but contributed nothing to the process leading up to it. It was the complex preliminary process—the scouting out of game by various means and the knowledge of where and when to capture it—that made hunting efficient and, consequently, successful. As for the rotation of hunting territories, it is difficult to say whether this is a product of the historic fur trade or not.[38] The point is hardly relevant to our purposes, however, since the Waswanipi, in common with other Eastern Canadian hunters, have traditionally held that wildlife are fully capable of protecting themselves against overexploitation through the application of various sanctions.

Hunters became deeply suspicious when they failed to locate their game. Feit found that the Waswanipi hunter retained his composure when no beaver appeared in his traps after three or four days, the usual explanation being that "'the beaver don't want to be caught yet.'" By the second week, however, the hunter became alarmed. "Then a hunter is not just confronting the whims of the animal, he is having 'bad luck.' Bad luck is a result of a decision on the part of *chuetenshu* or the animals that a man should not get what he wants—usually because he has failed to fulfil one or more of his responsibilities. One of the most important responsibilities is not to kill too many animals. Thus the hunter is often confronting the consequences of his own activity when he goes hunting, and this confrontation occurs through the will of *chuetenshu* and the animals." Feit reiterated this crucial point elsewhere. "It is . . . claimed that men have the skill and technology to kill many animals, too many, and it is part of the responsibility of the hunter not to kill more than he is given, not to 'play' with animals by killing them for fun or self-aggrandizement."[39, g] Hallowell's Saulteaux (Ojibwa) informants revealed

g. See part 2, chapter 3, footnote e on the probable aboriginality of this sentiment.

a similar anxiety, blaming either sorcery or offended game keepers
for their misfortune. "In other words," summarized Hallowell,
"according to native theory one *should* be able to make a living
unless something goes wrong, and, if something does go wrong,
it is *somebody's* fault."[40] "Somebody," of course, was either a
sorcerer, a game spirit, or a game keeper—all three being personified.

The clear implication is that hunters had a cautious respect
for their wildlife quarry. Indeed, there was a good deal of latent
antagonism between the hunter and the hunted[41]—an antagonism that might erupt into overt hostility, given the proper circumstances. Wildlife could punish man by simply avoiding him
—by starving him and making him destitute, in other words—or
by afflicting him with disease. In Speck's words: "The fatalities
of life are represented in starvation, freezing, accident, and disease
for which the animals, animal overlords, plant spirits, and demons
of nature, and monsters are responsible. The individual has only
to rely upon their benevolence for his welfare. His own soul is
his medium of power in the struggle against their force."[42] Diamond Jenness underscored the point in his study of the Parry
Island Ojibwa: illness came from several sources, including angered
wildlife, who inflicted disease on those "who speak ill of them,
or show them disrespect by throwing their bones to the dogs."[43]
And the same was true among the Saulteaux: "While it is necessary, of course, for men to kill animals in order to live," acknowledged Hallowell, "what is wrong is to cause them unneces-
sary suffering. I believe that the disease sanction is applicable to
the treatment of animals because cruelty to individual animals is
offensive to the 'persons' who are their 'masters.' "[44, h]

There was something intriguing about this idea, wrote Robert
Ritzenthaler, a specialist on Ojibwa health and disease. "In my
search through considerable literature dealing with the attitude
of Indians toward disease," he confessed, "I was struck by a

h. See Hallowell, "Ojibwa World View and Disease," in *Man's Image in
Medicine and Anthropology*, Monograph 4, edited by Iago Galdston, pp.
258-315, Institute of Social and Historical Medicine, New York Academy of
Medicine (New York: International Universities Press, 1963), pp. 278-279,
where he appears to contradict himself.

rather curious, but recurring phenomenon. Namely, that there is a tremendously widespread tendency among American Indians to associate animals with disease. Furthermore, . . . such associations are as prominent among agricultural tribes as among hunting tribes. . . . Judging from its widespread distribution and counterparts in Asia," he concluded, "this is an old belief. It is also a field of inquiry which would be an interesting one for further exploration."[45]

In the specialized terminology of epidemiologists, Ritzenthaler was addressing himself to the matter of zoonoses: infectious and parasitic diseases shared by man and other vertebrate species.[i] Ever since man first domesticated animals he has shared many of their ailments. Yet, in pre-Columbian North America, where domesticated animals were limited to the dog, perhaps the turkey, and a few beaver,[46] livestock diseases would have been practically negligible. Of much more importance, here, were a variety of occupational wildlife diseases which doubtless infected the hunter and gatherer and to a lesser degree, perhaps, the horticulturalist.[47] Commenting on one such malady, sylvatic plague, a team of wildlife biologists recently observed, "There seems little doubt, on theoretical grounds, that Indians have been subjected to plague during their long history since it is the present consensus that wild rodent plague has been entrenched in western North America and Mexico from prehistoric times."[48] Likewise, "tularemia is considered to be firmly entrenched in natural foci in the wild, probably has been for several thousand years and might be expected to continue." That this has been the case in North America, in particular, seems assured. "The distribution of the organism [*Pasteurella* or *Francisella tularensis*] and its adaptation to ectoparasites of rodents and lagomorphs [rabbits and hares] suggests that it has long been enzootic in wild animals in both the New World and the Old World, probably originating in the latter at the end of the Miocene or early Plio-

i. The following section is adapted from my article "Wildlife Diseases as a Factor in the Depopulation of the North American Indian," *Western Historical Quarterly* 7 (January 1976):47–62.

cene."[49] Judging from the widely held conviction that animals were disease-causing agents, one can surmise that the aboriginal Americans were indeed cognizant of zoonotic infection, however they rationalized its cause (usually punishment for taboo infraction) and mode of transmission.

A careful reading of the historic evidence for certain of these epizootics (wildlife epidemics, so to speak) and, in some cases, related (human) epidemics makes one suspicious of their reputed antiquity in the New World. For example, we read in Father Jerome Lalemant's *Relation* of 1647 that three distraught members of an Ottawa River tribe (the Weskarini, or Petite Nation) had recently arrived in Montréal with news of a mysterious outbreak among the woodland caribou. "There had arisen a certain disease among the Caribous," recorded the Jesuit, "which made them vomit blood through the throat, remaining quite still when they were pursued. They have seen as many as five, six, or seven fall stiff in death in a moment: that has so terrified them that they have resolved to leave their country in order to come and live near the French."[50] Perhaps slightly exaggerated as to the swiftness of death, this anecdote nonetheless conveys the impression that these people had never witnessed such a spectacle before. They were terrified by it, so much so that they fled their band territory to seek refuge with the French. The implication seems to be that caribou had never experienced such an affliction (showing pasteurellosis symptoms) within tribal memory; in other words, it was attendant upon white contact. I shall return to this provocative suggestion subsequently.

Fur trade records furnish further evidence of wildlife diseases. Probably the most detailed and numerous accounts come from the late eighteenth and early nineteenth centuries when there was an intriguing series of epizootics and epidemics in the Midwest and Plains region. In several cases there were in fact concurrent or sequential epizootics and epidemics, leading one to suspect a causal interrelationship.

The series got off with a bang during the autumn and winter months of 1781–1782 when the northern Plains and Upper Great Lakes were ravaged by a smallpox pandemic of appalling proportions. As far as Hudson's Bay Company factors could determine, the disease had made its debut the preceding summer when an unsuspecting party of Blackfoot contracted it while on a raid against a Snake encampment. Saukamappee, a Blackfoot participant, described the scene to David Thompson. "Next morning at the dawn of day, we attacked the Tents, and with our sharp flat daggers and knives, cut through the tents and entered for the fight; but our war whoop instantly stopt, our eyes were appaled [sic] with terror; there was no one to fight with but the dead and dying, each a mass of corruption." Two days later the disease broke out in the Blackfoot camp, "and spread from one tent to another as if the Bad Spirit carried it. We had no belief that one Man could give it to another, any more than a wounded Man could give his wound to another."[51]

From the Blackfoot the epidemic swept westward, across the Rocky Mountains, northward to the tundra, and eastward to Hudson Bay, with a mortality that was absolutely staggering. The Indians themselves placed it at more than one-half their population, whereas Mitchell Oman thought it was closer to three-fifths.[52] William Walker aptly depicted the grisly scene in a letter to William Tomison, dated December 4, 1781. "The small pox is rageing all around Us [at Hudson House] with great Violence, sparing very few that take it. . . ." He was especially apprehensive that the food provisions would dry up "when the Indians is dying Daily and them that has not taken the small pox, is frightened to look after any thing for fear of falling in with others that is bad. I had sent out five Men to the Barren Ground to Maintain themselves but on Saturday Decr. 2d they returned, all Starving, no Buffaloe to be found and the Indians all Dying by this Distemper that there is no getting a livelyhood, the Indians lying Dead about the Barren Ground like rotten sheep, their Tents left standing and the Wild beast Devouring them."[53]

Many of the dead and dying were indebted to the traders, who had loaned them supplies on credit. In a seemingly callous effort to recover their losses the traders instructed their men to search for Indian encampments and strip diseased corpses of their valuable beaver robes. The naked bodies were to be piously wrapped in duffel or covered with logs, to prevent the ravenous wolves and dogs from devouring the carcasses. Curiously, we are told that "all the Wolves and Dogs that fed on the bodies of those that died of Small Pox lost their hair especially on the sides and belly, and even for six years later many Wolves were found in this condition and their furr [sic] useless. The Dogs were mostly killed." It is questionable whether these scavengers were being infected by smallpox per se; perhaps they had fallen victim to some other disorder, one that was triggered by the variola.[54, j]

For some unaccountable reason the wildlife from Hudson Bay to the Rocky Mountains were likewise decimated, coincidentally with the smallpox epidemic. It was an unprecedented phenomenon, a puzzle to both veteran traders and Indians, both of whom undoubtedly recognized the rhythmic cycle of wildlife abundance (maxima) and scarcity (minima) still characteristic of the Canadian north.[55, k] There had been no apparent disease which could have explained the matter. "With the death of the Indians," acknowledged Thompson, "a circumstance took place which never has, and in all probability, never will be accounted for." While the Indians were being destroyed by the smallpox epidemic, "the numerous herds of Bison and Deer [caribou] also disappeared both in the Woods and in the Plains, and the Indians about Cumberland House declared the same of the Moose, and the Swans,

j. Monkeys are the only animals presently known susceptible to variola under natural conditions. Yet conditions in the present case were obviously abnormal: smallpox was a relatively new and enormously destructive disease, here, in the New World. Modern epidemiologists really have no conception of the effects of smallpox-death meat on carnivores under these circumstances, prompting Henry F. Dobyns (personal communication) to conclude that contemporary observations, in this case reports of scavenger infection, may indeed be credible. See Dobyns, "An Outline of Andean Epidemic History to 1720," *Bulletin of the History of Medicine* 37 (November-December 1963):499–500, 513.

k. See Diamond Jenness, *The Ojibwa Indians of Parry Island, Their Social and Religious Life*, Canada, Department of Mines, *National Museum of Canada, Bulletin No. 78*, Anthropological Series No. 17 (Ottawa, 1935), pp. 23–25, and Ruth Underhill, "Religion among American Indians," *Annals of the American Academy of Political and Social Science* 311 (May 1957):130, for the aboriginal explanation of wildlife fluctuations. Most furbearing species, excepting the wolverine, black bear, raccoon, otter, and beaver, have roughly a ten-year periodicity.

Geese and Ducks with the Gulls no longer frequented the Lakes in the same number they used to do; and where they had abundance of eggs during the early part of the Summer, they had now to search about to find them." The situation defied explanation. Mused Thompson, further on: "It is justly said, that as Mankind decrease, the Beasts of the earth increase, but in this calamity the natives saw all decrease but the Bears. . . . The enquiries of intelligent Traders into this state of the Animals from the Natives were to no purpose. They merely answered, that the Great Spirit having brought this calamity [i.e., smallpox epidemic] on them, had also taken away the Animals in the same proportion as they were not wanted, and intimating the Bisons and Deer were made and preserved solely for their use; and if there were no Men there would be no Animals."[56] And there the matter rested.

Thompson was on to something important; wildlife biologists have observed similar massive die-offs of unrelated species in recent years (although not involving humans and on a considerably smaller scale) which are often synchronous throughout the Canadian boreal zone. Wildlife build up to a certain peak in numbers, and then they plunge—nobody is quite sure why or how—only to build up to a maximum once more within a predictable number of years. There have been various theories suggested: random fluctuation theories, meteorological theories, and others.[57] One of the more attractive proposals, championed initially by Charles S. Elton, for years the foremost authority on the subject, is that diseases are the principal agent regulating this population explosion. And yet it was unclear to Elton and others since him precisely what epizootic diseases are implicated, although sylvatic plague and tularemia (identified in 1912) seem to be extremely common.[58,1] Both diseases, incidentally, are highly contagious to man.

1. Lloyd Keith, *Wildlife's Ten-Year Cycle* (Madison: University of Wisconsin Press, 1963), finds fault with all of these theories, including the disease theory. I am informed by Professor Jeanne Kay, of the University of Utah Department of Geography, that Keith is now inclined to view wildlife cycles as resulting from a complex set of conditions, including availability of browse vegetation and degree of predation, with weather somehow acting to synchronize the whole affair.

Fourteen years after the decimation of 1781–1782 there was another mysterious outbreak, this time among the beaver. On November 28, 1796, James Bird wrote the following memorandum to his superior, George Sutherland, from his post on the Assiniboine River. Bird began by apologizing for his paucity of beaver skins, but he was powerless to do anything about it, since "the Indians of this place have made no fall hunt worth mentioning. I have only traded about 300 beavers since you passed and have but a poor prospect of getting anything considerable this season owing to a scarcity of beaver (of which there is a universal complaint) and such a number of our traders having left this quarter . . . , as also to the improvements the Canadian [i.e., Northwest Company] traders have made in the quality of their goods."[59] The following April Sutherland himself registered the same complaint in a letter to Peter Fidler of Buckingham House. "The Indians have told me often of the great scarcity of beaver. Many of them have been in and brought but very few." Bird wrote Sutherland again, in May, once more grumbling about the lack of beaver.[60] An explanation was soon forthcoming. Sutherland's entry for May 3, 1797, reads as follows: "Wind and weather the same. Men employed as yesterday. The last of the Souther'd [Cree] Indians came in, brought but few furs. They informed me that there has been a distemper among the beaver of which great numbers have died as they are daily seen floating on the water since the breaking up of the ice."[61]

Beaver continued to be scarce in Cree country for three years thereafter.[62] The next year, 1801, smallpox was reported among the Atsina (Gros Ventre). "The Fall Indians," wrote agent Peter Fidler from the South Saskatchewan River, "have had the smallpox amongst them this summer and carried off upwards of 100 all young people, they received it from a few Tatood [Arapaho] Indians who comes far to [i.e., from] the south, and they are said to have got it from some other Indians that trade with the Europeans far down the Mis sis sury River. The Fall Indians, on account of the war and disease this summer cutting off such numbers of them, appears desperate, and is nearly ready to fall on anyone they can."[63] Could there have been some connection between the beaver epizootic (probably bacterial) and the small-pox (viral) epidemic? Only that a sharply curtailed intake of animal protein might have rendered these people more susceptible to infection with smallpox. Beyond that the state of epidemiological knowledge is too limited to allow us to establish more direct relationships.

In the captivity narrative of John Tanner, a white who was raised as an Ottawa (by adoption) living among the Ojibwa, we find a graphic and extremely valuable description of one such beaver epizootic. Circumstantial evidence leads us to believe that Tanner made his observations in the autumn of 1803, or thereabouts, somewhere in the corridor of land between Lake Superior and the Red River of the North. "I knew of more than twenty gangs of beaver in the country about my camp," he recalled for his army surgeon biographer some years later, "and I now went and began to break up the lodges, but I was much surprised to find nearly all of them empty. At last I found that some kind of distemper was prevailing among these animals, which destroyed them in vast numbers. I found them dead and dying in the water, on the ice, and on the land; sometimes I found one that, having cut a tree half down, had died at its roots; sometimes one who had drawn a stick of timber half way to his lodge, was lying dead by his burthen." Curiosity prompted him to perform an impromptu autopsy. "Many of them, which I opened, were red and bloody about the heart. Those in large rivers and running water suffered less; almost all of those that lived in ponds and stagnant water, died. Since that year the beaver have never been so plentiful in the country of Red River and Hudson's Bay, as they used formerly to be. Those animals which died of this sickness we were afraid to eat, but their skins were good." Evidently, not all beaver were taken ill with the disease, as he says he knew the whereabouts "of two gangs of beaver, that had escaped the prevailing sickness, and I took my traps and went in pursuit of them. In a day or two I had taken eight."[64]

We have a fair idea of the geographical range of this particular epizootic from a report filed by Peter Fidler. " 'Beaver formerly a well known Animal is now very scarce . . . ,' " he observed in 1820.

"Formerly more Packs of Beaver skins at 90 lb. weight was taken out of this District [Dauphin District] than are now got [in] single skins—about 19 years some disorder occasioned by the Change of the Air or Some other unknown cause suddenly reduced them to the very few that is now to be found. This was the Case South of the Athapescow [Athabasca River] all along the Coast of Hudson's Bay as far West as the Eastern borders of the Rocky—This unknown cause extended at the same time in the same direction to near Moose Factory, there and to the Northward of the Settlement the Disorder seems not to have extended its fatal effects."[65]

Returning to Tanner, he and his cautious friends were seemingly correct in their assessment of the disease: there proved to be no harm in collecting the beaver skins. This would rule out the possibility of an insect vector, assuming of course that the disease microorganism was infective for man as well as animals. The fact that they somehow knew to refrain from eating the meat, yet considered the skins safe to handle, would suggest a waterborne bacterial or viral infection.

Studies of the Canadian beaver (*Castor canadensis*) show it to be noncyclical in its fluctuations. This owing, perhaps in part anyway, to the cleansing virtues of its aquatic habitat and a vegetable diet (aspen and cottonwood bark preferred), both of which serve to remove it from the source of most enzootics: infected fleas and ticks and their wildlife hosts. This is certainly not the full explanation, however, since other herbivorous, aquatic species do cycle, most notably the muskrat. In this case drought and flooding appear to influence population fluctuations. Obviously there are other habitat relationships involved which animal ecologists do not as yet fully appreciate. Beaver are likewise relatively secure from predation; in pre-fur-trade times, before the advent of the steel trap baited with castoreum, the rodent had a very real capacity for becoming a pest. Wildlife biologists are now aware that beaver, in the wild, are subject to various sorts of endoparasitism (by trematodes) and ectoparasitism (by fleas, ticks, and beetles), although neither seems to contribute significantly to mortality. More important than these rather benign ailments, there are on record recent epizootics of pseudotuberculosis (*Pasteurella* or *Francisella pseudotuberculosis*) and tularemia (*Pasteurella* or *Francisella tularensis*), the symptoms of one resembling those of the other, except that the disease in the case of pseudotuberculosis is more prolonged, with spleen and liver abscesses being more pronounced than they are under tularemic conditions.

Several clues mentioned by Tanner—his observation of thoracic, peritoneal, and pericardial bloody fluid and the coincidence of stagnant water and the disease—would lead one to believe he was witness to a massive epizootic of tularemia. Indeed, the clinical signs he described, sketchy as they were, and the nature of the habitat correspond to what we know today as a classic case of tularemia infection.[66, m] Tanner's epizootic was evidently waterborne, a conjecture reinforced by current observation. "It appears possible that infection in beavers or other water-frequenting animals is a reflection of a concurrent epizootic among land-frequenting animals living in proximity to affected streams and, further, that some non-parasitic agency, water for example, may serve as a medium through which or by which infection can be conveyed from tularemia-infected land animals to water animals."[67] *F. tularensis* was shown by another, later, team of biologists to be viable in infected pond water (from which the diseased beaver carcasses had been removed) and pond mud for at least sixteen months. What is more, studies of mud samples yielded evidence that *F. tularensis* not only survives in a water-mud

m. Investigations by wildlife biologists have shown that beaver have succumbed to regional tularemia epizootics by at least the hundreds, and muskrats by the thousands (Anonymous, "Trappers Victims of Rodent Plague," *Fur Trade Journal of Canada* [August 1950]:6–7; R. R. Parker et al., "Contamination of Natural Waters and Mud with *Pasteurella tularensis* and Tularemia in Beavers and Muskrats in the Northwestern United States," *National Institutes of Health Bulletin* 193 [Washington, D.C., 1951]:25). In a recent epizootic among pen-raised beaver, where the medium of infection was definitely water, mortality stood at a formidable 70 percent, some of the survivors having been vaccinated against the disease (J. F. Bell et al., "Epizootic Tularemia in Pen-Raised Beavers, and Field Trials of Vaccines," *American Journal of Veterinary Research* 23 [July 1962]:884–887).

medium but actually thrives in it. Curiously, the infectivity of water and mud samples collected and tested in the autumn, four or five months after the epizootic had subsided, showed a marked increase over that of late summer samples.[68]

In all probability, then, there was a direct, causal relationship between this regional tularemia epizootic, witnessed by Tanner in the fall of 1803, and a fever showing definite tularemia symptoms which surfaced a year later. "While we were engaged in collecting and preparing the grain [wild rice]," he reminisced, "many among us were seized with a violent sickness. It commenced with cough and hoarseness, and sometimes bleeding from the mouth or nose. In a short time many died, and none were able to hunt." Hunting, Tanner recalled, could be done only on horseback, the contagion being so debilitating. Even when the hunters gave chase on horseback the game eluded them, frightened off by their loud, incessant coughing (bronchitis). Just at the point when he imagined himself to be recovering, Tanner remembered being seized by an excruciating earache, accompanied by excessive drainage. In this miserable condition he was comatose for days on end; when alert, he was absolutely deaf. Despondent and delirious, he resolved to end his life, but his friends anticipated and prevented his design.

Though my health soon became good, I did not recover my hearing [he actually had partial hearing after that], and it was several months before I could hunt as well as I had been able to do previous to my sickness; but I was not among those who suffered most severely by this terrible complaint. Of the Indians who survived, some were permanently deaf, others injured in their intellects, and some, in the fury occasioned by the disease, dashed themselves against trees and rocks, breaking their arms, or otherwise maiming themselves. Most of those who survived, had copious discharges from the ears, or in the earlier stages had bled profusely from the nose. This disease was entirely new to the Indians, and they attempted to use few or no remedies for it.[69]

The bronchitis, fever, hemorrhaging—in general, typhoid-like symptoms—and extreme prostration are all reminiscent of tularemia, which becomes even more suspect when we recall how this same geographic locale had been the scene of a tularemia epizootic within the preceding twelve months. Notice, furthermore,

Tanner's remark that the epidemic occurred while his people were harvesting the wild rice: tularemia can be either water-borne or tick-borne and is not directly transmissible between infected humans.[70, n]

Epidemiologists have identified four distinct varieties of the disease: ulceroglandular, oculoglandular, glandular, and typhoidal tularemia. The clinical signs of the last, typhoidal, form resemble very closely Tanner's detailed depiction of the illness. "The onset of typhoidal tularemia is abrupt and without warning, and is marked by chills, fever, headache, vomiting, sweating, prostration or joint pains." Continues this same physician:

There is an initial rise of temperature, followed by remission of the fever and symptoms for two or three days, then a return of the fever, which is constantly elevated or spiking, for from three to ten weeks, disappearing by lysis.

It is of interest that patients may retain a sense of well-being throughout the course of a typhoidal tularemia of several week's duration with persistent fever; however, prostration is usual. Nosebleeds during the second and third weeks are not uncommon. Headache may be severe or lacking. . . .

The mortality rate of the typhoidal type of tularemia [has been found] . . . to be approximately 40 per cent, nearly four times that of other clinical types, and the incidence of complicating pneumonia four times the average in the other three types.

Septicemia [in one study] . . . occurred in 1 out of every 17 cases without forewarning. The chief clinical signs of septicemia are progressive enlargement of the liver and spleen, sometimes with increasing jaundice and septic fever. Hyperpnea [rapid, deep respiration] and cyanosis [bluish skin coloration], meningeal and cerebral involvement, diarrhea, progressive bronchopneumonia, acute renal involvement, pleurisy, pericarditis, and peritonitis may appear. Septicemia is the chief cause of death attributable to tularemia alone, but pneumonic lesions were shown to be present in half of [a particular researcher's] . . . fatal cases.[71]

n. Tanner was more lucky than he was correct in his assessment of the potential danger posed by the beaver disease. Assuming that it was tularemia, he and his associates could very easily have contracted an ulceroglandular or oculoglandular form of the disease by, respectively, inadvertently inoculating an open wound (on the hand, most typically), or by rubbing a contaminated hand in the eye. There is at least one case on record where a trapper, by coincidence an Indian woman, skinned a diseased muskrat and managed to avoid infection (Parker et al., "Contamination of Natural Waters," p. 32).

The evidence seems strongly to suggest that these Ojibwa fell prey to a waterborne typhoidal tularemia epidemic which resulted from a slightly antecedent tularemia epizootic. What is striking about this epidemic and several of the other epizootics described above was their novelty. "This disease was entirely new to the Indians," asserted Tanner, "and they attempted to use few or no remedies for it"; the three Ottawa River Indians described by Father Lalemant were terrified by a caribou epizootic, leading one to suspect they had never witnessed such a spectacle before the coming of the French; and David Thompson's Indian informants of over a century later were seemingly baffled by the mysterious disappearance of various game species. Could it be possible that North American wildlife were being decimated by alien diseases somehow introduced by Europeans?[o] Tularemia is especially interesting in this regard. Russian and American epidemiologists are now convinced that

two basic types of tularemia organisms occur in nature distinguished by differences in virulence and biochemical reactions, and which occur in different habitats and are associated with different modes of transmission and different maintenance mechanisms. One type, termed *F. t. tularensis* or "Type A" is thought to be restricted in distribution to the New World, is highly virulent for laboratory animals . . . produces a higher fatality rate in untreated human cases (5–7%), . . . is associated with drier habitats, and with ticks, hares, rabbits, sheep and grouse; transmission is primarily through the tick vector which is also responsible for its long term perpetuation. The second type, termed *F. t. palearctica* or "Type B," occurs in both the Old and New World, is relatively avirulent for laboratory rabbits, produces fatality in less than one percent of untreated human cases, . . . is associated with wetland habitats and in North America is characteristic of rodents (beaver, muskrats, voles) and water. This type of tularemia is believed to be a single complex dependent on water and cannibalism for transmission and entirely independent of tick transmission.[72]

o. See Charles Elton, *The Ecology of Invasions by Animals and Plants* (1958; reprint ed., New York: John Wiley and Sons, 1966), for some thoughts on the grave consequences of species invasions of virgin areas. Referring, more specifically, to the Americas, the subject of Alfred W. Crosby, Jr., *The Columbian Exchange: Biological and Cultural Consequences of 1492* (Westport, Conn.: Greenwood Press, 1972), pp. 64–121, one may infer that many of these exotic Old World fauna would have brought with them their equally alien diseases.

Actually, the demarcation between the two strains is not as sharp as is here implied; one strain is quite capable of assuming the epidemiological profile of the other, for reasons which remain obscure.[73]

Conceivably, the Type A strain was brought ashore by early European visitors, carried by infected ticks which parasitized their livestock. Lescarbot confirmed that sheep were among the first livestock imported to Acadia, and sheep, according to the above source, are one of several animals associated with Type A. "We had but one sheep," he wrote in his account of the Port-Royal barnyard, "which enjoyed the best possible health. . . ."[74] The sheep ticks, in turn, being non-host-specific, could have abandoned their European hosts for New World hosts, infecting them in the process. Canadian Indians would then have inadvertently picked up the infection from diseased wildlife.[p]

A common stowaway on European vessels of the period were commensal rats—rats whose fleas no doubt often carried murine typhus and bubonic plague. Lescarbot apologized for including these vile creatures in his zoological inventory, yet despite his disgust they deserved recognition because of their vast numbers and audacious behavior. "The savages had no knowledge of these animals before our coming; but in our time they have been beset by them, since from our fort [Port-Royal] they went even to their lodges, a distance of over four hundred paces, to eat or suck their fish oils."[75] Here, in the Micmac villages, they no doubt transmitted their vermin, *Xenopsylla cheopis* and *Pulex irritans*, to the already vermin-infested natives.[76] The infected fleas would in turn inject the bacterium *Yersinia* (or *Pasteurella*) *pestis* into the victim during feeding, and in a few days (usually three) the patient would begin showing signs of bubonic plague: tender buboes, usually in the femoral or inguinal region, fever, confusion, nausea, and vomiting. From the bubonic form the disease might progress to the septicemic or extremely lethal pneumonic form. Pneumonic plague, once it has surfaced, is highly

p. The question is then raised: Why or how did the Type A strain disappear from western Europe—something I cannot answer.

contagious in aerosol form, its symptoms consisting of "abdom-
inal ileus and bladder distention . . . , apathy, confusion, fright
anxiety, oliguria [scant urination], anuria [terminated urination],
and fulminant bilateral pneumonia."[77] Death occurs within one
to three days in untreated patients, 95 to 100 percent of whom
succumb.[78]

Canadian Indians probably enhanced their susceptibility to
plague by biting and eating their fleas and lice, a fairly common
habit according to many early commentators. Vietnamese people
have been observed doing the same thing in recent years, as have
Ecuadorian Indians, both of whom have come down with plague
as a result.[79] Still, the most common mode of transmission was
undoubtedly by flea bite.

As for plague among the wild rodent population, it is entirely
possible that commensal rat fleas infected with Y. pestis conveyed
the disease to local furbearers, triggering an epizootic which
might then have re-circulated among the human population as a
plague epidemic.

All of this is plausible, but frankly conjectural. No one knows
whether it actually happened and, even though it probably did,
nobody can prove it. The point in my bringing it up is to show
that it was not only possible, but probable, that Europeans imported zoonotic diseases to Canada (tularemia and plague, for
instance)—diseases which seeded natural foci, where sylvatic
plague and tularemia (perhaps of a different, Type B strain) were
already entrenched (enzootic). We really have no idea whether
there was, or is, a New World and Old World strain of plague. If
there were genetic differences between the wild, sylvatic plague,
which we speculate was indigenous to the New World, and the
domestic variety brought over by Europeans, epidemiologists
are ignorant of them.

The fact remains, on the strength of the Ojibwa evidence
alone, that some Indian deaths were caused by animal infections.
Whether these epizootics originated with European sources or
were native to the area is unclear. Circumstantial evidence would
argue that North American wildlife and their insect parasites had

served as reservoirs of disease long before Europeans arrived, some of the diseases perhaps being unique to the New World while others had an Old World counterpart in the form of a slightly different strain. No one would seriously dispute this, it seems to me. Nor would anyone argue that pre-Columbian American Indians, in this case Eastern Canadian Indians, were immune to infection from these wildlife sources of disease. As to how many people died as a result of them is impossible to say. Yet when we consider that there have been cases in this century when literally hundreds of thousands of Russians have become ill with tularemia, because they drank or bathed in contaminated water, we justifiably suspect that the mortality rate was at times high, at least after contact and the introduction of an especially virulent strain. There are also cases on record where hundreds of water-rat hunters in the Soviet Union and an indeterminate number of muskrat and beaver trappers in America have come down with tularemia after having skinned or otherwise incautiously handled diseased carcasses.[80] This, too, would lend credence to a high incidence of the disease among Canadian hunter-gatherers, with an indeterminate death rate.

Speculation and conjecture aside, it is obvious that these Eastern Canadian and other North American Indians blamed wildlife for their diseases precisely because they were, indeed, the source of many of their ailments. There may have been something of a mythological and spiritual rationale as well—certainly these Canadian Indians rationalized the origin of their diseases in spiritual terms—yet this was an ideology which we must recognize as derived from actual experience.

One of the most pronounced themes of early contact history in this Eastern Canadian region is a sweeping and monumental despiritualization among the aboriginal population. Oddly enough, this movement toward secularization was not confined to the acculturated (or perhaps, more appropriately, deculturated) native groups. The feeling one gets from reading the contemporary testimony to this process is that it was not an acculturative phenomenon, although missionization and acculturation in general certainly speeded it up, but was a symptom of some internal spiritual malaise. There was, in other words, something awry in the native cosmology. Hearne detected this among the Chipewyan, a tribe which at that time was far beyond the pale of Christian influence. "Religion," he wrote, "has not yet begun to dawn among the Northern Indians; for though their conjurors do indeed sing songs, and make long speeches, to some beasts and birds of prey, as also to imaginary beings, which they say assist them in performing cures on the sick, yet they, as well as their credulous neighbours, are utterly destitute of every idea of practical religion." Yet, even in this unadulterated state there was something amiss. Continued Hearne:

It is true, some of them will reprimand their youth for talking disrespectfully of particular beasts and birds; but it is done with so little energy, as to be often retorted back in derision. Neither is this, nor their custom of not killing wolves and quiquehatches [wolverines, predators of the beaver], universally observed, and those who do it can only be viewed with more pity and contempt than the others; for I always found it arose merely from the greater degree of confidence which they had in the supernatural power of their conjurors, which induced them to believe, that talking lightly or disrespectfully of anything they seemed to approve, would materially affect their health and happiness in this world.[81]

It would appear that these as yet unacculturated Chipewyan were rejecting the traditional spiritual formula for the Good Life; they were now barely subscribing to the ritual and taboo that had traditionally given order and meaning to their universe. They were becoming infidels quite apart from Christian missionary teaching. David Thompson noted a similar behavior among the Cree. "I have found many of the Men," he observed, "especially those who had been much in company with white men, to be all half infidels, but the Women kept them in order; for they fear the Manito's [sic]. . . ."[82] Were they apostatizing for the sake of Christianity? Clearly they were not: the Jesuit experience proves that, as does the fact that many of these people had not as yet been exposed to Christian instruction. Besides, "infidel" is a designation meaning no religion whatsoever, and this is obviously the sense in which Thompson is using the term. Much the same sort of thing was observed among the Micmac: people were rejecting the traditional spiritual answers because they no longer proved satisfying. The corrosive element in each case was undoubtedly disease: European-derived disease. For not only were shamans incapable of curing the new diseases but initially, at least (before there was sustained contact with Europeans), they could not explain them. Or could they? Is it not reasonable to assume that these people, who were seemingly accustomed to blaming offended wildlife for their sicknesses, would have blamed them as well for the new contagions? It was precisely this suspicion—that animals were unduly punishing man with sickness—which triggered the secularization, or profanation, of the aboriginal spiritual world.

Never had the Indians experienced diseases of such magnitude and severity. We might hypothesize that after the initial outbreak, whenever it occurred, the distraught victims resorted to their usual methods of relief: herbal remedies, sweatbaths, bloodletting, and emetics. Finally the conjuror was directed to summon his potent spiritual powers. But this time the spirits in the shaking tent could give no cure, although they may have identified the source. Surely an epidemic so widespread could not have been caused by sorcery; anyway, even the suspected sorcerers were succumbing. Somehow the connection must have been made between the sickness that stalked the land and the animals that were overrunning the earth. Perhaps, in the Indian mind, like that of Thompson's and Henry's informants, the contagion was construed as part of a conspiracy of the beasts. In an attempt to extricate himself from their morbid grip, the Indian sought to destroy his wildlife tormentors: he went on a war of revenge, a war which soon became transformed into the historic fur trade. This would explain the strangely vindictive, hostile posture of Micmac, Cree, and Ojibwa sources, mentioned above, toward the beaver and other wildlife. Man stood helpless before their onslaught; the dialogue between man and Nature became acrimonious and eventually nonexistent, and shamans were powerless to mend the shattered universe.

As an epilogue it should be said that not all these Eastern Canadian hunters became unalterably hostile toward the spirit world. The deference and affection for the slain bear expressed by the Ojibwa Wawatam, and his kin, proves this. Likewise, the aged Cree who shared his hospitality and traditions with David Thompson was mournful over the passing of the beaver, and with good reason. When "the whole of these extensive countries were denuded of Beaver, the Natives became poor, and with difficulty procured the first necessaries of life, and in this state they remain, and probably for ever."[83] Little did Thompson know just how prophetic those tragic words would be.

The next several hundred years would find many of these people reverting to aboriginal beliefs, reaffirming their faith in the old ways of their pre-Columbian ancestors. The Wabeno cult of the late eighteenth century marked one such renaissance among the Ojibwa.[84] Another followed in the Shawnee revival under Tenskwatawa, Tecumseh's visionary brother. A good many Ojibwa subscribed to the messianic, redemptionist message of The Prophet (Tenskwatawa), as well as took part in the abortive rebellion. Far to the east, the coastal Micmac likewise experienced revitalization under a charismatic figure named Abistanaooch. Partly as a result of these movements the diligent ethnologist still finds vestiges of hunting magic, a belief in Nature spirits, and conjuring among the less acculturated Eastern Canadian bands, but knowledgeable and willing informants are becoming increasingly scarce.

Surveying this great panorama of early contact history, it is obvious that the fur trade overhauled the social and cultural configuration of the tribes involved. Many of these changes have been documented in the two preceding sections. But the real purpose of this investigation has been to determine what the trade meant to the Indian on his own terms. I have argued that the scholarly fraternity's infatuation with Western economic theory, combined with an unfamiliarity with the ethnography, have caused it to think of the trade essentially in supply-and-demand terms. From a Western standpoint the theory is admirable, but unfortunately it gives little thought as to how the Indian may have conceived of the experience.

The thesis, here, has been that the fur trade must be reconciled to the supernaturalistic world view of the Indian if it is to be seen as a two-dimensional experience. By reconstituting the native belief and value system as it functioned in late prehistoric times throughout Eastern Canada, we discerned a behavioral environment that encompassed wildlife and plant-life in a reciprocating relationship of courtesy. A kind of contractual agreement existed between man and animals: the one was not to ruin the other with the powerful sanctions each was possessed of. The Indian hunter, for example, had the right to harvest game, in return for which privilege he was to perform proper rituals of disposal and consumption and observe taboo. Yet from legend and ethnographic analogy one suspects there must have been discord within the system. Informants spoke darkly of a conspiracy of animals against man; there was a strange aura of bitterness in the hunting of commercially valuable game. It is my conviction that Old World diseases had a part in alienating aboriginal man from the game spirits. More specifically, because shamans lost their ability to cure diseases—diseases that were probably originally assigned to offended wildlife—the Indian lost faith in the traditional avenues of spiritual redress. Man thus became hostile toward an animal kingdom which he was convinced had broken faith with him. Surely Christian missionary teaching accented the alienation process by its criticism of shamanism and so-called superstitions and by the encouragement given by the Jesuits to the trade, but these corrosive forces did not initiate it.

As for the actual trade, it furnished the native with the means to vanquish his enemies, the treacherous wildlife, as well as improve his chances for living a leisurely existence—or so he deluded himself. This latter goal proved, of course, to be chimerical. As it happened, the Indian trader became locked, first, into an alien economy and, then, into a life-style which left him impoverished and, paradoxically, busier than ever. In the beginning, however, before this juggernaut quality was realized—when it was, it was too late to undo—the body ornaments and other baubles, clothing, liquor, and such domestic conveniences as the copper kettle were compelling inducements to barter. And yet these could not have been of themselves sufficiently alluring to prompt the Indian to renege on his spiritual commitments. The fact is that the spiritual edifice had already rotted from within by the time these became craved necessities. In order to procure them the Indian hunted and trapped recklessly—his conscience only slightly troubled. The fur-to-trade-goods exchange, although it exacerbated this spiritual decay, was thus more a symptom than its cause.

CHAPTER SIX

Conclusion

Fifty years ago, in the days when the term *primitive* could still be used in a nonpejorative sense, Lucien Lévy-Bruhl, the French anthropologist, entitled the book he had just written *Primitive Mentality*. Still a provocative work among cultural anthropologists, its thesis is basically that the mind of the non-literate is mystical, or magical, in its identification of causation. Behavioral patterns that have perplexed Western observers become perfectly clear when we accept the supernatural epistemology and phenomenology of the tribesmen, he argued. Only by divesting ourselves of our Western rationalism do we appreciate the true meaning of the ordeal, native land tenure, the nature of death, witchcraft, taboo, and the shattering consequences of European intrusion on such a closed and delicate universe.[1]

I have tried to interpret the Eastern Canadian fur trade within such a context. The "keepers of the game" were not mankind, Indian or white, but the spiritual wardens regulating wildlife. Regardless of how jarring that concept may be to Occidental thought, that was the cultural framework within which these Eastern Canadian hunters conducted their lives. And it is only by accepting the relative validity of the same spiritual premises that we may hope to understand and appreciate the aboriginal hunting complex: the magic, ritual, taboo, and technology of the chase. When Europeans arrived all of this did not just simply disappear; fragments of the aboriginal hunting and, broader yet, spiritual complex survive today) Additional proof comes from the testimony of early witnesses who recorded the death throes of the traditional belief system in the face of overwhelming cultural pressure. Yet it is my contention that this system was already collapsing from within, when the foundation of mutual cooperation on which it was predicated was repudiated, first by the animal kingdom and then by man. The hostility thus generated bequeathed to the historic fur trade an aspect of revenge which has eluded scholars until now.

Admitting, then, that we have seriously underestimated the significance of the spiritual factor, what were the principal and combined forces which motivated the Indian to barter furs for European wealth? In answering this question one should make it clear, to begin with, that Indians placed nowhere near the same value on skins and pelts as did the Europeans who came among them. Indeed, a recurring and noteworthy theme of Indian-white trade negotiations was the astonishment of the native at the fierce competition and greed among white traders for a few worn-out skins—in the case of the much prized *castor gras.* The avarice of individual traders registered profoundly in the minds of their Indian counterparts, who despised such baseness of character—and bluntly said so. The usual theory advanced by the incredulous natives, who found themselves spectators to European intrigue and bad manners, was that Europe must be impoverished of such-and-such an item. For what else could prompt these people to seek so desperately to provide themselves with such prodigious quantities of it for transshipment? The idea of material accumulation and hoarding in order to gain prestige was entirely foreign to the native way of thinking. Wealthy people disposed of their goods in native society; altruism took precedence over conspicuous affluence. By dispensing wealth, one gained prestige and social validation, while avoiding the stigma of being labeled a necromancer. There was thus no point, indeed a positive danger, in accumulating and hoarding quantities of material wealth.

When considering Indian views of Europeans, as we are doing here, it is well to remember that Native American societies, at least those treated here, were probably emotionally secure and confident entities on the eve of European contact. In most cases, it is safe to assume, these groups were devastated by alien European diseases carried inland by infected natives some time before the majority of them actually witnessed the white man. The resulting epidemics had the effect of demoralizing the community, insofar as their mysterious origin was frustratingly obscure and their cure beyond the healing arts of the shamans. This was the emotion-charged setting of internal despair and rage into which the Jesuit priest and trader-explorer-soldier came. And here one must depart from the usual explanation for what ensued: the Indian had little difficulty understanding and categorizing his white-complexioned visitors. Although initially he may have endowed them with special spiritual significance, he very soon realized that Europeans were flawed, sometimes seriously flawed in their character and culture, as the Indian became fond of pointing out. The idea that the native stood in rapt, prolonged awe of Europeans has been exaggerated. Consider, for example, the chronic frustration of the Jesuit fathers: Indian converts were difficult to make and even more difficult to preserve—apostatization was rampant. Those who had been ostensibly healed through prayer were only a little more easy of instruction and conversion, but they too soon fell away from the unadulterated Gospel.

Part of the problem lay in the Indian's penchant for hospitality, a point repeatedly affirmed by early chroniclers. And hospitality, in those days and among those people, was an all-out affair. Gifts, honors, and deference were showered on strangers. If a visitor of distinction wanted anything, he was given it. Of course there might often be something expected in return, either immediately or belatedly bestowed, but this does not alter the fact that the Indian mood of reception was warm and generous. Such generosity even extended to the abstract realm of ideas, theories, stories, news, and teachings; the native host prided himself on his ability to entertain and give assent to a variety of views, even if they were contrary to his better judgment, information, or personal inclinations. In this institutionalized hospitality lies the key to understanding the frustration of the priest, whose sweet converts one day were the relapsed heathens of the next. Conversion was often more a superficial courtesy than an eternal commitment, something the Jesuits simply could not fathom.

Added to this spirit of acquiescence (more often than not rooted in anxiety over offending someone else) and generosity was a shrewd and practiced business sense. This, too, was a source of surprised comment by whites, especially those whose dealings with the Indians were explicitly trade-oriented. All of these Eastern Canadian tribes had bartered with neighbors long before European landfall; the haggling and logistics of trade were hardly introduced *de novo* by whites.

The earliest proposals for trade were considered by the natives as somewhat whimsical (the old, worn-out skins idea), but also, more importantly, as a means of getting something desired (trade goods) in exchange for something of less value (skins and pelts). True enough, there was the obstacle of wildlife resentment that had to be removed. Beyond that, though, the Indian was convinced that he stood to benefit by far the most from the transaction. Le Jeune was thus accosted one day by an incredulous Montagnais who facetiously announced: " 'The Beaver does everything perfectly well, it makes kettles, hatchets, swords, knives, bread; and, in short, it makes everything.' He was making sport of us Europeans, who have such a fondness for the skin of this animal and who fight to see who will give the most to these Barbarians, to get it; they carry this to such an extent that my host said to me one day, showing me a very beautiful knife, 'The English have no sense; they give us twenty knives like this for one Beaver skin.' "[2] I think we can appreciate the man's point. After all, with liquor (rum and brandy were the usual fare) he could achieve spiritual ecstasy and a socially acceptable moral laxity; he could adorn himself and his women with the most pleasing ornaments; he could now enjoy the convenience of a copper kettle; he (or, more properly, his wife or mother) was partially relieved of the necessity of clothing the household after the introduction and (incomplete) adoption of European dress; European foodstuffs gave him more time for other pursuits; his valor soared as he vanquished his gunless enemies with this remarkable device; and numerous other chores and occupations were facilitated with the new trade items. Once the sanctions against overkilling game had been nullified, the way was opened to a more convenient life-style. This is what appealed to the Indian partner in the trade: the chance to make his traditional life-way more convenient, his traditional goals more attainable. He was not interested in improving his standard of living through bald material accumulation. Prosperity and affluence, for him, meant rather the judicious borrowing of certain material goods which, when used, would facilitate the traditional way of doing things. His goal was, therefore, enhanced convenience—without material encumbrance.

Taken all together, what we have here is a novel interpretation of the fur trade—from the Indian side of the issue. The process might have begun as follows: the initial willingness to procure and exchange furs for goods was an hospitable gesture combined with a business acumen that clearly recognized a good bargain. Slightly antedating this was the timely rationalization for wantonly slaughtering such unprecedented numbers of game. Man and animal were at war, and the rules of the usually amicable but guarded relationship were altered accordingly.

In a cultural ecological sense, I have suggested that European contact might appropriately be designated a trigger factor, meaning that it set in motion a series of forces leading to a profound change in the aboriginal ecosystem. Put simply, the spiritual infrastructure of aboriginal life was vigorously assailed by the combined forces of alien contact: disease, missionization, and the fur trade. In some cases it was completely jettisoned, but such complete repudiation must have been rare. More typically, it was modified to accommodate the new European reality: remnants of native ritual, taboo, and mythology were merged with or set alongside Christian ritual and doctrine; beleaguered victims became resigned to a life devastated by chronic disease; and, most importantly for us, the spiritual hunt was profaned.

Without question the most poignant and profound tragedy of white contact for these people was this despiritualization phenomenon. Indians themselves were acutely aware of it, as when a group of angry Algonkians confronted Le Jeune and denounced Christianity as a malefic influence. " 'It is a strange thing,' said they, 'that since prayer has come into our cabins, our former customs are no longer of any service; and yet we shall all die because we give them up.' 'I have seen the time,' said one of them, 'when my dreams were true; when I had seen Moose or Beavers in sleep, I would take some. When our Soothsayers felt the enemy coming, that came true; there was preparation to receive him. Now, our dreams and our prophecies are no longer true,—prayer has spoiled everything for us.' . . . The Father," we are told,

remonstrated with them, that if one did not teach them . . . they would burn eternally in Hell, and that the danger of their Salvation obliged us [Jesuits] to urge them. But the majority became still more obstinate, and were furious with spite against the Father, and said that he was a greater sorcerer than their own people; that the country must be cleared of such; that they had clubbed three sorcerers at the Island [Montréal? Alumette?], who had not done so much harm as he. There was some fear lest they should carry out their evil thought: but the Divine goodness did not permit it,—on the contrary, it drew great benefits from their malice.[3]

What is so pathetic about this scene is that we can understand and sympathize with both sides of the issue, the Indian and the equally earnest Jesuit.

Many years later Frank Speck witnessed a similarly tragic commentary on despiritualization. He had been interviewing a Naskapi, named Basil, on the ability of a certain drum to warn its owner of impending danger. "In commenting on this story, Basil . . . added his own views by saying, 'But I don't believe in that now. It all belongs to the olden times. It is what we are taught to call the devil, perhaps. The times have changed. With the coming of the whites and Christianity the demons of the bush have been pushed back to the north where there is no Christianity. And the conjuror does not exist any more with us, for there is no need of one. Nor is there need for the drum.' "[4] The conjuror and the drum became obsolete when Nature became inarticulate—despiritualized. Such was the atmosphere in which the historic fur trade was conducted in Eastern Canada. Wildlife were hounded without quarter not just because their hides were valuable for trading purposes but because they were now considered man's implacable enemy; they were deaf and dumb and treacherous.

If our histories of the North American fur trade are to be full and accurate they will have to reconcile themselves to the stark fact that once upon a time man and animals talked with one another on this continent. Why they ceased their conversation is a question for the ethnohistorian to ponder; whether they will ever do so again is a question for the prophets.

Epilogue: The Indian and the Ecology Movement[a]

Lᴀᴛᴇ ɪɴ ᴛʜᴇ 1960s the North American Indian acquired yet another stereotypic image in the popular mind: the erstwhile "savage," the "drunken" Indian, the "vanishing" Indian was conferred the title of the "ecological" (i.e., conservationist-minded) Indian. Propped up for everything that was environmentally sound, the Indian was introduced to the American public as the great high priest of the Ecology Cult. Depending upon one's point of reference, this might appear to be another crass commercial gimmick, a serious case of misread or ignored history, or a logical outgrowth of the conservation movement. Actually, it was some of all three. The idea would never have taken hold had it not been that conservationists needed a spiritual leader at that particular point in time, and the Indian, given the contemporary fervor and theology of environmentalism, seemed the logical choice.

The man perhaps most responsible for this peculiar choice was Aldo Leopold, a wildlife biologist now considered to be one of

a. The following chapter is based in part on my article "The Ecological Effects of Indian-White Relations: Major Euroamerican Influences," in the *Handbook of North American Indians*, edited by William C. Sturtevant, vol. 4 (Washington, D.C.: Smithsonian Institution, 1976–), which is in press.

the major theoreticians of the movement. Writing in the 1940s, Leopold, incensed at man's arrogance toward other life-forms, proposed that the time had now come to extend our ethics from man-to-man to man-to-land. He called his novel idea a "land ethic."[1] Contained within this remarkable bit of insight was the germ of a new perspective on conservationism, a movement well underway by Leopold's time.

Intellectuals, such as the Transcendentalists Henry David Thoreau, Ralph Waldo Emerson, and John Muir, and a variety of landscape painters (e.g., Thomas Cole and Ashur B. Durand) had many years before preached an aesthetic view of Nature. To their way of thinking, Nature, which included wilderness, was to be enjoyed and preserved not for its own sake—that was Leopold's notion—but for the spiritual benefit man derived from it. Juxtaposed to this, the aesthetic school of thought, was the utilitarianism of George Perkins Marsh, the Bureau of Reclamation, Gifford Pinchot, and others, for whom conservationism meant the efficient, regulated use of natural resources. First there were the utilitarian and the aesthetic views, and then, with Leopold, there evolved the ecological perspective. Leopold, in sum, gave the spiritual conscience of John Muir and the engineering mentality of Muir's contemporaries a moral twist.[2]

As a national panacea "ecology" began to tantalize the American public in the early sixties. Rachel Carson sounded the alarm in 1962 with her unsettling *Silent Spring*. Readers were appalled at the revelation that we were systematically poisoning our continental ecosystem. Public confidence was shaken on another front when Paul Ehrlich's *Population Bomb* was published a few years later. There were too many of us, coolly observed the Stanford biologist, and if we did not act now to limit our population spiral the near future would be without a doubt catastrophic. Ehrlich left little to the imagination as he spelled out the possibilities in macabre scenarios. The same decade witnessed the enactment of federal clean air and water legislation, the passage of the Wilderness Act, and a cosmetic campaign to beautify America.

From the sixties and on into the seventies, one had only to look around to see for oneself that we were in the grip of an ecological crisis. Molecular biologists warned that unrestrained atomic testing might wreak genetic havoc. Smog, getting progressively worse, now became more than a literal eyesore; it was shown to be a cause for the fatal respiratory disease emphysema. Urban sprawl was suddenly unseemly and ominous: the strip of southern California coastline from San Diego to Santa Barbara was irreverently dubbed SanSan; Boston to Washington, Boswash. It was a period of cute, ironic slogans. Cigarette smoking was found definitely to cause lung cancer; food additives became suspect as carcinogenic agents; a casual assay of several tuna fish tins turned up inordinate quantities of mercury—a neurotoxin, among other things. The national mood was jittery. A multi-million-dollar health business cashed in on the nation's paranoia about eating "right." On the beaches, the concern over the sinking of the oil tanker *Torrey Canyon* was mild compared to the howl raised over the Santa Barbara oil spill. The guilty oil firm in the latter case must have cursed its bad luck: to have a well blow out on the beaches of a Sierra Club stronghold. Youth caught the beat of the movement in the lyrics of Bob Dylan and his imitators. Disenchantment—with the Indochina War, with environmental degradation, with racism—needed a vent. Utilitarian, aesthetic, and ecological conservationism found their fulfillment, and more, in this fashionable anxiety and outrage known as the Gospel of Ecology.[b]

The cant was partly mystical, impatiently and self-righteously moral. Nature was to be revered in her own right; she must be gently caressed into yielding her fruits, not raped. But alas, so we were told, the correct, or in the contemporary idiom, "ecological," attitude is alien to the Western mind. The Jeremiahs of the movement directed us to our own past to confirm that pronouncement.[3] Western man desperately needed a model, a hero, a guru to teach him: the American Indian, so it was decreed.

b. All of the foregoing was derived from lectures given by Roderick Nash at the University of California, Santa Barbara.

In a speech delivered before a collegiate audience in Lynchburg, Virginia, Rennard Strickland declared emphatically, "The idea of ecology demands the ideal of the Indian." *"It is not an accident,"* he reminded his youthful listeners, *"that the idea of ecology and the ideal of the Indian should emerge simultaneously as national issues* [emphasis his]."[4] A decade ago Stewart L. Udall found it "ironical that today the conservation movement finds itself turning back to ancient Indian land ideas, to the Indian understanding that we are not outside of nature, but of it." More recently, the former secretary of the interior avowed that "the Indians were, in truth, the pioneer ecologists of this country."[5] European-Americans allegedly held a crass view of Nature, in contrast to the Indian's reverence for Mother Earth; the former attitude has fostered despoliation, the latter the conservation of our natural resources. Indeed, this conservationist ethic was shared by the Indians of all the Americas, claimed Terence Grieder, who detected a lesson herein for modern man. Perhaps the best way to preserve our wildlife would be to develop a sense of "subrational supernatural regulation" like that of the ancient shamans.[6]

N. Scott Momaday, a Pulitzer prize–winning Kiowa novelist, has taken Grieder's sentiments slightly further, forecasting certain disaster should we fail to learn wise land-use from our Indian brethren.[7] The most strident advocate of this latter principle is the Indian activist Vine Deloria, Jr., a Standing Rock Sioux. "The Indian," solemnly vouchsafes Deloria, "lived with his land. He feared to destroy it by changing its natural shape because he realized that it was more than a useful tool for exploitation. It sustained all life, and without other forms of life, man himself could not survive. . . . All of this understanding was ruthlessly wiped out to make room for the white man so that civilization could progress according to God's divine plan." *"The white man destroyed his land,"* exclaims Deloria, *"he destroyed the planet earth* [emphasis his]." Deloria sees only one avenue of escape. "To survive, white society must return the land to the Indians in the sense that it restores the land to the condition it was in before the white man came." Or again, "The only answer [to the white man's environmental problems] will be to adopt Indian ways to survive. For the white man even to exist, he must adopt a total Indian way of life. That is really what he had to do when he came to this land. It is what he will have to do before he leaves it once again."[8]

At least one recent historian has incorporated a more cerebral and informed variant of this idea in his work. In the respected opinion of Wilbur R. Jacobs, the frontier thesis of Frederick Jackson Turner and company is bankrupt on the matter of the Indian. Jacobs has dismissed the stereotype of the heroic, patriotic frontiersman-fur-trapper as a fabrication, created and perpetuated by romantics. Let us dispense with this noble claptrap, he has urged, and expose the frontiersman for the despoiler that he in fact was. The real hero of the wilderness drama was the Indian, as Jacobs plays on the familiar theme of the native as conservator of natural resources. He pleads for modern America to give heed to the Indian's cosmic vision so as to restore the balance of Nature that was once hers.[9]

One finds a kindred sentiment expressed in William Faulkner's *The Bear*. Old Ben, the mysterious bear, and Sam Fathers, the aged Indian, are symbols of the American wilderness in the novel—symbols of a wilderness that is being developed into oblivion, to Faulkner's dismay. Other American writers have been likewise fascinated by the Indian's sympathetic relationship with the land. James Fenimore Cooper, in his *Leatherstocking Tales*, and especially Francis Parkman, in his epic *France and England in North America* and in *The Oregon Trail*, tenderly linked the Indian with the wilderness and mourned their mutual passing. There reposes a comparable fascination in Melville's *Moby Dick*, Cather's *Death Comes for the Archbishop*, and Hemingway's Nick Adams stories. Clearly the *bon sauvage*-attuned-to-Nature idea has long been a favorite device in American literature.

Antecedents to contemporary eco-Indian literature can also be found in the writings of a handful of social scientists who flourished a generation or so ago. In the late 1930s, within two years of one another, the historian William Christie MacLeod and the ethnologist Frank G. Speck, both of the University of Pennsylvania, published nearly identical articles on "Conservation Among Primitive Hunting Peoples" and "Aboriginal Conservators."[10] Both articles, as their titles suggest, argued for an aboriginal conservationist ethic among select North American tribes. Some years later William A. Ritchie, state archaeologist for New York, phrased it in present-sounding terms. "We may say, in sharp contrast to the white man's way, that the Indian trod lightly through his natural environment, merging himself sympathetically into the world of living and even non-living things."[11] The message was identical to that of the late sixties, but Americans were not as yet prepared to make an issue of it. Today the pronouncements of these scholars have been incorporated into the larger rhetoric of the American Environmental Movement, and the Indian has emerged as its ambiguous hero.

Not surprisingly, there are dissenters who dismiss most of this as sentimental nonsense. It is no mere coincidence that many of this latter sort are ethnologists who have for years been scrutinizing the Indian in the field, their experience with him being something less than enchanting. Thus Bernard J. James, studying the Lac Court Oreilles Ojibwa, wryly observed that there was some empirical evidence to support the local white claim "that 'all you need to do to find their towns is to drive onto the reservation and follow the beer cans.' . . . It was possible in 1952 to count from a moving vehicle over three hundred discarded beer cartons per mile (discounting those obscured by grass and undergrowth) on some stretches of reservation road. I observed nothing comparable near local White communities."[12] One can understand this sort of behavior in the subculture of poverty and inferiority in which these people are mired. Emanating from this is a good deal of hostility and resentment toward the white majority, the reservation Ojibwa expressing their rage and frustration through violent drinking bouts and other means. They have been made to bear a series of white negative stereotypes, observed James—"drunken," "lazy," "dirty," and so on—stereotypes which they deeply resent, yet accept. Hence the strewn beer cans.

Unfortunately, not all scholars have been so sensitive and discriminating in their study of contemporary or historic Indian attitudes toward the land. For example, John Greenway, a musicologist with some training in cultural anthropology, several years ago published a swashbuckling article flippantly entitled, "Will the Indians Get Whitey?" The Indian, said he in effect, is a knave—an incorrigibly murderous bum who today raids the conscience and pocketbook of the nation with scandalous impunity and success.[13] Among other things, he doubtless had in mind the current apotheosis of the Native American to ecological mentor. Only slightly more circumspect was the frontier historian W. H. Hutchinson, who likewise felt compelled to deliver himself of a diatribe: "The Remaking of the Amerind: A Dissenting Voice Raised Against the Resurrection of the Myth of the Noble Savage." Hutchinson's acerbic prose assailed the dewy-eyed romantics who claim for the Indian such a delicate ecological conscience "as to make the Sierra Club seem an association of strip miners by comparison." Nature "is *not* a benign bovine with a teat for every questing mouth!"[14] The Indian revered Nature because he had no other choice, flatly declared Hutchinson. To him Nature was controlled by supernatural powers whom he was obliged to propitiate if he hoped for success in life; failure to perform the proper rituals, adhere to taboos, and conduct ceremonials was tantamount to inviting disaster. We ought to recognize that the Indian was above all a pragmatist when it came to land-use.

This final point has found its most compelling spokesman in Clifford C. Presnall of the United States Fish and Wildlife Service. American Indians have traditionally conceived of game as a utility, theorized Presnall in an article in the *Journal of Mammalogy*, and since time out of memory they have geared their hunting practices to be as economical as possible. In his words:

To the Indian the pursuit of game is a vocation; to us it is an avocation. The Indian regards wildlife as necessary to his existence, so much so that he worships it; he propitiates it with prayers before killing it, in order that future success in the hunt may be assured; he does not abhor the waste of game *per se*, but is opposed to a scarcity of game because that will force him to work harder; he objects to killing purely for sport, believing that it will anger the animal deities who will then hinder his business of hunting for food. . . . The Indian in sport may think nothing of gambling away his wife, but will avoid waste of energy in his business enterprise—his hunting; and he will hunt in certain ways because of superstitious fears about his future. The basic concepts of the two races are not very different; the Indian has merely applied vocation concepts to wildlife and we think of it as an avocation.

If given the opportunity, Indians will not hesitate to overkill wildlife if it suits their purposes: "Any primitive race," Presnall was confident, "would be expected" to overexploit wildlife in times of abundance, assuming of course they had the means to do it.[15] Game was abundant in late prehistoric times simply because the Indians were too few, too poorly equipped, and without sufficient incentive to harvest more than the surplus. The introduction and adaptation to the European marketplace and technology removed two of the three obstacles to overkilling, and we might add, the Indian was quick to respond.

The diaries and reminiscences of explorers, traders, captives, settlers, missionaries, and other first-hand observers of post-contact Indian society offer incontrovertible, although qualified, evidence that this was in fact so. I have already alluded to such evidence in the previous chapters, but that forms only a fraction of the record. John Dunn, employee of the Hudson's Bay Company and resident of the Oregon Territory for eight years, described the Company's propaganda campaign to encourage regulated hunting of beaver among the natives. "But the attempt will be easily understood to be one of extreme difficulty," he lamented, "in consequence of the passion for depriving the animal creation of life so strongly implanted in the breast of the North American Indian, that it costs him a pang to pass bird, beast, or fish, without an effort to destroy it, whether he stands in need of it or not. The tendency to destructiveness is a vehement instinct of their nature."[16] Alexander Ross upbraided the natives for regarding animals " 'with more of a butcher's than a herdsman's eye.' "[17] Dunn himself was an appalled spectator to the wholesale slaughter of a migrating herd of caribou as it strove to cross the Hayes

River (near York factory, on Hudson Bay) in the summer of 1831. Only a fraction of the meat was rescued for present use, he ruefully observed, the rest being abandoned to rot on the banks or float downstream.[18]

We find references to a similar remorseless attitude throughout Samuel Hearne's journal. Time and again he commented that his Chipewyan guides would seemingly kill far more caribou and muskox than they could use. Cutting out the tongue, fat, and other choice portions, they left the remainder of the carcass to rot, much to the Englishman's disgust.

To induce them to desist from this practice, I often interested myself, and endeavoured, as much as possible, to convince them in the clearest terms of which I was master, of the great impropriety of such waste; particularly at a time of the year when their skins could not be of any use for clothing [this particular incident occurred in June 1771], and when the anxiety to proceed on our journey would not permit us to stay long enough in one place to eat up half the spoils of their hunting. As national customs, however, are not easily overcome, my remonstrances proved ineffectual; and I was always answered, that it was certainly right to kill plenty, and live on the best, when and where it was to be got, for that it would be impossible to do it where every thing was scarce: and they insisted on it, that killing plenty of deer and other game in one part of the country, could never make them scarcer in another. Indeed, they were so accustomed to kill every thing that came within their reach, that few of them could pass by a small bird's nest, without slaying the young ones, or destroying the eggs.[19]

Over a century later, the ethnologist Alanson Skinner remarked that the Northern Saulteaux, Ojibwa, slaughtered numerous moose each year. "The natives are exceedingly wasteful of them. . . . One of the most redeeming qualities of the Northern Saulteaux is their exceedingly poor marksmanship, for they seek to slay every living animal they see, whether it can be of any use to them or not."[20] And one could go on.

The record seems emphatic on this issue: the post-contact Indian wasted game with gusto. On the Great Plains he and his forefathers tumbled scores of buffalo over escarpments to their death, leaving most of the carcasses there to putrify; in the barren grounds to the north he apparently senselessly decimated the migrating caribou herds; in the boreal zone in between he over-hunted the moose; and on innumerable watercourses throughout the continent he trapped out the beaver completely. How, in the face of such incriminating evidence, can the Indian be held up as a "pioneer" ecologist? Where is the Indian's so-called reverence for Nature in the confused mass of a bison heap or the stillness of an empty beaver pond? Strickland begged the question by extolling the "ideal" of the Indian; Udall lamely admitted, else-where, that once he had been exposed to European material goods, "the Indian, too, became a raider of the American earth."[21] The others seem to have ignored the issue altogether.

The problem with the two points of view on the Indian-land relationship is that each one serves as a rallying point for a much larger ideological debate centering on the place of the Indian in American history and contemporary society. The question of the Indian's ecological proclivities thus becomes an acutely sen-sitive, if not volatile, issue, which is further bedeviled by the fact that evidence on the subject is extremely complex and quite often either ambiguous or outrightly contradictory. It is, in short, a hazardous area of inquiry which has become stalemated in glib, opposing arguments founded on over-generalized data often interpreted out of context—the most graphic illustration being the one which I have purposely constructed in the preceding paragraph. "Where is the Indian's so-called reverence for Nature in the confused mass of a bison heap or the stillness of an empty beaver pond?" The question assumes that the Indian's "reverence for Nature" is nonexistent, according to the slender evidence which has preceded it. The assumption is, however, premature.

In the pages which follow I propose to answer that question in a round-about and limited sort of way. Specifically, I propose to examine with a biologist's eye those episodes of prehistoric and historic Indian land-use which have attracted the greatest atten-tion, in part because they appear to be the most damning of the Indian: the part played by the Paleoindian in Pleistocene extinc-tions, the role of the Indian in the extinguishment of various wildlife species under the aegis of the historic fur trade, the place of the Indian in the extermination of the historic bison herds, and the Indian's use of fire throughout the continent.

As it happens, the ecological impact and sentiments of the Indian in each instance are rather difficult to interpret—especially his sentiments. Nevertheless, after reviewing what he did to the land and the ecological consequences of those acts, I have attempted to identify the lowest common denominator of all historic Indian peoples' sentiments toward the land, where those sentiments were or have remained unimpaired by white influence. The question of "the Indian's so-called reverence for Nature" is thus circuitously answered, although doubtless somewhat less definitively than some would like, which is a reflection on the complicated nature of the subject.

Situated about one hundred forty miles southeast of the city of Denver is one of the most remarkable monuments to paleolithic man's hunting prowess: the Olsen-Chubbock site, in the standard archaeological directory. Here, some eighty-five hundred years ago, very likely on a late May or early June day when the wind was out of the south, a herd of two hundred buffalo (all of them now extinct *Bison bison occidentalis*) was stampeded over a bluff to its death in the arroyo below. Appealing to historical analogy, archaeologists have estimated that there must have been a hundred or so people who participated in the kill and butchering, the process having yielded enough meat and fat to feed a band of one hundred fifty men, women, and children for at least a month.

The hunters were Plano Culture people, deriving their name from their distinctive projectile point style: the elongated, large, unfluted, lanceolate-shaped Plano point. Plano people, together with their Llano (also known as Clovis and Folsom) predecessors, have been traditionally thought of as big game hunters. Archaeologists refer to all three groups as the Paleoindians, bearers of the first readily identified culture of North America: the Big Game Tradition. These early Americans seemingly ran down the mightiest game the virgin continent had to offer—the mammoth, mastodon, bison, and others—trailing the wounded, now crippled, beast as its life's blood ran out through channels grooved into the faces of primitive spear points. Early man made his voice heard on this continent, not with a whimper but with a shout of triumph; he was a conqueror of the biggest Nature had available. Perhaps, though, he was too much of a conqueror.

For some obscure reason, or reasons, there was an unprecedented, global extinction of faunal genera during the last ice age, the Pleistocene. The perplexing thing is that fauna had been rendered extinct during and after previous ice ages; in each case, however, they had been replaced by similarly adapted genera. This was not so in Pleistocene times, when extinction occurred without replacement. The chronology of the extinctions is revealing. "In continental North America, the only major episode of generic extinction in the Pleistocene occurred close to eleven thousand years ago. Provisional stages for the start of major extinction episodes elsewhere are: South America 10,000 B.P.; West Indies, mid-postglacial; Australia, 13,000 B.P.; New Zealand, 900 B.P.; Madagascar, very late postglacial (800 B.P.); northern Eurasia (four genera only), 13,000 to 11,000 B.P.; Africa and probably Southeast Asia, before 40,000 to 50,000 B.P."[22]

Extinctions were obviously occurring before, during, and after post-glacial climatic change. This, and the fact that only large land mammals (except on islands) were affected, makes one initially skeptical of climate as the agent of destruction. Anyway, there had always been climatic changes associated with previous ice ages, yet these had evidently never precipitated such a massive and irreversible die-off of wildlife. The only new element in the extinction equation was man, whose dispersion throughout the globe bears a sinister correspondence to the above extinction timetable. How could he have done it, with his primitive tools and scant population? One probable means was through the use of deliberately set fires, or cultural fires, as they are known. Fire drives have been implicated in Africa, for instance, where fossil sites are often associated with charcoal. In the Americas, archaeologists have theorized that gregarious and fearless megafauna were for the first time—twelve, fifteen, maybe twenty thousand years ago—confronted by spear- and fire-equipped man, the Clovis hunter, whose hunting with these nonselective tools was inherently wasteful. In effect, then, the Paleoindian was a super-predator. "The thought that prehistoric hunters ten to fifteen thousand years ago (and in Africa over forty thousand years ago) exterminated far more large animals than has modern man with modern weapons and advanced technology is certainly provocative and perhaps even deeply disturbing," suggests Paul S. Martin, the foremost advocate of the "overkill" idea. "Have we dismissed too casually the possibility of prehistoric overkill? The late-Pleistocene extinction pattern leaves little room for any other explanation."[23]

"Overkill" has a certain theatrical quality to it: the big game of the continents and other major landforms fell like dominos before the relentless onslaught of man. Those species which survived managed to do so only by fleeing to the remote and less hospitable reaches of the continents. Thus, for the muskox of the North American tundra, a fortuitous barrier of ice interposed between the most northerly extension of the herds and the Clovis hunter. By the time the ice had melted the Paleoindian was long gone, and so too were the southern herds; the survivors were now free to extend their range westward, unmolested by predaceous man.

The Overkill Thesis is flawed, however. Skeptics are quick to point out that it is almost totally conjectural, there being little explicit archaeological evidence to support it. Signs of charcoal, for example, do not confirm human activity; it is impossible to distinguish in these instances between cultural and natural (lightning) fires. Moreover, in North America, where the mammoth and bison were the only large game hunted to any appreciable degree, the bison continues to thrive. "In 25 of the 34 documented sites bison was the exclusive or predominant game found," points out one researcher, "mammoths ran a poor second as the sole or major game in 7, and at only 2 were various other animals emphasized."[24] Evidently those bison that were extinguished, such as the *Bison antiquus* and *B. bison occidentalis*, must have fallen victim to some catastrophe other than the famed buffalo drive (which includes the buffalo jump and the buffalo pound). We surmise this from the fact that its relative, the *Bison bison*, remains, yet all three types were seemingly hunted using the same means—a means which (for the buffalo jump, anyway) appears not to have been used "earlier than 9,000 years ago, somewhat too late to have been involved in most of the major extinctions."[25] The cliff drive must therefore not have been as wasteful as is often thought. Another criticism of Martin's theory is that in Europe, where kill sites are more abundant than they are in North America, there were far fewer mammalian extinctions. All of these are serious objections to the "overkill" idea.

These days scholars are inclined to diminish the Overkill Theory somewhat by combining it with a climatological theory, thus soft-pedaling the significance of human predation.[26] In the case of North America, for example, it appears as though the majority of extinctions took place around eleven thousand years ago, in early post-Pleistocene times, as the climate rather abruptly turned warmer and drier. The result was that the Great Plains were rendered an inhospitable environment for many large herbivores (the horse, camel, ground sloth, and mammoths), whose fate was sealed when they were prevented from migrating elsewhere by geographical and floristic barriers. Just as their grassland habitat could not move, neither could they. Trapped in what was now a desert, victims of overspecialization and their enormous nutritional requirements, many of these genera perished altogether—forever. Granted, Paleoindian man may have pushed the few survivors over the brink to extinction—that much is possible—but it would be naive to think he was the prime agent in the matter. Man was the principal cause only under neolithic circumstances, as in India and the Near East, when as farmer he outbid these herbivorous species for the necessities of life: food, water, and cover. We might add that extinction was not as wholesale in the park-like eastern woodlands, since there were fewer megaherbivores here to begin with. Some, like the mastodon, a browser in pine-spruce forests, became extinguished as the forest canopy closed over them, preventing sufficient insolation from reaching the forest floor and thus eliminating vital understory forage.

An analogous ecological entrapment occurred in Argentina, as the Pampas (the equivalent of the North American Great Plains) were likewise unable to shift to another region. Confined to a habitat that was becoming progressively intolerable, large herbivores eventually passed out of existence. The only species to survive were browsers and a grazer of mountain origins which presumably weathered the catastrophe by retreating to the highlands. Down on the plains, the large herbivores were fragmented into small groups, precariously balanced on the edge of extinction. Once again, there is every possibility that Paleoindian man delivered the final, decisive blow—the coup de grâce.

There must have been quite a different situation prevailing in North Africa, however. Post-glacial desiccation here prompted the Saharan savanna, together with the resident megafauna, to migrate north, east, and south. Those mammals which moved northward were seemingly extirpated as a result of man's pastoral and agricultural activities, while those which retreated southward and eastward to the higher, more temperate regions managed to survive even into recent times in the new savannas and grasslands. Significantly, they thrived in spite of hunting man's presence. Witness the teeming, genera-rich grasslands of Africa in modern times, with man and animal in predator-prey balance. Evidence of this sort leads one to believe that post-Pleistocene extinctions, at least, were caused more by a climate which destroyed subhabitats and ecological niches than by overly predaceous man.[27]

A variation of the climatological theory has it that man was inadvertently responsible for megafaunal extinctions through the elimination of carnivorous species. The crucial point, here, is that man was a more efficient hunter than these other carnivores. Animal carnivores typically bring down the old, the young, and the infirm of their prey; man the hunter, on the other hand, is less age selective with his prey: he tends to harvest game of all ages. The outcome is that those herbivores which were singled out by the Paleoindian as his principal quarry—under less pressure from predation by animal carnivores—were conferred a greater chance of survival up to the critical reproductive years than they had enjoyed previously. Or, to phrase it another way, they actually experienced something of a population explosion, now that they were able to reproduce in much greater numbers than before. As their numbers multiplied, they increasingly monopolized the forage, water, and plant cover which competitive species also relied on, ultimately eliminating these other large herbivores, along with their specialized predators, simply because there were more of them.[28]

In addition to its being suspiciously reductionist and at times incredible, the Overkill Theory is vitiated in its emphasis on large game to the exclusion of small game. Who is to say the Paleoindian hunter was any more of a big game hunter than he was a small game hunter—and forager? Overall, one gets the impression that man's role in Pleistocene extinctions was not as critical and sinister as some have argued.

Quite a different set of circumstances prevailed on this North American continent under the aegis of the historic fur trade. By then the Big Game Tradition was long gone, and the focus of most aboriginal subsistence activities was now on small game, wild plant gathering, fishing, or maize-beans-squash agriculture.

Across the ocean, in western Europe, fur fashions had been fluctuating for centuries. In the thirteenth and fourteenth centuries English tastes had been inclined toward squirrel; in the next century it was marten. Then, in the sixteenth, the bottom fell out of the fur industry throughout the whole of western Europe as furbearers became increasingly scarce, wholesale prices soared, and political instability cast a pall over the international trade. Once again, it was probably the fashion world which delivered the hardest blow, for styles had changed from fur linings and facings to the soft fabrics of silk, velvets, and other precious cloths. In the midst of this inexorable cycle of events two developments in particular deserve close attention. Beaver, on whose pelts the fur empires of North America were later erected, were ominously scarce by the time of Columbus. They were virtually extinct in southern Europe and, along with many other furbearing species, were becoming exceedingly scarce throughout greater Europe—including the vast northern Russian forests. The second development is that Moscow, which up until that point had been the fur capital of western Europe, now turned from a depressed market in the West to a lucrative one in the Orient.[29]

It took a change in clothing fashions to reverse the declining fortunes of the trade and inaugurate an unprecedented run on North American furs—a business that was to last, gathering and abating in momentum, for the next three centuries. More specifically, it was the seemingly trivial advent of the beaver hat and its popularity late in the sixteenth century which triggered a take-off in the trade.[30]

Beaver, marten, fisher, otter, mink, and muskrat were the staples of the trade, with beaver far outranking the others in importance. Supplementing these were the skins and hides of large herbivores: moose, Virginia deer, antelope, elk, bison, and caribou (both the woodland and barren ground varieties). It is fair to say that by the time the fur business had run its course, all of these species had been overly exploited, with attendant shrinking of their range, a decreased pressure on their habitual forage (causing secondary effects on plant growth and species dominance), and the disruption of the normal food chains of which they were members.[31] Because of its vital role in the trade, the case of the beaver merits special consideration.

When Europeans first arrived on this continent beaver were ubiquitous except for pockets in the arid Southwest where water was insufficient to maintain them. Concentrated most heavily around Hudson Bay and the western Great Lakes, the Mackenzie, Yukon, and Fraser rivers in the far north, the tributaries of the Columbia and the headwaters of the Missouri and Saskatchewan, the beaver and his works must have been a familiar sight across the land. Beaver in such formidable numbers—the naturalist, Ernest Thompson Seton, has estimated there were about 60 million in 1492[32]—were without question an ecological factor of major proportions. Certainly their dams flooded untold hundreds of thousands of acres, creating ponds for the lodge and facilitating the transport of woody vegetation used for food. Archaeologists have determined that some dams had been used for centuries, being kept in constant repair by subsequent generations.

The dams must have had a salutary effect on water relations, for in regulating stream flow they kept numberless streams and creeks running throughout the dry season. They also conserved the water from heavy rains, preventing excess runoff and flooding downstream. As tons of topsoil were washed down from hillsides they were retained behind the earthworks of the structure, forming a deep, mineral-rich bed of alluvium at the bottom of the pond which became exposed as a fertile, grassy meadow once the pond was abandoned and the water drained off. An additional benefit was that ground-water table levels were raised nearer the surface as a result of damming. And, where ponds were at a sufficiently high altitude and deep enough to remain cool, they served as marvelous trout ponds. Moreover, we can conclude that most everywhere the dams facilitated travel by their extensive flooding upstream and regulation of water volume downstream.

The heavy exploitation of these nongregarious rodents for the fur trade released countless tons of water from an equally indeterminate number of ponds, resulting in lowered water tables, increased stream bank erosion and runoff from storms, and the irretrievable loss of tons of stored-up topsoil that were washed to the sea. On a less dismal note, the meadows exposed in the process proved a boon to the frontier farmer, who for years enjoyed their remarkable fertility.[33]

Even though he was responsible for much of this overkill and must bear a corresponding share of the blame for its ecological results, the Indian was by no means alone in his abuse of hunting and trapping. Whatever European and American hunters lacked in numbers relative to the Indian they made up for in enthusiasm and energy. Thus twenty trappers took 5,000 beaver in 212 traps in the 1823–1824 season in the Bitterroot Mountains, marveled

Alexander Ross; James O. Pattie captured 250 beaver in two weeks spent on the San Francisco River, Arizona, in 1825; John James Audubon and an associate claimed that Rocky Mountain trappers in the mid-nineteenth century could harvest up to 500 beaver in a year; and so on.[34] On the strength of statistics such as these, Ernest Thompson Seton has estimated that some 1 million beaver were either trapped or died of natural causes in the ten-year period 1860–1870 throughout North America.[35] And he is probably not far wrong. Another way to look at these grim data is to approach them from a lifetime of hunting. In 1865, in his sixty-fourth year, one such frontier hero named John Hutchins of Manlius, New York, unabashedly announced that he had "caught in traps, or otherwise destroyed . . . 100 moose; 1000 deer; 10 caribou; 100 bears; 50 wolves; 500 foxes; 100 raccoons; 25 wild cats; 100 lynx; 150 otter; 600 beaver; 400 fishers; mink and marten by the thousands; muskrats by the ten thousands."[36] Hutchins' grisly obituary is poignant testimony to the frontier syndrome that resources were limitless. And, judging from his behavior, the Indian seemingly concurred.

One curious offshoot of the fur trade was the emergence of a form of land tenure known collectively as the Algonkian family hunting territory system. Prior to the publication of Eleanor Leacock's monograph "The Montagnais 'Hunting Territory' and the Fur Trade," scholars used to argue over whether the system, still operating in many parts of Canada, is pre- or post-Columbian in origin.[37] Today the debate has been pretty much laid to rest: the family hunting territory system appears definitely to have been a post-contact phenomenon.

Broadly speaking, disregarding regional differences of evolution and variety, the aboriginal mode of social organization and proprietorship for many hunting-and-gathering Canadian Algonkian bands changed sometime during the historic period from large groups of families hunting and trapping communally held areas to small groups of families hunting and trapping discrete, exclusive territories within the tribal boundaries. The characteristic features of the system are patrilineal inheritance, ownership by the family patriarch, and a strong proprietary sense over commercially valuable furbearers. It would thus seem that the profit motive has spawned a strong sense of conservation among such families, who endeavor to farm their nonmigratory fur-bearers on a sustained yield basis.[38] The game farming takes the form of regulated hunting of some sort, generally through the use of a rotational system whereby all or part of the territory is rested periodically, as I have already discussed for the Waswanipi Cree. Again, as I alluded to there, there is no reason to doubt the pre-Columbian authenticity of the hunter's respect for wild-life just because his mode of land tenure, with its accompanying profit-motivated conservationism, may be white-induced. The critical point in all of this is that traditional sentiments toward game have been revived and applied within a new context. There exist, therefore, two compelling incentives to conserve furbearers: the one commercial (a result of acculturation) and the other spir-itual (and essentially aboriginal). It is my conviction that the second motive, the spiritual sense of obligation and fear of retri-bution, in the absence of a compelling commercial incentive in late prehistoric times, was adequate to ensure the effective con-servation of game resources. What we are witnessing today, among the Waswanipi Cree for example, is the recrudescence of a kind of aboriginal land ethic—a sentiment which has stood opposed to the excessive slaughter of wildlife for whatever pur-pose, whether for commercial gain or vendetta. Thus it lay dor-mant throughout the period of heavy exploitation. In a cultural context where traditional spiritual beliefs were sapped of their vitality, the mutual obligation–mutual courtesy hunting ethic of the Algonkian Indian languished—languished, that is, until game conservation became feasible and desirable with the adop-tion of the family hunting territory system, originally a commer-cially adapted institution. Over the subsequent years the family hunting territory has become much more than a commercially oriented affair for these people; it has become, among other things, a repository for a revitalized conservationist ethic of pre-Columbian origins.

One animal that never figured prominently in the Canadian fur trade was the bison, the returns from the sale of robes and hides being considered by Hudson's Bay Company officials not worth the high costs of transportation. Instead, they paid Plains Indians and mixed-blood Métis to harvest the beast for its fat and meat only, to provision the company posts. Possessed of a certain entrepreneurial ingenuity the Métis turned around and marketed the spurned robes in St. Paul, for as it turned out American merchants had no trouble making a handsome profit from the animal's pelt.[39]

At the time of early contact buffalo occupied a huge range centering on the Great Plains and extending as far east as the Appalachian piedmont and south into northeastern Mexico. Closely related to this plains variety was a wood buffalo, found scattered from the Great Slave Lake southwest throughout the intermountain region to the Central Valley of California and beyond to Sonora province. Altogether there may have been as many as 30 million head carpeting much of the North American continent.[40] It is not uncommon to read this figure doubled or even trebled—we just do not know how many millions there were.

From contemporary accounts of the vast herds, it seems self-evident that until the coming of whites, natural predators, disease, and other natural calamities were never severe enough in their combined activities to deplete the bison drastically. Wolves, the grizzly bear, and man—even using the celebrated buffalo jump—seem to have hardly made a dent in their numbers. The implication seems to be that pre-equestrian bison hunters harvested the animal on a sustained yield basis. Whether this sort of game management was intentional or not, we cannot say. Be that as it may, the evidence seems conclusive that bison, which had survived for millennia in the presence of predaceous man, were never seriously threatened until the early decades of the last century, when the process of systematic extermination got under way. Between 1830 and 1900 tens of millions of these beasts were slaughtered for sport and commerce or just plain expediency. Man's cupidity and avarice, a declared military policy of extermination, and governmental lethargy conspired to reduce the herd to a pitiful 541 survivors by the turn of the century.[41] In seventy years the gigantic Plains herd (or herds—there may have been four of them) was split by the railroad into a distinct northern and southern segment. The latter was extirpated in the last quarter of the century, and only a relic of the former herd was spared the same fate. Today these and other Plains herbivores and carnivores are thriving on big game preserves and a handful of private ranches scattered throughout their original domain, most of them preserved by governmental fiat.

In what way was the Plains Indian implicated in all of this, and what effect did the acquisition of the horse have on numbers of bison slain? We know that the horse, introduced by the Spanish in the early sixteenth century, had reached the Plains, Prairie, and Great Basin provinces by the seventeenth century—when in the century is unclear. And in the process it set in motion forces that were to transfigure native society and culture: prairie tribes and bands began moving out onto the short grass plains, giving up village farming for a more nomadic life and big game economy; native population soared; male prosperity became linked with polygyny—more wives tanned more hides for the traders; intertribal hostilities were accelerated as tribes jostled each other for prime hunting ranges; and militarism flourished as horse thieving gained in prestige and popularity.[42, c] Prehistoric pedestrian impounding and surrounding (including jumping) techniques were now outmoded as buffalo running came to replace them in selective advantage and sheer glory. And yet, contrary to what one might think, bison were not seriously threatened with the advent of the horse; even under pressure from the fur trade, intimates Frank Gilbert Roe, the equestrian Indian was restrained in hunting the beast. If the horse changed anything in the numbers of bison slaughtered, Roe has argued, it caused a reduction. Horsed hunters could now hunt more economically (i.e., selectively) than ever before, and enhanced selectivity placed considerably less pressure on the herds than there had been formerly, in the dog days.[43]

c. Richard G. Forbis, "The Old Women's Buffalo Jump, Alberta," *Contributions to Anthropology, 1960, Part 1, National Museum of Canada, Bulletin No. 180*, Anthropological Series No. 57 (Ottawa, 1962), pp. 56–123, and Clark Wissler, "The Influence of the Horse in the Development of Plains Culture," *American Anthropologist*, n.s. 16 (January–March 1914):1–25, play down the horse-inspired social and cultural revolution, arguing that the horse served to intensify and expand upon preexisting institutions rather than create them *de novo*.

Paradoxically, the horse may have led to the depletion of the bison in an indirect fashion. It is well known to scholars of the Plains Indian Wars that the horse gave the Indian warrior a very real edge over the United States troops sent against him. In the early phase of this series of campaigns, lasting from the 1860s to the 1890s, the military command sought to preserve the herds as a cheap and convenient means of provisioning the subdued hostiles. However, an undistinguished military record soon made it apparent that as long as the buffalo survived, the parasitical Indian would flourish and effectively defy reservationism. Buffalo policy thus did an about-face. Legislators and military tacticians now looked the other way as hidemen, in league with the railroads, orgiastically destroyed the strategically placed buffalo in order to bring the horse Indians to their knees.[44] Unfortunately for both the Indian and the buffalo, the plan worked.

Contemporaneous with the extermination of the bison was a popular fascination with its treeless range, the so-called Great American Desert. This distinct and expansive mid-latitude grassland—the home of the buffalo, elk, antelope, deer, wolf, grizzly, prairie dog, and numerous other wildlife—had long felt the impact of man and animals.[45] Current doctrine has it that fires, including cultural (man-set) fires, exerted a definitive influence on the establishment and maintenance of plant species throughout aboriginal North America, particularly in those marginal zones where other environmental factors (i.e., climate, soil, and animal activity) would tend to support a variety of vegetation. Apparently this was so in the Great Plains, the California Central Valley, and the Palouse region of the state of Washington. The upshot is that plant ecologists view the short grass plains (or steppes) of the Great Plains as a floristic disclimax produced by a combination of climatic pressures, periodic fires, soil type, heavy grazing (by bison and other herbivores), and the consumption of grass by invertebrates and rodents. How much weight to assign to each of these environmental forces remains problematic.[46]

Upon reflection, Omer C. Stewart pronounced burning to be a "universal culture pattern" among Indians of the continental United States, and one could say the same for Canadian Indians.

Stewart was deeply impressed by the fact that he had stumbled across more than two hundred references to Indian burning during his years of research—burning whose most common use was to facilitate hunting, by encircling, stampeding, or rousing the game. Less frequently, burning was also used to "improve pasture, improve visibility, collect insects, increase yield of seeds, increase yield of berries, increase other wild vegetable foods, make vegetable food available, remove or thin trees to allow other growth, clear land for planting, stimulate growth of wild tobacco, aid in warfare, facilitate travel, produce a spectacle, . . . reduce danger from snakes, insects, etc.," and, not surprisingly, was at times a result of sheer carelessness.[47] There can be no doubt the Indian fully understood fire as an effective instrument of land management.

Had they been deprived of Indian fires, Stewart has further reasoned, the Great Plains would most likely have presented a forested prospect to early European-American explorers. Softwood forests from the north and Rocky Mountains would have reached south and east to join with eastern hardwoods and southwestern mesquite, juniper, and pine. In the high, dry plains, where soil and precipitation are not conducive to tree growth, shrubs and bushes would have predominated, shading off into savannas of grass and open forest.[48] But not everyone agrees.

The most ardent critic of the so-called (Carl) Sauer-Stewart hypothesis—that the central North American grassland is essentially pyrogenic—is Waldo Wedel of the Smithsonian Institution, who has argued for a climatological theory of origin and maintenance. In the course of developing his counterposition, Wedel has strenuously disputed Stewart's proposition that forests would follow the elimination of fires. Even if fires were completely suppressed, he maintains, climatic pressures would be pervasive enough to thwart a successful forest invasion.[49]

To the east of the Mississippi, the evidence seems more conclusive that fires were in great measure responsible for the open, park-like structure of much of the eastern deciduous forest. Fires, likewise, appear to have created the cathedral-like aspect of many redwood and sequoia groves along the California coast

and inland, in the Sierras, while they selected for longleaf pine dominance in the Southeast and ponderosa pine dominance in the Southwest. Hillsides of chaparral and valley grasses were likewise fire-induced and fire-maintained throughout California.[50] In all of this, one must bear in mind that the majority of these cultural fires were light, surface or ground fires which burned cool and posed no threat to soil fertility and mature woody vegetation. Frequent fires (whether lightning- or man-caused) consumed whatever forest litter was left over from the Indians' firewood gathering activities, thus precluding the accumulation of potentially dangerous fuel.[51]

It is obvious that the Indian influenced flora in other ways besides the employment of fire. Altogether, a great portion of the East was cleared of forest to plant crops (maize, beans, pumpkins, squash, gourds, sunflowers, and tobacco being the most common), opening the forest canopy and increasing the amount of insolation absorbed by soil and ground vegetation. Shrubs and herbs found a compatible niche along the forest edge and in turn provided habitat and forage for wildlife in what was now a distinct community. Called ecotones, these edge communities attracted the most life-supporting of man's faunal and floral resources. In their swidden (slash-and-burn) activities, native farmers were in addition prone to let certain useful trees, such as walnuts and hickories, remain standing, offering them a reproductive advantage over other, adventive species when fields were eventually abandoned or fallowed. Furthermore, wild grasses, seeds, fruits, berries, and herbs gathered and prized by Indians for one reason or another were given a much broader dispersal than they would otherwise have enjoyed.[52]

Things changed dramatically under the white regime as fires, now considered a threat to livestock and colonial settlement, were vigorously suppressed whenever feasible and the fire-using Indian was displaced or somehow eliminated. Almost imperceptibly, woody vegetation began to creep onto the grassy plains where formerly it had been excluded as a result of frequent burning. Tall grass prairies along the eastern border of the Great Plains were replaced by short grass species as fires occurred less often and domestic livestock continued to graze where the dwindling bison herds had left off. The rare gound fire which now swept through the region was now incapable of harming the young adventive woody species that soon made their appearance. Eventually the forest became dominant throughout much of the prairie zone—a zone where cultural fires had seemingly exerted a profound effect on floristic composition. Elsewhere, in those forests where fires had once been a regular occurrence, undergrowth flourished if sunlight permitted, litter accumulated, and climax vegetation was forced to compete for space, water, and insolation with other species now released from the pyric bondage. When fires did occur, under the white regime, they were far more deleterious than before, frequently crowning into intense wildfires destructive to plants and animals alike. Meanwhile, throughout the horticultural East, abandoned Indian fields were becoming overgrown, reverting to a unique ecological niche known as "old" fields.[d]

Farther to the west, in California, chaparral began invading grassland as fires were here, too, cut back. As the years passed by and livestock began seriously to over-graze the range, as exotic Mediterranean grasses were introduced, the Indian removed as an agent in seed dissemination, and the land developed, the fastidious native grasses were eliminated altogether. In their stead were wild oats, wild mustards, and wild radishes, all foreign species. The transhumance cycle capped off this tragic shift in floristic composition by permanently removing minerals from montane and upland forage (impoverishing soil and vegetation alike), while overgrazing caused severe erosion, gullying, and ultimately flooding of rain-swollen rivers whose stream-beds had been dangerously elevated by sedimentation.[53] California, like the rest of the New World, was experiencing the new dispensation.

d. See Marvin Dodge, "Forest Fuel Accumulation—A Growing Problem," *Science* 177 (July 1972):139–142, for a forester's assessment of the forest fuel accumulation problem and the role of prescribed burns in eliminating this debris and precluding holocausts.

Years ago an ethnographer named Cora Du Bois was made privy to a strange Wintu eschatology. "People talk a lot about the world ending," began her informant, Kate Luckie,

but this world will stay as long as Indians live. When the Indians all die, then God will let the water come down from the north. Everyone will drown. That is because the white people never cared for land or deer or bear. When we Indians kill meat, we eat it all up. When we dig roots, we make little holes. When we build houses, we make little holes. When we burn grass for grasshopper, we don't ruin things. We shake down acorns and pine nuts. We don't chop down the trees. We only use dead wood. But the white people plow up the ground, pull up the trees, kill everything. . . . The spirit of the land hates them. . . . The Indians never hurt anything, but the white people destroy all. They blast rocks and scatter them on the earth. . . . When the Indians use rocks, they take little round ones for their cooking. The white people dig deep tunnels. They make roads. They dig as much as they wish. They don't care how much the ground cries out. How can the spirit of the earth like the white man? That is why God will upset the world—because it is sore all over. Everywhere the white man has touched it, it is sore. It looks sick. . . . But eventually the water will come.[54]

Has the Indian always cared "for land or deer or bear," or is this just wishful thinking? Certainly the case against the Paleo-indian big game hunter is flimsy. The "overkill" idea is simply too tentative to use against the Indian or, more explicitly, his Paleoindian ancestor. There is really no substantial empirical evidence to confirm, or even suggest for that matter, that paleo-lithic man in North America was a "super-predator." The evidence which does exist is clearly subject to a number of interpretations. Aside from whatever ecological damage he may have caused, as is revealed in the archaeological record, there is of course no way of getting at the Paleoindian's hunting sentiments. We are at this stage therefore incapable of determining whether the Paleoindian progenitor of the modern Indian functioned as a conservationist of game resources, and we shall never know what went on in his head.

Thousands of years later the eighteenth- and nineteenth-cen-tury descendants of these paleolithic big game hunters were still pursuing bison on the Great Plains, pursuing them on recently acquired horses—one of the animals which had been rendered extinct in the Western hemisphere in early post-Pleistocene times. What can we say about their hunting practices? Was the Plains Indian responsible for the decimation of those vast herds? Only in part, and certainly not in large part. Hide-hunters, sport hunters, provisioners, and other trigger-happy types, including among their ranks certain Indians, were the culprits—along with the railroad and domestic livestock. As is obvious from reading *The Oregon Trail*, for instance, the majority of Plains tribes seem to have been acutely aware of their absolute dependence on the bison. Perhaps, at times, they hunted them improvidently. Yet, given the chaos of the period, a turmoil which expressed itself in repeated epidemics, warfare, and displacement, it is hardly surprising that Indian bands might have had difficulty and little incentive to regulate their harvest. They recognized that the bison were becoming more and more inaccessible, and they also recognized that if they did not act now to slay the beast they might never have the opportunity again. In short, their traditional hunting practices were predicated on abundance; in a period of scarcity and uncertainty—for which the Plains Indians were not initially to blame—these practices could easily have become overly exploitive. Given the events of the time, and their complex and sometimes conflicting implications for Plains hunters, it would be rash to pass judgment on them as guilty for an ecological crime to which they may have been unwitting or forced accessories.

And one could probably make the same excuse for those Indians who participated in the more conventional fur trade. The only trouble with this is that in parts of Eastern Canada, at least, native hunters seemed oddly predisposed to promote the trade. One calls to mind Cartier's experience in Chaleur Bay, for example. This manifest enthusiasm does not of itself establish a predisposition to overkill furbearers, certainly, although I have speculated that such a sentiment preceded a later, commercial impetus to barter furs. In Eastern Canada, anyway, and quite possibly in other areas of the continent where the trade was prosecuted with comparable vigor, a long-standing compact between the animal kingdom and man was evidently disrupted; the mutual obligation–mutual courtesy relationship was dissolved, first as a result of the spiritually disintegrative effects of exotic diseases and, later on, Christian proselytization and the trade itself. Once this constraint was removed or compromised the Eastern Canadian hunter-gatherer became a likely candidate for overkill. We can conclude, then, that Eastern Canadian hunters were not conservationist-minded during the heyday of the fur trade, that indeed they were baldly exploitive, because their traditional incentives to conserve wildlife were rendered inoperative.

Granting this much, could one extend the "holy war" thesis to include the horticultural tribes which also participated in the trade: the Huron, League Iroquois, Susquehanna, Cherokee, and so forth? Probably somewhat less confidently, it seems to me. Horticulturalists, especially the five tribes which dominated the trade in the late sixteenth–early seventeenth century (Huron, Iroquois, Susquehanna, Powhatan, and Cherokee), were likely to be less concerned with the spiritual ramifications of wildlife extermination because: (a) hunting was for them subsidiary to fishing, gardening, and gathering, and consequently less mythologized; (b) they appear to have had fewer furbearers to begin with, which would again have discouraged mythologizing, especially a "conspiracy" idea; (c) fewer furbearers probably meant fewer diseases contracted from these beasts, hence there would be less tendency to blame anomalous maladies on angered or treacherous wildlife; and (d) the bulk of the furs they procured seem to have been either stolen or traded from hunter-gatherers who spearheaded the extermination campaign. For these and perhaps other reasons the coastal and interior horticultural tribes were quite possibly less compromised in their role as hunters and traders than were their hunter-gatherer colleagues and competitors.

On the question of cultural fires it seems evident that native practitioners conducted themselves wisely, even precociously. Given what we know, today, about the salutary effects of these fires and the circumspect manner in which they employed them, we can no longer sustain the idea that the Indian was "by nature

an incendiary, and forest burning was . . . [his] besetting sin."
There was nothing especially "wasteful and destructive" in his
use of forest products.[55] Certainly there were times when waste
and destruction occurred, but the point is that these were aber-
rations—deviations from the norm. On the whole, the North
American Indian earns high marks for his cautious use of plant
resources.

   This by no means exhausts the subject of pre- and post-contact
Indian land-use in North America: Navajo sheep farming, Alas-
kan Eskimo reindeer herding, and the fur seal and sea otter trade
are other possible topics for consideration. Those covered here
are only the most noteworthy and popularly known episodes.
Even from this limited perspective, however, one sees a pattern
of behavior and sentiment emerging. What we are dealing with
are two issues: the ideology of Indian land-use and the practical
results of that ideology. Actually, there was a great diversity of
ideologies, reflecting distinct cultural and ecological contexts. It
is thus more than a little artificial to identify a single, monolithic
ideology, as though all Native Americans were traditionally in-
spired by a universal ethos. Still, there were certain elements
which many if not all of these ideologies seemed to share, the
most outstanding being a genuine respect for the welfare of other
life-forms. Nature was to be cautiously and solicitously manipu-
lated to fulfill man's needs—cautiously because she could strike
back against abuse—solicitously because, in addition to a sense
of fear and awe and mystery, aboriginal man felt a genuine kinship and often affection for wildlife and plant-life. And here is
where Clifford Presnall's analysis of Indian land-use is flawed.
He infers a cynical spirituality where there was, instead, a genuine spirituality. Wildlife were revered and propitiated not only
out of fear that their favors might be withheld, although there
was some sense of that, but also because they were felt to be
inherently deserving of such regard. Admittedly, mankind needed
their goodwill to survive—to be physically nourished—yet he
also appealed to them for spiritual and aesthetic sustenance. And
they evidently furnished it. As long as this courteous relationship lasted—man and Nature fulfilling each other's needs and

respecting one another's boundaries—the two must have lived in harmony, and man and Nature were, practically speaking, conservationist one toward the other. Land-use was therefore not so much a moral issue for the Indian as it was technique animated by spiritual-social obligations and understandings. Ethics were invoked only when either party broke regulations, if even then; certainly they did not form the basis of the man-animal pact. As expressed by Frank Speck, writing about the Naskapi:

Requirements of conduct toward animals exist . . . which have to be known and carried out by the hunter. His success depends upon this knowledge, and, they argue, since no one can know everything and act to perfection, the subject of magico-religious science becomes, even from the native point of view, an inexhaustible one. Therefore, failure on the chase, the disappearance of the game from the hunter's districts, with ensuing famine, starvation, weakness, sickness, and death, are all attributed to the hunter's ignorance of some hidden principles of be-havior toward the animals, or to his wilful disregard of them. The for-mer is ignorance. The latter is sin.[56]

There is nothing here to suggest morality; certainly there is nothing to suggest the presumptuous, condescending extension of ethics from man-to-man to man-to-land, as the Leopoldian land ethic implies. Nature, for virtually all North American In-dians, was sensate, animate, and capable of aggressive behavior toward mankind. When Indians referred to other animal species as "people"—just a different sort of person from man—they were not being quaint. Nature was a community of such "people" —"people" for whom man had a great deal of genuine regard and with whom he had a contractual relationship to protect one another's interests and fulfill mutual needs. Man and Nature, in short, were joined by compact—not by ethical ties—a compact predicated on mutual esteem. This was the essence of the tradi-tional Indian-land relationship.

There is something immensely attractive about such a view of Nature. Yet it would be naive to think that Western man could himself subscribe to it, and so cure his environmental miseries. If the Judeo-Christian tradition has taught us anything, it has convinced us that Yahweh is one God. Nature, in the Christian realm, is anything but animated. It was above all else an articulate universe which formed the matrix of the traditional Indian-land relationship. Thus, even if we absolve him of his ambiguous culpability in certain episodes of despoliation, invoking instead his pristine sentiments toward Nature, the Indian still remains a misfit guru. Even if he were capable of leading us, we could never follow him. The Indian's was a profoundly different cosmic vision when it came to interpreting Nature—a vision Western man would never adjust to. There can therefore be no salvation in the Indian's traditional conception of Nature for the troubled environmentalist. Some day, perhaps, he will realize that he must look to someone else other than the American Indian for realistic spiritual inspiration.[e]

e. I realize that this final position, on the incompatibility of these two perspectives on Nature, is a debatable one; certainly not all social scientists would agree with me in this.

The reader should bear in mind that I am not attacking the principle of cultural borrowing and rejection. Ralph Linton, *The Study of Man: An Introduction* (New York: D. Appleton-Century Company, 1936), chapter 23; Homer G. Barnett, "Culture Processes," *American Anthropologist*, n.s. 42 (January-March 1940):21–48; Barnett, "Invention and Cultural Change," *American Anthropologist* 44 (January-March 1942):14–30; and Melville J. Herskovits, *Man and His Works: The Science of Cultural Anthropology* (New York: Alfred A. Knopf, 1948), chapter 32, have worked out a clever and useful scheme showing how the process works or fails to work, but what they say bears little relation to the issue here, it seems to me. We are confronting here an alien ideology of land-use which is antithetical to the central dogmas of Christianity. And I simply cannot imagine how the two views are capable of reconciliation.

Barnett, incidentally, makes the point that in most cases the receptor society will tend to keep the alien form, or the "whole new complex of principle, form, meaning and function," separate from an indigenous and analogous form, or complex (Barnett, "Invention," p. 24). What I gather from reading Barnett is that although a few Western iconoclasts might embrace the native ideology of land-use, one would expect that most individuals would instead add the alien ideology of land-use to the existing, Western ideology of land-use; the former would not be substituted for the latter, but would, at best, exist alongside it. Hence, at best, we might witness a cofunctioning of two ideologies of land-use— that is, we might if they were mutually compatible, which they are not. Which brings me back to my point above, that the traditional native ideology of land-use will not be acceptable to, and is incapable of adoption by, Western man, at least as long as he remains a Christian.

Notes

Prologue: The Paradox

1. Peter Jones, *History of the Ojebway Indians; with Especial Reference to Their Conversion to Christianity* (London: A. W. Bennett, 1861), p. 84.

2. Dale L. Morgan, "The Fur Trade and Its Historians," *American West* 3 (Spring 1966):92.

3. Oscar Lewis, *The Effects of White Contact upon Blackfoot Culture, with Special Reference to the Rôle of the Fur Trade*, Monographs of the American Ethnological Society (Seattle: University of Washington Press, 1942); E. E. Rich, "Trade Habits and Economic Motivation among the Indians of North America," *Canadian Journal of Economics and Political Science* 26 (February 1960):35–53; Preston Holder, "The Fur Trade as Seen from the Indian Point of View," in *The Frontier Reexamined*, edited by John Francis McDermott, pp. 129–139 (Urbana: University of Illinois Press, 1967); Wilcomb E. Washburn, "Symbol, Utility, and Aesthetics in the Indian Fur Trade," in *Aspects of the Fur Trade: Selected Papers of the 1965 North American Fur Trade Conference*, edited by Russell W. Fridley, pp. 50–54 (St. Paul: Minnesota Historical Society, 1967); John C. Ewers, "Influence of the Fur Trade upon Indians of the Northern Plains," in *People and Pelts: Selected Papers of the Second North American Fur Trade Conference*, edited by Malvina Bolus, pp. 1–26 (Winnipeg: Peguis Publishers for the Hudson's Bay Company, 1972); Harold Hickerson, "Fur Trade Colonialism and the North American Indian," *Journal of Ethnic Studies* 1 (Summer 1973):15–44; Arthur J. Ray, *Indians in the Fur Trade: Their Role as*

Trappers, Hunters, and Middlemen in the Lands Southwest of Hudson Bay, 1660–1870 (Toronto: University of Toronto Press, 1974).

4. John M. Cooper, "The Northern Algonquian Supreme Being," *Primitive Man* 6 (July and October 1933):84–87.

5. Charles A. Bishop, *The Northern Ojibwa and the Fur Trade: An Historical and Ecological Study* (Toronto: Holt, Rinehart and Winston of Canada, 1974), p. 342; Bishop, "The Emergence of the Northern Ojibwa: Social and Economic Consequences," *American Ethnologist* 3 (February 1976):39–54; Bishop and M. Estellie Smith, "Early Historic Populations in Northwestern Ontario: Archaeological and Ethnohistorical Interpretations," *American Antiquity* 40 (January 1975):54–63.

6. Douglas Byers, "The Environment of the Northeast," in *Man in Northeastern North America*, edited by Frederick Johnson, Papers of the Robert S. Peabody Foundation for Archaeology, vol. 3, pp. 3–32 (Andover, Mass.: Phillips Academy, 1946); Victor E. Shelford, *The Ecology of North America* (Urbana: University of Illinois Press, 1963), pp. 120–151, 17–55.

7. A. D. Fisher, "The Cree of Canada: Some Ecological and Evolutionary Considerations," *Western Canadian Journal of Anthropology* 1, no. 1 (1969):7–19; June Helm and Eleanor Burke Leacock, "The Hunting Tribes of Subarctic Canada," in *North American Indians in Historical Perspective*, edited by Eleanor Burke Leacock and Nancy Oestreich Lurie, pp. 343–374 (New York: Random House, 1971).

8. Bishop, *Northern Ojibwa*; Bishop, "Emergence of Northern Ojibwa"; Harold Hickerson, "The Feast of the Dead Among the Seventeenth Century Algonkians of the Upper Great Lakes," *American Anthropologist* 62 (February 1960):81–107; Hickerson, "The Sociohistorical Significance of Two Chippewa Ceremonials," *American Anthropologist* 65 (February 1963):67–85; Hickerson, "Some Implications of the Theory of the Particularity, or 'Atomism,' of Northern Algonkians," *Current Anthropology* 8 (October 1967):313–343; Hickerson, *The Chippewa and Their Neighbors: A Study in Ethnohistory* (New York: Holt, Rinehart and Winston, 1970); Hickerson, "The Chippewa of the Upper Great Lakes: A Study in Sociopolitical Change," in *North American Indians in Historical Perspective*, ed. Leacock and Lurie, pp. 169–199; June Helm, *The Indians of the Subarctic: A Critical Bibliography* (Bloomington: Indiana University Press for the Newberry Library, 1976), p. 39.

9. Dean R. Snow, "Wabanaki 'Family Hunting Territories,'" *American Anthropologist* 70 (December 1968):1143–1151; Snow, "The Changing Prey of Maine's Early Hunters," *Natural History* (November 1974):15–24; Calvin Martin, "The Four Lives of a Micmac Copper Pot," *Ethnohistory* 22 (Spring 1975):111–133; John M. Cooper, "The Culture

of the Northeastern Indian Hunters: A Reconstructive Interpretation," in *Man in Northeastern North America*, ed. Johnson, pp. 272-305; Regina Flannery, "The Culture of the Northeastern Indian Hunters: A Descriptive Survey," in *Man in Northeastern North America*, ed. Johnson, pp. 263-271; Margaret W. Fisher, "The Mythology of the Northern and Northeastern Algonkians in Reference to Algonkian Mythology as a Whole," in *Man in Northeastern North America*, ed. Johnson, pp. 226-262; Roland Burrage Dixon, "The Mythology of the Central and Eastern Algonkins," *Journal of American Folk-Lore* 22 (January 1909): 1-9; Fred Eggan, "Northern Woodland Ethnology," in *The Philadelphia Anthropological Society: Papers Presented on Its Golden Anniversary*, edited by Jacob W. Gruber, pp. 107-124 (New York: Columbia University Press for Temple University Publications, 1967).

10. Calvin Martin, "Ethnohistory: A Better Way to Write Indian History," *Western Historical Quarterly* 9 (January 1978), in press.

11. Bernard G. Hoffman, "Souriquois, Etechemin, and Kwĕdĕch: A Lost Chapter in American Ethnography," *Ethnohistory* 2 (Winter 1955): 65-87; Henry Percival Biggar, ed., "The First Voyage, 1534," in *The Voyages of Jacques Cartier*, Publications of the Public Archives of Canada No. 11 (Ottawa: F. A. Acland, 1924), pp. 49-56.

12. Alfred Goldsworthy Bailey, *The Conflict of European and Eastern Algonkian Cultures, 1504-1700: A Study in Canadian Civilization*, Publications of the New Brunswick Museum, Monographic Series No. 2 (St. John, New Brunswick, 1937), p. 6.

13. Peter Farb, *Man's Rise to Civilization as Shown by the Indians of North America from Primeval Times to the Coming of the Industrial State* (New York: E. P. Dutton and Company, 1968), pp. 83, 82.

14. Hickerson, "Fur Trade Colonialism," p. 24.

15. Marshall D. Sahlins, *Stone Age Economics* (Chicago: Aldine/Atherton, 1972), p. 4.

16. W. H. Hutchinson, "The Remaking of the Amerind: A Dissenting Voice Raised Against the Resurrection of the Myth of the Noble Savage," *Westways* (October 1972):94.

17. Harold A. Innis, *The Fur Trade in Canada: An Introduction to Canadian Economic History*, rev. ed. (Toronto: University of Toronto Press, 1970), p. 5. See Henry Percival Biggar, *The Early Trading Companies of New France: A Contribution to the History of Commerce and Discovery in North America* (Toronto: University of Toronto Library, 1901), pp. 28-29; and Harold Demsetz, "Toward a Theory of Property Rights," *American Economic Review* 57 (May 1967):347-359.

18. Daniel B. Fusfeld, "Economic Theory Misplaced: Livelihood in Primitive Society," in *Trade and Market in the Early Empires: Economies in History and Theory*, edited by Karl Polanyi, Conrad M. Arensberg,

and Harry W. Pearson, pp. 342–355 (New York: Macmillan, Free Press, 1957), p. 345.

19. George Dalton, "Economic Theory and Primitive Society," *American Anthropologist* 63 (February 1961):21. See Stillman Bradfield, "Economic Anthropology," in *Introduction to Cultural Anthropology: Essays in the Scope and Methods of the Science of Man,* edited by James A. Clifton, pp. 183–199 (Boston: Houghton Mifflin Company, 1968), p. 192.

20. Sahlins, *Stone Age Economics,* p. 186, note.

21. Karl Polanyi, "The Economy as Instituted Process," pp. 243–270 in *Trade and Market in Early Empires,* ed. Polanyi, Arensberg, and Pearson, pp. 243–244.

22. Scott Cook, "Economic Anthropology: Problems in Theory, Method, and Analysis," in *Handbook of Social and Cultural Anthropology,* edited by John J. Honigmann, pp. 795–860 (Chicago: Rand McNally and Company, 1973), p. 809.

23. John McManus, "An Economic Analysis of Indian Behavior in the North American Fur Trade," *Journal of Economic History* 32 (March 1972):36–53.

24. See Julius E. Lips, "Public Opinion and Mutual Assistance among the Montagnais-Naskapi," *American Anthropologist,* n.s. 39 (April–June 1937):222–228.

25. Sahlins, *Stone Age Economics,* p. 14.

26. Marshall D. Sahlins, "Notes on the Original Affluent Society," in *Man the Hunter,* edited by Richard B. Lee and Irven DeVore, pp. 85–89 (Chicago: Aldine Publishing Company, 1968), p. 85; Sahlins, *Stone Age Economics,* pp. 1–39; Robert McC. Netting, "The Ecological Approach in Cultural Study," Addison-Wesley Modular Publications, Module No. 6 (1971), pp. 5–6; Lewis R. Binford, "Post-Pleistocene Adaptations," in *New Perspectives in Archeology,* edited by Sally R. Binford and Lewis R. Binford, pp. 313–341 (Chicago: Aldine Publishing Company, 1968), pp. 327–328.

27. Sahlins, *Stone Age Economics,* pp. 1–2.

28. Ibid., pp. 14, 5.

29. Don E. Dumond, "The Limitation of Human Population: A Natural History," *Science* 187 (February 1975):713–721; Brian Hayden, "Population Control among Hunter/Gatherers," *World Archaeology* 4 (October 1972):205–221.

30. Otis T. Mason, "Traps of the American Indian—A Study in Psychology and Invention," in the *Annual Report of the Smithsonian Institution* (1901), pp. 461–473 (Washington, D.C., 1902); John M. Cooper, "Snares, Deadfalls, and Other Traps of the Northern Algonquians and Northern Athapaskans," *Catholic University of America, Anthropological Series No. 5* (Washington, D.C.: Catholic University

of America, 1938); James W. VanStone, *Athapaskan Adaptations: Hunters and Fishermen of the Subarctic Forests* (Chicago: Aldine Publishing Company, 1974), p. 24.

31. Robin F. Wells, "Castoreum and Steel Traps in Eastern North America," *American Anthropologist* 74 (June 1972):479–483.

32. Arthur J. Ray, "Some Conservation Schemes of the Hudson's Bay Company, 1821–50: An Examination of the Problems of Resource Management in the Fur Trade," *Journal of Historical Geography* 1, no. 1 (1975):49–68; Ray, *Indians in the Fur Trade*, pp. 195–216.

33. See Harvey A. Feit, "The Ethno-Ecology of the Waswanipi Cree; or How Hunters Can Manage Their Resources," in *Cultural Ecology: Readings on the Canadian Indians and Eskimos*, edited by Bruce Cox, pp. 115–125 (Toronto: McClelland and Stewart, 1973), pp. 116–117; and Feit, "Twilight of the Cree Hunting Nation," *Natural History* (August-September 1973):48–57, 72.

34. VanStone, *Athapaskan Adaptations*, p. 102.

35. See Madeleine Rousseau and Jacques Rousseau, "Le Dualisme religieux des peuplades de la forêt boréale," in *Proceedings and Selected Papers of the 29th International Congress of Americanists: Acculturation in the Americas*, edited by Sol Tax, vol. 2, pp. 118–126 (Chicago: University of Chicago Press, 1952) and J. Rousseau, "Persistances païennes chez les Amérindiens de la forêt boréale," *Cahiers des Dix*, no. 17 (1952):183–208.

36. Werner Müller, "North America in 1600," in *Pre-Columbian American Religions*, by Walter Krickeberg et al., pp. 147–229 (New York: Holt, Rinehart and Winston, 1968), p. 160.

Chapter One: The Protohistoric Indian-Land Relationship

1. Reuben Gold Thwaites, ed., *The Jesuit Relations and Allied Documents: Travels and Explorations of the Jesuit Missionaries in New France, 1610–1791*, 73 vols. (Cleveland: The Burrows Brothers Company, 1896–1901), 8:57, hereafter cited as *Jesuit Relations*.

2. Baron de Lahontan, *New Voyages to North-America* (1703), edited by Reuben Gold Thwaites, 2 vols. (Chicago: A. C. McClurg and Company, 1905), 1:82.

3. *Jesuit Relations*, 5:25; 6:297–299; 8:57; 40:151; 68:47, 109–111; 69:95, 99–113.

4. Ibid., 8:41.

5. Nicolas Denys, *The Description and Natural History of the Coasts of North America (Acadia)* (1672), translated and edited by William F. Ganong (Toronto: The Champlain Society, 1908), pp. 187, 199, 209, 219–220.

6. Ibid., pp. 432, 450.

7. Father Chrestien Le Clercq, *New Relation of Gaspesia, with the Customs and Religion of the Gaspesian Indians* (1691), translated and edited by William F. Ganong (Toronto: The Champlain Society, 1910), pp. 212–213; Frank G. Speck and Ralph W. Dexter, "Utilization of Animals and Plants by the Micmac Indians of New Brunswick," *Journal of the Washington Academy of Sciences* 41 (August 1951):250–259; Harlan I. Smith and W. J. Wintemberg, "Some Shell-Heaps in Nova Scotia," Canada, Department of Mines, *National Museum of Canada, Bulletin No. 47*, Anthropological Series No. 9 (Ottawa, 1929), pp. 17, 36; *Jesuit Relations*, 3:77; Marc Lescarbot, *The History of New France* (1618; first published 1609), translated by W. L. Grant, 3 vols. (Toronto: The Champlain Society, 1907–1914), 3:93, 194–195.

8. Wilson D. Wallis and Ruth Sawtell Wallis, *The Micmac Indians of Eastern Canada* (Minneapolis: University of Minnesota Press, 1955), p. 19. See D. W. Moodie and Barry Kaye, "The Northern Limit of Indian Agriculture in North America," *Geographical Review* 59 (October 1969):513–529.

9. Lescarbot, *History of New France*, 2:323–325; 3:158.

10. *Jesuit Relations*, 3:79.

11. Bruce J. Bourque, "Aboriginal Settlement and Subsistence on the Maine Coast," *Man in the Northeast*, no. 6 (Fall 1973):7.

12. *Jesuit Relations*, 3:79; Denys, *Description and Natural History*, p. 403; Lescarbot, *History of New France*, 3:80; Le Clercq, *New Relation of Gaspesia*, pp. 88–89, 93; Le Sieur de Dièreville, *Relation of the Voyage to Port Royal in Acadia of New France* (1708), translated by Mrs. Clarence Webster and edited by John Clarence Webster (Toronto: The Champlain Society, 1933), p. 146.

13. *Jesuit Relations*, 3:79.

14. Lescarbot, *History of New France*, 3:219–220.

15. *Jesuit Relations*, 3:79.

16. Lescarbot, *History of New France*, 3:222–224; Le Clercq, *New Relation of Gaspesia*, pp. 276–280; Dièreville, *Relation of Voyage*, pp. 133–134; Denys, *Description and Natural History*, pp. 429–433.

17. Lescarbot, *History of New France*, 3:220–222; Denys, *Description and Natural History*, pp. 426–429; Le Clercq, *New Relation of Gaspesia*, pp. 274–276.

18. Le Clercq, *New Relation of Gaspesia*, pp. 118–119.

19. Ibid., pp. 93–94; Denys, *Description and Natural History*, p. 412; Lescarbot, *History of New France*, 3:133; Speck and Dexter, "Utilization of Animals and Plants," p. 255.

20. Speck and Dexter, "Utilization of Animals and Plants," p. 255.

21. Le Clercq, *New Relation of Gaspesia*, pp. 116, 119; Dièreville, *Relation of Voyage*, p. 131; *Jesuit Relations*, 3:107–109.

22. Denys, *Description and Natural History*, pp. 433–434.

23. *Jesuit Relations*, 3:79.

24. Smith and Wintemberg, "Shell-Heaps in Nova Scotia," pp. 16–17, 113, 127; Speck and Dexter, "Utilization of Animals and Plants," pp. 251–254; *Jesuit Relations*, 3:81.

25. Lescarbot, *History of New France*, 3:236–237; Denys, *Description and Natural History*, pp. 436–437.

26. Le Clercq, *New Relation of Gaspesia*, pp. 92, 137; Lescarbot, *History of New France*, 3:230–231; Denys, *Description and Natural History*, pp. 435–436.

27. *Jesuit Relations*, 3:83.

28. Ibid.

29. Le Clercq, *New Relation of Gaspesia*, pp. 109–110, 283; Denys, *Description and Natural History*, pp. 389, 434.

30. Denys, *Description and Natural History*, pp. 402–403, 426.

31. Roy A. Rappaport, *Pigs for the Ancestors: Ritual in the Ecology of a New Guinea People* (New Haven: Yale University Press, 1968), pp. 237–238; Andrew P. Vayda and Roy A. Rappaport, "Ecology, Cultural and Noncultural," in *Introduction to Cultural Anthropology: Essays in the Scope and Methods of the Science of Man*, edited by James A. Clifton, pp. 477–497 (Boston: Houghton Mifflin Company, 1968), p. 491.

32. William A. Ritchie, "The Indian and His Environment," *Conservationist* (December–January 1955/56):27. See Frank G. Speck, "Aboriginal Conservators," *Audubon Magazine* (July 1938):258–261; Speck, *Naskapi: The Savage Hunters of the Labrador Peninsula* (Norman: University of Oklahoma Press, 1935); John Witthoft, "The American Indian as Hunter" (Harrisburg: Pennsylvania Historical and Museum Commission, 1967); George S. Snyderman, "Concepts of Land Ownership Among the Iroquois and Their Neighbors," *Bureau of American Ethnology Bulletin 149*, edited by William N. Fenton (Washington, D.C., 1951); Robert F. Heizer, "Primitive Man as an Ecologic Factor," *Kroeber Anthropological Society, Papers*, no. 13 (Fall 1955):1–31; Gordon M. Day, "The Indian as an Ecological Factor in the Northeastern Forest," *Ecology* 34 (April 1953):329–346; William Christie MacLeod, "Conservation Among Primitive Hunting Peoples," *Scientific Monthly* 43 (December 1936):562–566; John M. Cooper, "Field Notes on Northern Algonkian Magic," *Proceedings of the Twenty-Third International Congress of Americanists*, New York, September 1928 (1930): 513–518; Cooper, "The Relations Between Religion and Morality in Primitive Culture," *Primitive Man* 4 (July 1931):33–48; Cooper, "The Northern Algonquian Supreme Being," *Primitive Man* 6 (July and October 1933):41–112; Ruth Underhill, "Religion among American

Indians," *Annals of the American Academy of Political and Social Science* 311 (May 1957):127-136.

33. Murray Wax, "Religion and Magic," pp. 225-242 in *Introduction to Cultural Anthropology*, ed. Clifton, p. 235.

34. Rosalie Wax and Murray Wax, "The Magical World View," *Journal for the Scientific Study of Religion* 1 (Spring 1962):181.

35. See William Jones, "The Algonkin Manitou," *Journal of American Folk-Lore* 28 (July-September 1905):183-190; Wax and Wax, "The Magical World View," pp. 182, 183; Frederick Johnson, "Notes on Micmac Shamanism," *Primitive Man* 16 (July and October 1943):58-59.

36. Wax and Wax, "The Magical World View," pp. 182, 183, 185; Underhill, "Religion among American Indians," pp. 128, 130; Margaret W. Fisher, "The Mythology of the Northern and Northeastern Algonkians in Reference to Algonkian Mythology as a Whole," in *Man in Northeastern North America*, edited by Frederick Johnson, Papers of the Robert S. Peabody Foundation for Archaeology, vol. 3, pp. 226-262 (Andover, Mass.: Phillips Academy, 1946), pp. 233-234.

37. Le Clercq, *New Relation of Gaspesia*, pp. 187, 209, 212-214; Denys, *Description and Natural History*, pp. 117, 442.

38. Dièreville, *Relation of Voyage*, p. 139; Le Clercq, *New Relation of Gaspesia*, pp. 225-229, 276-277.

39. Le Clercq, *New Relation of Gaspesia*, pp. 225-229.

40. Ibid., pp. 226, 227-229.

41. A. Irving Hallowell, "Bear Ceremonialism in the Northern Hemisphere," *American Anthropologist*, n.s. 28 (1926):1-175; Witthoft, "The American Indian as Hunter," p. 19; Edward S. Rogers, *The Quest for Food and Furs : The Mistassini Cree, 1953-1954*, National Museum of Man, Publications in Ethnology No. 5 (Ottawa, 1973), p. 10; Robert J. Sullivan, *The Ten'a Food Quest*, Catholic University of America, Anthropological Series No. 11 (Washington, D.C.: Catholic University of America Press, 1942), pp. 83-88; Adrian Tanner, "Bringing Home Animals: Religious Ideology and Mode of Production of the Mistassini Cree Hunters" (Ph.D. diss., University of Toronto, 1976), pp. 259-262.

42. Le Clercq, *New Relation of Gaspesia*, p. 227.

43. Denys, *Description and Natural History*, pp. 430, 442; Le Clercq, *New Relation of Gaspesia*, pp. 192-193.

44. Erwin H. Ackerknecht, "The Shaman and Primitive Psychopathology in General," in *Medicine and Ethnology: Selected Essays*, edited by H. H. Walser and H. M. Koelbing, pp. 57-89 (Baltimore: The Johns Hopkins Press, 1971), p. 62.

45. Bruno Klopper and Bryce L. Boyer, "Notes on the Personality Structure of a North American Indian Shaman: Rorschach Interpretation," *Journal of Projective Techniques* 25 (June 1961):170.

46. Ackerknecht, "Shaman and Primitive Psychopathology," p. 77.
47. *Jesuit Relations*, 2:75; Le Clercq, *New Relation of Gaspesia*, pp. 215–218, 296–299; Johnson, "Notes on Micmac Shamanism," pp. 71–72; Denys, *Description and Natural History*, pp. 415, 417–418; Stansbury Hagar, "Micmac Magic and Medicine," *Journal of American Folk-Lore* 9 (July-September 1896):170–177. See Wilson D. Wallis, "Medicines Used by the Micmac Indians," *American Anthropologist*, n.s. 24 (January-March 1922):24–30; and Arthur F. Van Wart, "The Indians of the Maritime Provinces, Their Diseases and Native Cures," *Canadian Medical Association Journal* 59 (December 1948):573–577.

Chapter Two: Early Contact and the Deterioration of the Environmental Ethos

1. Carl Ortwin Sauer, *Northern Mists* (Berkeley and Los Angeles: University of California Press, 1968), pp. 36, 56–57; Sauer, *Sixteenth Century North America: The Land and the People as Seen by the Europeans* (Berkeley and Los Angeles: University of California Press, 1971), pp. 297–298; David Beers Quinn, *England and the Discovery of America, 1481–1620. From the Bristol Voyages of the Fifteenth Century to the Pilgrim Settlement at Plymouth: The Exploration, Exploitation, and Trial-and-Error Colonization of North America by the English* (New York: Alfred A. Knopf, 1974), pp. 49, 8–14, 74, 85–86.
2. John Witthoft, "Archaeology as a Key to the Colonial Fur Trade," *Minnesota History* 40 (Winter 1966):204.
3. Bernard G. Hoffman, *Cabot to Cartier: Sources for a Historical Ethnography of Northeastern North America, 1497–1550* (Toronto: University of Toronto Press, 1961), pp. 197, 198.
4. Henry Percival Biggar, *The Early Trading Companies of New France: A Contribution to the History of Commerce and Discovery in North America* (Toronto: University of Toronto Library, 1901), pp. 28–29, 32; Hoffman, *Cabot to Cartier*, pp. 198–200, 201.
5. Witthoft, "Archaeology as a Key," pp. 204–205.
6. John Witthoft, "Indian Prehistory of Pennsylvania" (Harrisburg: Pennsylvania Historical and Museum Commission, 1965), p. 28. See Alfred W. Crosby, Jr., *The Columbian Exchange: Biological and Cultural Consequences of 1492* (Westport, Conn.: Greenwood Press, 1972), pp. 35–63.
7. Henry F. Dobyns, "Estimating Aboriginal American Population: An Appraisal of Techniques with a New Hemispheric Estimate," *Current Anthropology* 7 (October 1966):395–412.
8. Alfred L. Kroeber, *Cultural and Natural Areas of Native North America* (1939) (Berkeley and Los Angeles: University of California

Press, 1963), pp. 166, 134; James Mooney, "The Aboriginal Population of America North of Mexico," *Smithsonian Miscellaneous Collections* 80 (February 1928):33; Woodrow Borah, "The Historical Demography of Aboriginal and Colonial America: An Attempt at Perspective," in *The Native Population of the Americas in 1492*, edited by William M. Denevan, pp. 13–34 (Madison: University of Wisconsin Press, 1976), p. 15.

9. Dobyns, "Estimating Aboriginal American Population."

10. Henry F. Dobyns, "An Outline of Andean Epidemic History to 1720," *Bulletin of the History of Medicine* 37 (November-December 1963):494.

11. Sherburne F. Cook, "Demographic Consequences of European Contact with Primitive Peoples," *Annals of the American Academy of Political and Social Science* 237 (January 1945):107–111; Thomas Dale Stewart, *The People of America* (New York: Charles Scribner's Sons, 1973), p. 36.

12. Woodrow Borah, "America as Model: The Demographic Impact of European Expansion upon the Non-European World," in *Actas y Memorias, XXXV Congreso Internacional de Americanistas* [*Proceedings of the International Congress of Americanists*], *Mexico 1962*, 3 vols., 3:379–387 (Mexico: Editorial Libros de Mexico, 1962), pp. 380–382; Borah, "Historical Demography of Aboriginal and Colonial America," pp. 17–18, 31–32; William M. Denevan, "Introduction," in *The Native Population of the Americas in 1492*, ed. Denevan, p. 3; Dobyns, "Estimating Aboriginal American Population," pp. 412–414; Dobyns, Review of *Essays in Population History: Mexico and the Caribbean, Volume One*, by Sherburne F. Cook and Woodrow Borah (Berkeley and Los Angeles: University of California Press, 1971), *Ethnohistory* 20 (Summer 1973):293–294; Dobyns, *Native American Historical Demography: A Critical Bibliography* (Bloomington: Indiana University Press for the Newberry Library, 1976), pp. 15–16, 40.

13. Cook, "Demographic Consequences of European Contact"; Borah, "America as Model," pp. 381–382.

14. Sherburne F. Cook, "Interracial Warfare and Population Decline Among the New England Indians," *Ethnohistory* 20 (Winter 1973):1–24; Cook, "The Significance of Disease in the Extinction of the New England Indians," *Human Biology* 45 (September 1973):485–508.

15. Dobyns, "Estimating Aboriginal American Population," pp. 412–415; Denevan, "Introduction," p. 3; Borah, "America as Model," pp. 381–382; Borah, "Historical Demography of Aboriginal and Colonial America," pp. 17, 31–32; Sherburne F. Cook and Woodrow Borah, *Essays in Population History: Mexico and the Caribbean*, 2 vols. (Berkeley and Los Angeles: University of California Press, 1971–1974).

16. Stewart, *People of America*, pp. 43–48; Sherburne F. Cook, "The

Incidence and Significance of Disease among the Aztecs and Related Tribes," *Hispanic American Historical Review* 26 (August 1946):335; Denevan, "Introduction," p. 5; Crosby, *Columbian Exchange,* pp. 122–164; Francisco Cuerra, "The Problem of Syphilis," in *First Images of America: The Impact of the New World on the Old,* edited by Fredi Chiappelli, vol. 2, pp. 845–851 (Berkeley and Los Angeles: University of California Press, 1976), p. 850; Saul Jarcho, "Some Observations on Disease in Prehistoric North America," *Bulletin of the History of Medicine* 38 (January-February 1964):1–19; Ronald Hare, "The Antiquity of Diseases Caused by Bacteria and Viruses, A Review of the Problem from a Bacteriologist's Point of View," in *Diseases in Antiquity: A Survey of the Diseases, Injuries and Surgery of Early Populations,* compiled and edited by Don Brothwell and A. T. Sandison, pp. 115–131 (Springfield, Ill.: Charles C. Thomas, 1967), p. 123; Stephen J. Kunitz and Robert C. Euler, "Aspects of Southwestern Paleoepidemiology," *Prescott College Anthropological Reports No. 2* (1972); Frederick L. Dunn, "Epidemiological Factors: Health and Disease in Hunter-Gatherers," in *Man the Hunter,* edited by Richard B. Lee and Irven DeVore, pp. 221–228 (Chicago: Aldine Publishing Company, 1968), pp. 222, 223–228.

17. Stewart, *People of America,* pp. 19–20.

18. Borah, "America as Model," pp. 386–387; Dobyns, *Native American Historical Demography,* p. 1; Stewart, *People of America,* pp. 43–44; Calvin Martin, "Wildlife Diseases as a Factor in the Depopulation of the North American Indian," *Western Historical Quarterly* 7 (January 1976):47–62.

19. Borah, "America as Model," p. 381; Cook, "Incidence and Significance of Disease among Aztecs," p. 335; Cook, "Human Sacrifice and Warfare as Factors in the Demography of Pre-colonial Mexico," *Human Biology* 18 (May 1946):81–102; Cook, *Soil Erosion and Population in Central Mexico,* Ibero-Americana, No. 34 (Berkeley and Los Angeles: University of California Press, 1949); Cook, *Erosion Morphology and Occupation History in Western Mexico,* Anthropological Records 17 (1963):281–334 (Berkeley and Los Angeles: University of California Press, 1963); Stewart, *People of America,* p. 35.

20. Alfred W. Crosby, Jr., "Virgin Soil Epidemics as a Factor in the Aboriginal Depopulation in America," *William and Mary Quarterly* 33 (April 1976):289–299; Crosby, *Columbian Exchange,* pp. 35–63; Dobyns, "Outline of Andean Epidemic History."

21. Sauer, *Sixteenth Century North America,* pp. 90–91.

22. Father Chrestien Le Clercq, *New Relation of Gaspesia, with the Customs and Religion of the Gaspesian Indians* (1691), translated and edited by William F. Ganong (Toronto: The Champlain Society, 1910), pp. 146–152.

23. Alfred Goldsworthy Bailey, *The Conflict of European and Eastern Algonkian Cultures, 1504-1700: A Study in Canadian Civilization,* Publications of the New Brunswick Museum, Monographic Series No. 2 (St. John, New Brunswick, 1937), p. 83; Diamond Jenness, *The Indians of Canada,* 6th ed., *National Museum of Canada, Bulletin No. 65,* Anthropological Series No. 15 (Ottawa, 1963), pp. 258-259.

24. See *Jesuit Relations,* 2:75-77; 3:131-135.

25. Nicolas Denys, *The Description and Natural History of the Coasts of North America (Acadia)* (1672), translated and edited by William F. Ganong (Toronto: The Champlain Society, 1908), p. 415; *Jesuit Relations,* 3:105.

26. *Jesuit Relations,* 1:177.

27. Ibid., 3:105-107.

28. Ibid., 3:107, 111, 109; 2:73.

29. Brian Hayden, "Population Control among Hunter/Gatherers," *World Archaeology* 4 (October 1972):212; Don E. Dumond, "The Limitation of Human Population: A Natural History," *Science* 187 (February 1975):713-721.

30. *Jesuit Relations,* 1:173; 3:75.

31. Le Clercq, *New Relation of Gaspesia,* pp. 104-108.

32. *Jesuit Relations,* 1:183.

33. Ibid., 2:75-77; 3:123; Le Clercq, *New Relation of Gaspesia,* pp. 193, 220, 224-225, 227, 239, 253; J. H. Kennedy, *Jesuit and Savage in New France* (New Haven: Yale University Press, 1950), pp. 57-79, 97-132, 175-191; George R. Healy, "The French Jesuits and the Idea of the Noble Savage," *William and Mary Quarterly* 15 (April 1958):143-167; James P. Ronda, "European Indian: Jesuit Civilization Planning in New France," *Church History* 41 (September 1972):385-395; Ronda, " 'We Are Well As We Are': An Indian Critique of Seventeenth-Century Christian Missions," *William and Mary Quarterly* 34 (January 1977): 66-82; Cornelius J. Jaenen, "Amerindian Views of French Culture in the Seventeenth Century," *Canadian Historical Review* 55 (September 1974):263; Jaenen, *Friend and Foe: Aspects of French-Amerindian Cultural Contact in the Sixteenth and Seventeenth Centuries* (New York: Columbia University Press, 1976). See also Denys, *Description and Natural History,* pp. 117, 430, 442.

34. See Le Clercq, *New Relation of Gaspesia,* pp. 206, 227; Marc Lescarbot, *The History of New France* (1618; first published 1609), translated by W. L. Grant, 3 vols. (Toronto: The Champlain Society, 1907-1914), 3:94-95.

35. Jean Baptiste de la Croix Chevrières de Saint-Vallier, *Estat présent de l'Eglise et de la Colonie Françoise dans la Nouvelle France, par M. l'Evêque de Québec* (Paris, 1688), pp. 36-37; *Jesuit Relations,* 2:75-77.

36. Bailey, *Conflict of European and Eastern Algonkian Cultures,*

p. 145; Madeleine Rousseau and Jacques Rousseau, "Le Dualisme religieux des peuplades de la forêt boréale," in *Proceedings and Selected Papers of the 29th International Congress of Americanists: Acculturation in the Americas,* edited by Sol Tax, vol. 2, pp. 118–126 (Chicago: University of Chicago Press, 1952).

37. Lescarbot, *History of New France,* 3:128; Le Clercq, *New Relation of Gaspesia,* pp. 133, 135.

38. Le Clercq, *New Relation of Gaspesia,* pp. 187, 209, 212–214, 238–239, 303; Bailey, *Conflict of European and Eastern Algonkian Cultures,* p. 47; Denys, *Description and Natural History,* pp. 437–439; Lescarbot, *History of New France,* 3:279, 285; *Jesuit Relations,* 1:169; Sieur de Dièreville, *Relation of the Voyage to Port Royal in Acadia of New France* (1708), translated by Mrs. Clarence Webster and edited by John Clarence Webster (Toronto: The Champlain Society, 1933), p. 161.

39. Denys, *Description and Natural History,* pp. 439–441.

40. LeClercq, *New Relation of Gaspesia,* pp. 125, 193; *Jesuit Relations,* 1:165.

41. Denys, *Description and Natural History,* p. 430.

42. Bailey, *Conflict of European and Eastern Algonkian Cultures,* p. 145.

43. Denys, *Description and Natural History,* pp. 440–441.

44. Le Clercq, *New Relation of Gaspesia,* pp. 276–277.

45. Dièreville, *Relation of Voyage,* p. 139.

46. Ibid., p. 161.

47. Lescarbot, *History of New France,* 3:191–192; Denys, *Description and Natural History,* pp. 399, 442–443.

48. Calvin Martin, "The Four Lives of a Micmac Copper Pot," *Ethnohistory* 22 (Spring 1975):111–133.

49. Dièreville, *Relation of Voyage,* p. 174; Denys, *Description and Natural History,* pp. 172, 443–452.

50. Saint-Vallier, *Estat présent,* pp. 36–37, 42; *Jesuit Relations,* 3: 105–109; Denys, *Description and Natural History,* pp. 443–452; Dièreville, *Relation of Voyage,* p. 166; Le Clercq, *New Relation of Gaspesia,* pp. 244–245, 254–257; George F. G. Stanley, "The Indians and the Brandy Trade during the *Ancien Régime," Revue d'Histoire de l'Amérique Française* 6 (March 1953): 489–505; Bailey, *Conflict of European and Eastern Algonkian Cultures,* pp. 66–74; Jaenen, *Friend and Foe,* pp. 110–115.

51. W. D. Billings, *Plants, Man, and the Ecosystem,* 2nd ed. (Belmont, Calif.: Wadsworth Publishing Company, 1970), pp. 37–38.

Chapter Three: Pimadaziwin: The Good Life

1. Samuel Hearne, *A Journey from Prince of Wales's Fort in Hudson's Bay to the Northern Ocean, 1769, 1770, 1771, 1772* (1795), edited

with an introduction by Richard Glover (Toronto: Macmillan Company of Canada, 1958), pp. 219–220.

2. David Thompson, *Narrative, 1784–1812,* edited with an introduction and notes by Richard Glover (Toronto: The Champlain Society, 1962), pp. 77–78.

3. Thompson, *Narrative,* pp. 92, 154–155; Peter Jones, *History of the Ojebway Indians; with Especial Reference to Their Conversion to Christianity* (London: A. W. Bennett, 1861), p. 71; Alexander Henry, *Travels and Adventures in Canada and the Indian Territories Between the Years 1760 and 1776* (1809), edited with an introduction and notes by Milo Milton Quaife (Chicago: The Lakeside Press, R. R. Donnelley and Sons Company, 1921), p. 128; *Jesuit Relations,* 50:289; Sister Bernard Coleman, "The Religion of the Ojibwa of Northern Minnesota," *Primitive Man* 10 (July and October 1937):54.

4. See Roland Burrage Dixon, "The Mythology of the Central and Eastern Algonkins," *Journal of American Folk-Lore* 22 (January 1909): 1–9; James W. VanStone, *Athapaskan Adaptations: Hunters and Fishermen of the Subarctic Forests* (Chicago: Aldine Publishing Company, 1974).

5. Diamond Jenness, *The Ojibwa Indians of Parry Island, Their Social and Religious Life,* Canada, Department of Mines, *National Museum of Canada, Bulletin No. 78,* Anthropological Series No. 17 (Ottawa, 1935), pp. 22–23; Daniel Williams Harmon, *A Journal of Voyages and Travels in the Interiour of North America, . . . During a Residence of Nineteen Years, in Different Parts of the Country . . . ,* transcribed by Daniel Haskell (Andover: Flagg and Gould, 1820), pp. 363–364; Jones, *History of Ojebway Indians,* p. 84; Thompson, *Narrative,* pp. 74–76, 88.

6. George Copway, *The Traditional History and Characteristic Sketches of the Ojibway Nation* (London: Charles Gilpin, 1850), p. 153.

7. Ruth Landes, *Ojibwa Religion and the Midéwiwin* (Madison: University of Wisconsin Press, 1968), p. 24.

8. J. C. Beltrami, *A Pilgrimage in Europe and America, Leading to the Discovery of the Sources of the Mississippi and Bloody River; with a Description of the Whole Course of the Former, and of the Ohio,* 2 vols. (London: C. H. Reynall, 1828), 2:298; George Copway, *The life, history, and travels, of Kah-Ge-Ga-Gah-Bowh (George Copway), a young Indian chief of the Ojebwa nation, a convert to the Christian faith, and a missionary to his people for twelve years; with a sketch of the present state of the Ojebwa nation, in regard to Christianity and their future prospects . . .* (Albany: Weed and Parsons, 1847), pp. 36–37; Copway, *Traditional History,* pp. 152–153, 164–165; Peter Grant, *The Sauteux Indians* (written ca. 1804), in *Les Bourgeois de la Com-*

pagnie du Nord-Ouest, edited by L. R. Masson, series 2, pp. 303–366 (Québec: De l'Imprimerie Générale A. Coté et Compagnie, 1890), pp. 353–354, 356; Harmon, *Journal of Voyages and Travels,* pp. 363–364; Hearne, *Journey from Prince of Wales's Fort,* p. 222; Edwin James, ed., *A Narrative of the Captivity and Adventures of John Tanner (U.S. Interpreter at the Saut de Ste. Marie,) During Thirty Years Residence Among the Indians in the Interior of North America* (London: Baldwin and Cradock, 1830), p. 137; Jones, *History of Ojebway Indians,* p. 84; Nicolas Perrot, *Memoir on the Manners, Customs, and Religion of the Savages of North America* (written sometime between 1680 and 1718), in *The Indian Tribes of the Upper Mississippi Valley and Region of the Great Lakes,* edited by Emma Helen Blair, vol. 1, pp. 23–272 (Cleveland: The Arthur H. Clark Company, 1911), pp. 48–49; Thompson, *Narrative,* pp. 74–76; *Jesuit Relations,* 50:285–289; Sister M. Bernard, "Religion and Magic Among Cass Lake Ojibwa," *Primitive Man* 2 (July and October 1929):53; A. F. Chamberlain, "Notes on the History, Customs, and Beliefs of the Mississauga Indians," *Journal of American Folk-Lore* 1 (July–September 1888):157; Henry R. Schoolcraft, "Mythology, Superstitions and Languages of the North American Indians," *Literary and Theological Review* (New York) 2 (March 1835):103.

9. Jenness, *Ojibwa Indians of Parry Island,* pp. 18–20.

10. A. Irving Hallowell, "Ojibwa Ontology, Behavior, and World View," in *Culture in History: Essays in Honor of Paul Radin,* edited by Stanley Diamond, pp. 19–52 (New York: Columbia University Press, 1960), p. 45; Hallowell, "Sin, Sex and Sickness in Saulteaux Belief," *British Journal of Medical Psychology* 18, part 2 (1939):191–197; Hallowell, *Culture and Experience* (Philadelphia: University of Pennsylvania Press, 1955), pp. 291–305; Hallowell, "Ojibwa World View and Disease," in *Man's Image in Medicine and Anthropology,* Monograph 4, edited by Iago Galdston, pp. 258–315, Institute of Social and Historical Medicine, New York Academy of Medicine (New York: International Universities Press, 1963), pp. 274, 293.

11. Hearne, *Journey from Prince of Wales's Fort,* p. 221.

12. Hallowell, "Ojibwa World View and Disease," pp. 264–265, 269–270, 271–274, 283, 310; Hallowell, *Culture and Experience,* p. 145; Hallowell, "Ojibwa Ontology," p. 45.

13. Hallowell, "Sin, Sex and Sickness"; Hallowell, "Ojibwa World View and Disease."

14. Thompson, *Narrative,* p. 155; Hearne, *Journey from Prince of Wales's Fort,* p. 232; A. Irving Hallowell, "Bear Ceremonialism in the Northern Hemisphere," *American Anthropologist,* n.s. 28 (1926): 1–175; Hallowell, "Ojibwa World View and Disease," pp. 271–272, 283; Landes, *Ojibwa Religion,* pp. 27–28; Alanson Buck Skinner, "Notes

on the Eastern Cree and Northern Saulteaux," *Anthropological Papers of the American Museum of Natural History* 9, part 1 (New York, 1911): 69–73, 76, 162–164.

15. Schoolcraft, "Mythology, Superstitions and Languages," p. 105; VanStone, *Athapaskan Adaptations*, pp. 88–89, 122; Landes, *Ojibwa Religion*, p. 25.

16. Copway, *life, history, and travels*, pp. 51, 27; Grey Owl, *Pilgrims of the Wild* (London: Lovat Dickson and Thompson, 1935), p. 24; Jenness, *Ojibwa Indians of Parry Island*, p. 80; Bernard, "Religion and Magic," p. 55.

17. Copway, *life, history, and travels*, p. 27; Copway, *Traditional History*, pp. 130–131; Hearne, *Journey from Prince of Wales's Fort*, p. 220; Thompson, *Narrative*, p. 75.

18. Jenness, *Ojibwa Indians of Parry Island*, p. 80; Hallowell, "Ojibwa World View and Disease," pp. 278–279, 286.

19. Landes, *Ojibwa Religion*, p. 22.

20. Ibid., pp. 21, 8.

21. Duncan Cameron, *The Nipigon Country* (written between 1804 and 1805), pp. 229–300 in *Les Bourgeois de la Compagnie du Nord-Ouest*, ed. Masson, pp. 260–261; Copway, *life, history, and travels*, pp. 48–51; Copway, *Traditional History*, p. 154; Grant, *Sauteaux Indians*, pp. 356, 357; Thompson, *Narrative*, p. 81; *Jesuit Relations*, 50:291; 54:139–143.

22. Hallowell, *Culture and Experience*, p. 361.

23. Harvey A. Feit, "The Ethno-Ecology of the Waswanipi Cree; or How Hunters Can Manage Their Resources," in *Cultural Ecology: Readings on the Canadian Indians and Eskimos*, edited by Bruce Cox, pp. 115–125 (Toronto: McClelland and Stewart, 1973).

24. Hallowell, "Bear Ceremonialism," pp. 10–11; Jones, *History of Ojebway Indians*, p. 72.

25. Hearne, *Journey from Prince of Wales's Fort*, pp. 211–212.

26. Ibid., p. 212.

27. Jenness, *Ojibwa Indians of Parry Island*, pp. 22, 7; Henry, *Travels and Adventures*, p. 115; Perrot, *Memoir*, pp. 127–129.

28. Coleman, "Religion of Ojibwa," p. 55; Henry, *Travels and Adventures*, p. 115; Hearne, *Journey from Prince of Wales's Fort*, p. 44; Grant, *Sauteux Indians*, p. 331.

29. Henry, *Travels and Adventures*, pp. 125–126.

30. Ibid., pp. 130–131, 145–146; Lucien Lévy-Bruhl, *Primitive Mentality* (1923), translated by Lilian A. Clare (Boston: Beacon Press, 1966), pp. 212–213.

31. Bernard, "Religion and Magic," p. 55; John M. Cooper, "Field Notes on Northern Algonkian Magic," *Proceedings of the Twenty-*

Third International Congress of Americanists, New York, September 1928 (1930):513–516.

32. James, ed., *Narrative of Captivity*, pp. 192–193.

33. Martha Coleman Bray, ed., *The Journals of Joseph N. Nicollet: A Scientist on the Mississippi Headwaters with Notes on Indian Life, 1836–1837*, translated by André Fertey (St. Paul: Minnesota Historical Society, 1970), p. 211.

34. Ibid., pp. 211–216; James, ed., *Narrative of Captivity*, pp. 72, 174, 189; Cameron, *Nipigon Country*, p. 262.

35. Henry, *Travels and Adventures*, p. 139.

36. Ibid., p. 140.

37. Jenness, *Ojibwa Indians of Parry Island*, p. 24.

38. Perrot, *Memoir*, p. 131.

39. Henry, *Travels and Adventures*, pp. 194–195; Adrian Tanner, "The Elementary Feast and Its Transformations: Old and New Data from Quebec-Labrador" (Paper delivered at the Annual Meetings of the Canadian Sociology and Anthropology Association, Toronto, August 24, 1974).

40. Jenness, *Ojibwa Indians of Parry Island*, pp. 23–25.

41. *Jesuit Relations*, 50:289.

42. Morton I. Teicher, *Windigo Psychosis: A Study of a Relationship between Belief and Behavior among the Indians of Northeastern Canada*, Proceedings of the 1960 Annual Spring Meeting of the American Ethnological Society, edited by Verne F. Ray (Seattle and London: Distributed by the University of Washington Press, 1960); Seymour Parker, "The Wittiko Psychosis in the Context of Ojibwa Personality and Culture," *American Anthropologist* 62 (August 1960):603–623; Landes, *Ojibwa Religion*, pp. 12–14.

43. Robert E. Ritzenthaler, "Chippewa Preoccupation with Health: Change in a Traditional Attitude Resulting From Modern Health Problems," *Bulletin of the Public Museum of the City of Milwaukee* 19 (December 1953):223.

44. Harold Hickerson, *The Chippewa and Their Neighbors: A Study in Ethnohistory* (New York: Holt, Rinehart and Winston, 1970), p. 52.

45. Harold Hickerson, "Notes on the Post-Contact Origin of the Midewiwin," *Ethnohistory* 9 (Fall 1962):406; Hickerson, *Chippewa and Their Neighbors*, pp. 51–63.

46. Harold Hickerson, "The Feast of the Dead Among the Seventeenth Century Algonkians of the Upper Great Lakes," *American Anthropologist* 62 (February 1960):81–107; Hickerson, "Notes on Post-Contact Origin of Midewiwin"; Hickerson, "The Sociohistorical Significance of Two Chippewa Ceremonials," *American Anthropologist* 65 (February 1963):67–85; Hickerson, "The Chippewa of the Upper Great

Lakes: A Study in Sociopolitical Change," in *North American Indians in Historical Perspective*, edited by Eleanor Burke Leacock and Nancy Oestreich Lurie, pp. 169–199 (New York: Random House, 1971), pp. 176–178.

47. Hickerson, "Sociohistorical Significance of Two Chippewa Ceremonials," p. 79.

48. Selwyn Dewdney, *The Sacred Scrolls of the Southern Ojibway* (Toronto: University of Toronto Press for the Glenbow-Alberta Institute, 1975), pp. 21–22, 57–58, 60–71.

49. William W. Warren, *History of the Ojibways, Based upon Traditions and Oral Statements* (1853), in the *Collections of the Minnesota Historical Society*, vol. 5, pp. 21–394 (St. Paul, Minn.: Published by the Society, 1885), pp. 78–80.

50. Charles A. Bishop and Victor Barnouw, personal communication.

51. James V. Wright, "An Archaeological Survey along the North Shore of Lake Superior," Ottawa, *National Museum of Canada, Anthropology Papers*, no. 3 (March 1963); Wright, "A Regional Examination of Ojibwa Culture History," *Anthropologica*, n.s. 7, no. 2 (1965):189–227; Wright, "The Pic River Site: A Stratified Late Woodland Site on the North Shore of Lake Superior," *Contributions to Anthropology V: Archaeology and Physical Anthropology, National Museum of Canada, Bulletin No. 206*, Anthropological Series No. 72 (Ottawa, 1967) pp. 54–99; Wright, "The Application of the Direct Historical Approach to the Iroquois and Ojibwa," *Ethnohistory* 15 (Winter 1968):96–111; Wright, "Michipicoten Site," *Contributions to Anthropology VI: Archaeology and Physical Anthropology, National Museum of Canada, Bulletin No. 224*, Anthropological Series No. 83 (Ottawa, 1969), pp. 1–85; Charles A. Bishop, *The Northern Ojibwa and the Fur Trade: An Historical and Ecological Study* (Toronto: Holt, Rinehart and Winston of Canada, 1974), pp. 4–7; Bishop and M. Estellie Smith, "Early Historic Populations in Northwestern Ontario: Archaeological and Ethnohistorical Interpretations," *American Antiquity* 40 (January 1975):54–63; Bishop, "The Emergence of the Northern Ojibwa: Social and Economic Consequences," *American Ethnologist* 3 (February 1976):39–54.

52. Dixon, "Mythology of Central and Eastern Algonkins," pp. 8–9.

53. Roland Burrage Dixon, "The Early Migrations of the Indians of New England and the Maritime Provinces," *Proceedings of the American Antiquarian Society*, n.s. 24 (April 1914):74.

54. Father Chrestien Le Clercq, *New Relation of Gaspesia, with the Customs and Religion of the Gaspesian Indians* (1691), translated and edited by William F. Ganong (Toronto: The Champlain Society, 1910), pp. 146–152.

55. Dewdney, *Sacred Scrolls*, pp. 167, 170–176.

56. W. J. Hoffman, "The Midé Wiwin or 'Grand Medicine Society' of the Ojibwa," *Seventh Annual Report of the Bureau of Ethnology, 1885/86*, pp. 143–300 (Washington, D.C., 1891), pp. 262, 261.

57. See Dewdney, *Sacred Scrolls*, pp. 94–96, 110–111, 140, 122–130.

58. Ritzenthaler, "Chippewa Preoccupation with Health," pp. 190–192.

59. *Jesuit Relations*, 50:301; Bray, *Journals of Joseph Nicollet*, p. 218.

60. Cameron, *Nipigon Country*, p. 262; Grant, *Sauteux Indians*, p. 364.

61. Bray, *Journals of Joseph Nicollet*, pp. 218–222.

62. Henry, *Travels and Adventures*, pp. 117–120.

63. Hearne, *Journey from Prince of Wales's Fort*, pp. 123–126.

64. A. Irving Hallowell, *The Role of Conjuring in Saulteaux Society*, Publications of the Philadelphia Anthropological Society, vol. 2 (Philadelphia: University of Pennsylvania Press, 1942), p. 5.

Chapter Four: Contact and Nature's Conspiracy

1. Claude Charles le Roy, Bacqueville de la Potherie, "History of the Savage Peoples Who Are Allies of New France," taken from his *Histoire de l'Amérique septentrionale* (1753; first published 1716), in *The Indian Tribes of the Upper Mississippi Valley and Region of the Great Lakes*, edited by Emma Helen Blair, vol. 1, pp. 273–372; vol. 2, pp. 13–136 (Cleveland: The Arthur H. Clark Company, 1911), 1:278–280.

2. Nicolas Perrot, *Memoir on the Manners, Customs, and Religion of the Savages of North America* (written sometime between 1680 and 1718), vol. 1, pp. 23–272 in *The Indian Tribes of the Upper Mississippi Valley and Region of the Great Lakes*, ed. Blair, pp. 102–103; Peter Grant, *The Sauteux Indians* (written ca. 1804), in *Les Bourgeois de la Compagnie du Nord-Ouest*, edited by L. R. Masson, series 2, pp. 303–366 (Québec: De l'Imprimerie Générale A. Coté et Compagnie, 1890), p. 330; James V. Wright, "The Application of the Direct Historical Approach to the Iroquois and Ojibwa," *Ethnohistory* 15 (Winter 1968): 107–108; Lois Kay Lippold, "Aboriginal Animal Resource Utilization in Woodland Wisconsin" (Ph.D. diss., University of Wisconsin, Madison, 1971), p. 168; Charles A. Bishop, *The Northern Ojibwa and the Fur Trade: An Historical and Ecological Study* (Toronto: Holt, Rinehart and Winston of Canada, 1974), pp. 4–8, 328, 342, 347.

3. Grant, *Sauteux Indians*, p. 309.

4. Martha Coleman Bray, ed., *The Journals of Joseph N. Nicollet: A Scientist on the Mississippi Headwaters with Notes on Indian Life*,

1836–1837, translated by André Fertey (St. Paul: Minnesota Historical Society, 1970), p. 253; Duncan Cameron, *The Nipigon Country* (written between 1804 and 1805), pp. 229–300 in *Les Bourgeois de la Compagnie du Nord-Ouest*, ed. Masson, p. 274; George Copway, *The life, history, and travels, of Kah-Ge-Ga-Gah-Bowh (George Copway), a young Indian chief of the Ojebwa nation, a convert to the Christian faith, and a missionary to his people for twelve years; with a sketch of the present state of the Ojebwa nation, in regard to Christianity and their future prospects* . . . (Albany: Weed and Parsons, 1847), pp. 12, 19–20; Grant, *Sauteux Indians*, p. 326; Daniel Williams Harmon, *A Journal of Voyages and Travels in the Interiour of North America, . . . During a Residence of Nineteen Years, in Different Parts of the Country* . . . , transcribed by Daniel Haskell (Andover: Flagg and Gould, 1820), pp. 379–380; Alexander Henry, *Travels and Adventures in Canada and the Indian Territories Between the Years 1760 and 1776* (1809), edited with an introduction and notes by Milo Milton Quaife (Chicago: The Lakeside Press, R. R. Donnelley and Sons Company, 1921), pp. 24–25, 123, 143–144, 206–207; Edwin James, ed., *A Narrative of the Captivity and Adventures of John Tanner (U.S. Interpreter at the Saut de Ste. Marie,) During Thirty Years Residence Among the Indians in the Interior of North America* (London: Baldwin and Cradock, 1830), pp. 103–104; Peter Jones, *History of the Ojebway Indians; with Especial Reference to Their Conversion to Christianity* (London: A. W. Bennett, 1861), p. 71; David Thompson, *Narrative, 1784–1812*, edited with an introduction and notes by Richard Glover (Toronto: The Champlain Society, 1962), p. 79; Bishop, *Northern Ojibwa*, pp. 7–8, 11, 328, 342, 344–345; Wright, "Application of Direct Historical Approach," pp. 107–108; Harold Hickerson, "The Chippewa of the Upper Great Lakes: A Study in Sociopolitical Change," in *North American Indians in Historical Perspective*, edited by Eleanor Burke Leacock and Nancy Oestreich Lurie, pp. 169–199 (New York: Random House, 1971), pp. 169–178.

    5. Cameron, *Nipigon Country*, pp. 254–255; Grant, *Sauteux Indians*, p. 330; Henry, *Travels and Adventures*, pp. 131–132, 141–142.

    6. Henry, *Travels and Adventures*, pp. 143–144.

    7. Grant, *Sauteux Indians*, pp. 345–346.

    8. Henry, *Travels and Adventures*, p. 61.

    9. Perrot, *Memoir*, pp. 102–103.

    10. *Jesuit Relations*, 1:33.

    11. Ibid., 50:297.

    12. Ibid., 51:23, 50:277.

    13. Ibid., 55:125.

    14. Ibid., 55:117, 127, 129–131; 56:113.

    15. Ibid., 55:123–125, 127–129.

16. Ibid., 50:307–309.

17. Ibid., 51:21; 50:305.

18. Ibid., 66:283.

19. Alexander Henry, *Journal* (1824), in *The Manuscript Journals of Alexander Henry . . . and of David Thompson . . . , 1799–1814,* edited by Elliott Coues, in 3 vols. (New York: Francis P. Harper, 1897), 1:46.

20. John Duffy, "Smallpox and the Indians in the American Colonies," *Bulletin of the History of Medicine* 25 (July–August 1951):324–341.

21. Potherie, "History of Savage Peoples," 1:339–341.

22. George T. Hunt, *The Wars of the Iroquois: A Study in Intertribal Trade Relations* (Madison: University of Wisconsin Press, 1940); Allen W. Trelease, "The Iroquois and the Western Fur Trade: A Problem in Interpretation," *Mississippi Valley Historical Review* 49 (June 1962):32–51.

23. *Jesuit Relations,* 68:283.

24. Ibid., 57:21.

25. Potherie, "History of Savage Peoples," 1:309–310.

26. John Dunn, *The Oregon Territory, and the British North American Fur Trade; with an Account of the Habits and Customs of the Principal Native Tribes on the Northern Continent* (Philadelphia: G. B. Zieber and Company, 1845), pp. 57–58, 65; James, ed., *Narrative of Captivity,* pp. 10–11.

27. *Jesuit Relations,* 50:307.

28. Potherie, "History of Savage Peoples," 1:281.

29. Henry, *Journal,* 1:60–61.

30. Cameron, *Nipigon Country,* pp. 245, 288.

31. Ibid., pp. 296–297.

32. Ibid., pp. 254–255, 258, 275, 277, 281.

33. Samuel Hearne, *A Journey from Prince of Wales's Fort in Hudson's Bay to the Northern Ocean, 1769, 1770, 1771, 1772* (1795), edited with an introduction by Richard Glover (Toronto: Macmillan Company of Canada, 1958), pp. 115–116.

34. Harmon, *Journal of Voyages and Travels,* p. 268.

35. Thompson, *Narrative,* pp. 149, 229.

36. Bishop, *Northern Ojibwa,* pp. 11–12, 107, 184–190, 229, 232–235, 246–247, 249, 254, 255, 264–266, 277–278, 281–283, 296–298, 344–345.

37. James, ed., *Narrative of Captivity,* pp. 228–229, 236; Hearne, *Journey from Prince of Wales's Fort,* pp. 212–213.

38. Marshall T. Newman, "Ecology and Nutritional Stress in Man," *American Anthropologist* 64 (February 1962):22–34.

39. Cameron, *Nipigon Country*, p. 298; *Jesuit Relations*, 55:135; Perrot, *Memoir*, pp. 102–103; Grant, *Sauteux Indians*, p. 331.

40. Thompson, *Narrative*, p. 151.

41. Ibid., pp. 151–152.

42. Ibid., p. 75.

43. Ibid., p. 155.

44. Henry, *Travels and Adventures*, pp. 204, 128.

45. Thompson, *Narrative*, pp. 95–96.

46. Ibid., pp. 152, 95, 153–154, 156.

47. Potherie, "History of Savage Peoples," 1:309–311; Hearne, *Journey from Prince of Wales's Fort*, pp. 75–76.

Chapter Five: The Hunter's Relationship with the Hunted

1. Frank G. Speck, *Naskapi: The Savage Hunters of the Labrador Peninsula* (Norman: University of Oklahoma Press, 1935), pp. 76, 20.

2. Ibid., p. 76.

3. A. Irving Hallowell, "Bear Ceremonialism in the Northern Hemisphere," *American Anthropologist*, n.s. 28 (1926):10.

4. Speck, *Naskapi*, p. 82.

5. John Witthoft, "The American Indian as Hunter" (Harrisburg: Pennsylvania Historical and Museum Commission, 1967), p. 6; Adrian Tanner, "Bringing Home Animals: Religious Ideology and Mode of Production of the Mistassini Cree Hunters" (Ph.D. diss., University of Toronto, 1976).

6. Frank G. Speck, "Penobscot Tales and Religious Beliefs," *Journal of American Folk-Lore* 48 (January-March 1935):22–23.

7. Tanner, "Bringing Home Animals," pp. 230, 306–307, 275.

8. Speck, *Naskapi*, p. 113. See A. Irving Hallowell, "Ojibwa World View and Disease," in *Man's Image in Medicine and Anthropology*, Monograph 4, edited by Iago Galdston, pp. 258–315, Institute of Social and Historical Medicine, New York Academy of Medicine (New York: International Universities Press, 1963), pp. 271–272.

9. Speck, *Naskapi*, p. 97.

10. Tanner, "Bringing Home Animals," pp. 260–261.

11. Alanson Buck Skinner, "Notes on the Eastern Cree and Northern Saulteaux," *Anthropological Papers of the American Museum of Natural History* 9, part 1 (New York, 1911):73, 76; Ruth Landes, *Ojibwa Religion and the Midéwiwin* (Madison: University of Wisconsin Press, 1968), pp. 27–28.

12. Speck, *Naskapi*, pp. 82–94, 117–121.

13. Ibid., p. 41.

14. Ibid., pp. 43–44, 48–49.

15. Ibid., pp. 49, 218.

16. Tanner, "Bringing Home Animals," pp. 370, 329–371; Tanner, "The Significance of Hunting Territories Today," in *Cultural Ecology: Readings on the Canadian Indians and Eskimos*, edited by Bruce Cox, pp. 101–114 (Toronto: McClelland and Stewart, 1973); Julius E. Lips, "Notes on Montagnais-Naskapi Economy," *Ethnos* 12 (January–June 1947):6–7.

17. Landes, *Ojibwa Religion*, p. 7.

18. Tanner, "Significance of Hunting Territories," p. 110; Tanner, "Bringing Home Animals," pp. 246, 248–250.

19. Speck, *Naskapi*, p. 181; Landes, *Ojibwa Religion*, p. 25.

20. Speck, *Naskapi*, p. 94; John M. Cooper, "Field Notes on Northern Algonkian Magic," *Proceedings of the Twenty-Third International Congress of Americanists*, New York, September 1928 (1930):514.

21. Speck, *Naskapi*, p. 212; Tanner, "Bringing Home Animals," pp. 203–204.

22. *Jesuit Relations*, 6:215.

23. Speck, *Naskapi*, p. 150.

24. Ibid., pp. 139, 167–168; Edward S. Rogers, *The Quest for Food and Furs: The Mistassini Cree, 1953–1954*, National Museum of Man, Publications in Ethnology No. 5 (Ottawa, 1973), pp. 11–14.

25. James W. VanStone, *Athapaskan Adaptations: Hunters and Fishermen of the Subarctic Forests* (Chicago: Aldine Publishing Company, 1974), p. 65.

26. Adrian Tanner, "Decision and Cognition: A Restudy of Naskapi Divination" (Paper delivered at the Annual Meeting of the Northeast Anthropological Association, Burlington, Vermont, April 27–29, 1973), pp. 11–13; Tanner, "Bringing Home Animals," pp. 212–219, 234–237, 240–241, 61–62, 78, 82–83.

27. Adrian Tanner, "The Effect of Climate on Mistassini Cree Hunters" (Paper delivered at the Cultural Ecology Session of the Annual Meetings of the Canadian Sociology and Anthropology Association, Montreal, May 30, 1972), p. 8; Tanner, "Bringing Home Animals," pp. 158–172.

28. Cooper, "Field Notes," pp. 515, 516.

29. Ibid., p. 515.

30. Speck, *Naskapi*, p. 190.

31. Henry R. Schoolcraft, "Mythology, Superstitions and Languages of the North American Indians," *Literary and Theological Review* (New York) 2 (March 1835):105.

32. Speck, *Naskapi*, pp. 77–78.

33. Harvey A. Feit, "The Ethno-Ecology of the Waswanipi Cree; or How Hunters Can Manage Their Resources," pp. 115–125 in *Cultural Ecology*, ed. Cox, pp. 118–120.

34. Harvey A. Feit, "Twilight of the Cree Hunting Nation," *Natural History* (August-September 1973):53; Feit, "Ethno-Ecology of Waswanipi Cree," p. 118.

35. Feit, "Ethno-Ecology of Waswanipi Cree," p. 120.

36. Feit, "Twilight of Cree Hunting Nation," pp. 54-56; Feit, "Ethno-Ecology of Waswanipi Cree," p. 121.

37. Feit, "Ethno-Ecology of Waswanipi Cree," p. 122; Tanner, "Bringing Home Animals," pp. 61-62.

38. See Arthur J. Ray, "Some Conservation Schemes of the Hudson's Bay Company, 1821-50: An Examination of the Problems of Resource Management in the Fur Trade," *Journal of Historical Geography* 1, no. 1 (1975):49-68.

39. Feit, "Ethno-Ecology of Waswanipi Cree," p. 117; Feit, "Twilight of Cree Hunting Nation," p. 72; Speck, *Naskapi*, p. 151.

40. A. Irving Hallowell, *Culture and Experience* (Philadelphia: University of Pennsylvania Press, 1955), pp. 144-145.

41. VanStone, *Athapaskan Adaptations*, pp. 88-89, 122; Adrian Tanner, "The Elementary Feast and Its Transformations: Old and New Data from Quebec-Labrador" (Paper delivered at the Annual Meetings of the Canadian Sociology and Anthropology Association, Toronto, August 24, 1974), pp. 22-23; Tanner, "Bringing Home Animals," pp. 265-272, 313-315; Frederica de Laguna, "The Atna of the Copper River, Alaska: The World of Men and Animals," *Folk* (Dansk Ethnografisk Tidsskrift) 11/12 (1969/70):23-24.

42. Speck, *Naskapi*, p. 81.

43. Diamond Jenness, *The Ojibwa Indians of Parry Island, Their Social and Religious Life,* Canada, Department of Mines, *National Museum of Canada, Bulletin No. 78,* Anthropological Series No. 17 (Ottawa, 1935), p. 89.

44. Hallowell, "Ojibwa World View and Disease," p. 286; Hallowell, *Culture and Experience,* p. 268; Robert J. Sullivan, *The Ten'a Food Quest,* Catholic University of America, Anthropological Series No. 11 (Washington, D.C.: Catholic University of America Press, 1942), pp. 18-19, 32, 78, 80, 86, 103-104, 108, 112; De Laguna, "Atna of Copper River," pp. 23-24.

45. Robert E. Ritzenthaler, "Chippewa Preoccupation with Health: Change in a Traditional Attitude Resulting From Modern Health Problems," *Bulletin of the Public Museum of the City of Milwaukee* 19 (December 1953):243-244.

46. Baron de Lahontan, *New Voyages to North-America* (1703), edited by Reuben Gold Thwaites, 2 vols. (Chicago: A. C. McClurg and Company, 1905), 1:170-171, 192.

47. Mark V. Barrow, Jerry D. Niswander, and Robert Fortuine, comps., *Health and Disease of American Indians North of Mexico: A*

Bibliography, 1800–1969 (Gainesville: University of Florida Press, 1972), pp. 74–79.

48. Leo Kartman, Martin I. Goldenberg, and William T. Hubbert, "Recent Observations on the Epidemiology of Plague in the United States," *American Journal of Public Health and the Nation's Health* 56 (September 1966):1566.

49. Peter F. Olsen, "Tularemia," in *Diseases Transmitted from Animals to Man*, compiled and edited by William T. Hubbert, William F. McCulloch, and Paul R. Schnurrenberger, 6th ed., pp. 191–223 (Springfield, Ill.: Charles C. Thomas, 1975), pp. 196, 191.

50. *Jesuit Relations*, 30:281–283.

51. David Thompson, *Narrative, 1784–1812*, edited with an introduction and notes by Richard Glover (Toronto: The Champlain Society, 1962), p. 246.

52. Ibid., p. 236.

53. E. E. Rich, ed., *Cumberland House Journals and Inland Journals, 1775–82: Second Series, 1779–82*, introduction by Richard Glover, Publications of the Hudson's Bay Record Society, vol. 15 (London: The Hudson's Bay Record Society, 1952), pp. 225–226, 223–242, 262–279; Alexander Henry, *Journal* (1824), in *The Manuscript Journals of Alexander Henry . . . and of David Thompson . . . , 1799–1814*, edited by Elliott Coues, in 3 vols. (New York: Francis P. Harper, 1897), 1:46.

54. Thompson, *Narrative*, p. 237.

55. Charles S. Elton, "Periodic Fluctuations in the Numbers of Animals: Their Causes and Effects," *British Journal of Experimental Biology* 2 (October 1924):119–163; Elton, "Plague and the Regulation of Numbers in Wild Mammals," *Journal of Hygiene* 24 (October 1925):138–163; Elton, "The Study of Epidemic Diseases among Wild Animals," *Journal of Hygiene* 31 (October 1931):435–456; Elton and Mary Nicholson, "Fluctuations in Numbers of the Muskrat (*Ondatra zibethica*) in Canada," *Journal of Animal Ecology* 11 (May 1942):96–126; C. Gordon Hewitt, *The Conservation of the Wild Life of Canada* (New York: Charles Scribner's Sons, 1921), pp. 213–234; Lloyd B. Keith, *Wildlife's Ten-Year Cycle* (Madison: University of Wisconsin Press, 1963).

56. Thompson, *Narrative*, pp. 237, 238, 93.

57. Keith, *Wildlife's Ten-Year Cycle*.

58. Elton, "Study of Epidemic Diseases"; Elton, "Plague and Regulation of Numbers"; R. G. Green, "Disease—A Factor in Wild Life Management," *Minnesota Conservationist* 3 (August 1933):14–15, 25–26; Green and J. E. Shillinger, "Relation of Disease to Wildlife Cycles," *Transactions of the American Game Conference* (November 28–30, 1932) 19 (1933):432–436.

59. Alice M. Johnson, ed., *Saskatchewan Journals and Correspondence: Edmonton House, 1795–1800; Chesterfield House, 1800–1802*, introduction by Alice M. Johnson, Publications of the Hudson's Bay Record Society, vol. 26 (London: The Hudson's Bay Record Society, 1967), p. 78.

60. Ibid., pp. 91; 94, n. 2.

61. Ibid., p. 92.

62. Ibid., pp. 241; 242, n. 2.

63. Ibid., pp. 294, 316.

64. Edwin James, ed., *A Narrative of the Captivity and Adventures of John Tanner (U.S. Interpreter at the Saut de Ste. Marie,) During Thirty Years Residence Among the Indians in the Interior of North America* (London: Baldwin and Cradock, 1830), pp. 104–105.

65. Arthur J. Ray, *Indians in the Fur Trade: Their Role as Trappers, Hunters, and Middlemen in the Lands Southwest of Hudson Bay, 1660–1870* (Toronto: University of Toronto Press, 1974), p. 119.

66. H. L. Hammersland and E. M. Joneschild, "Tularemia in a Beaver," *Journal of the American Veterinary Medical Association* 96 (January 1940):96–97; William L. Jellison et al., "Epizootic Tularemia in the Beaver, *Castor Canadensis*, and the Contamination of Stream Water with *Pasteurella Tularensis*," *American Journal of Hygiene* 36 (September 1942):168–182.

67. Jellison et al., "Epizootic Tularemia," p. 179; R. R. Parker et al., "Contamination of Natural Waters and Mud with *Pasteurella tularensis* and Tularemia in Beavers and Muskrats in the Northwestern United States," *National Institutes of Health Bulletin* 193 (Washington, D.C., 1951):55; Olsen, "Tularemia," p. 210.

68. Parker et al., "Contamination of Natural Waters," pp. 56, 59; Olsen, "Tularemia," p. 210.

69. James, ed., *Narrative of Captivity*, pp. 110–113.

70. Jellison et al., "Epizootic Tularemia," p. 182; Parker et al., "Contamination of Natural Waters," pp. 2, 3; Theodore L. Badger, "Tularemia: Report of a Case of the Typhoidal Form," *New England Journal of Medicine* 220 (February 1939):190; Olsen, "Tularemia," pp. 207, 193; John E. Gordon, *Control of Communicable Diseases in Man*, 10th ed. (New York: American Public Health Association, 1965), p. 256.

71. Badger, "Tularemia," pp. 189–190; Olsen, "Tularemia," pp. 192, 193–194.

72. Olsen, "Tularemia," p. 208.

73. Ibid., p. 209.

74. Marc Lescarbot, *The History of New France* (1618; first published 1609), translated by W. L. Grant, 3 vols. (Toronto: The Champlain Society, 1907–1914), 3:226; 2:229.

75. Ibid., 3:226–227.

76. D. H. S. Davis, A. F. Hallett, and Margaretha Isaacson, "Plague," pp. 147–173 in *Diseases Transmitted from Animals to Man*, comp. and ed. Hubbert, McCulloch, and Schnurrenberger, p. 157.

77. Fred G. Conrad, Frank R. LeCocq, and Robert Krain, "A Recent Epidemic of Plague in Vietnam," *Archives of Internal Medicine* 122 (September 1968):197, 196.

78. Davis, Hallett, Isaacson, "Plague," p. 149.

79. Conrad, Le Cocq, Krain, "Recent Epidemic of Plague," p. 196.

80. Parker et al., "Contamination of Natural Waters," pp. 1–3, 25–37, 59.

81. Samuel Hearne, *A Journey from Prince of Wales's Fort in Hudson's Bay to the Northern Ocean, 1769, 1770, 1771, 1772* (1795), edited with an introduction by Richard Glover (Toronto: Macmillan Company of Canada, 1958), p. 220.

82. Thompson, *Narrative*, p. 81.

83. Ibid., pp. 157, 155; Grey Owl, *Pilgrims of the Wild* (London: Lovat Dickson and Thompson, 1935), pp. 47–51, 203.

84. Thompson, *Narrative*, pp. 191–193; James, ed., *Narrative of Captivity*, pp. 135–136, 287.

Chapter Six: Conclusion

1. Lucien Lévy-Bruhl, *Primitive Mentality* (1923), translated by Lilian A. Clare (Boston: Beacon Press, 1966).

2. *Jesuit Relations*, 6:297–299.

3. Ibid., 24:209–213.

4. Frank G. Speck, *Naskapi: The Savage Hunters of the Labrador Peninsula* (Norman: University of Oklahoma Press, 1935), p. 172. See David Merrill Smith, *Inkonze: Magico-Religious Beliefs of Contact-Traditional Chipewyan Trading at Fort Resolution, NWT, Canada*, National Museum of Man, Ethnology Division, Paper No. 6, Mercury Series, Ottawa (June 1973):12, 20; Robert J. Sullivan, *The Ten'a Food Quest*, Catholic University of America, Anthropological Series No. 11 (Washington, D.C.: Catholic University of America Press, 1942), pp. 75, 79, 120–121, 133.

Epilogue: The Indian and the Ecology Movement

1. Aldo Leopold, *A Sand County Almanac and Sketches Here and There* (New York: Oxford University Press, 1949), pp. 201–226; Roderick Nash, *Wilderness and the American Mind*, rev. ed. (New Haven: Yale University Press, 1973), pp. 182–199.

2. Nash, *Wilderness*; Donald Fleming, "Roots of the New Conservation Movement," *Perspectives in American History* 6 (1972):7–91.

3. Lynn White, Jr., "The Historical Roots of Our Ecologic Crisis," *Science* 155 (March 1967):1203–1207; Garret Hardin, "The Tragedy of the Commons," *Science* 162 (December 1968):1243–1248.

4. Rennard Strickland, "The Idea of Environment and the Ideal of the Indian," *Journal of American Indian Education* 10 (October 1970): 14, 9.

5. Stewart L. Udall, *The Quiet Crisis* (New York: Avon Books, 1963), p. 24; Udall, "The Indians," *American Way* (May 1971):9.

6. Terence Grieder, "Ecology Before Columbus," *Américas* (May 1970):28.

7. N. Scott Momaday, "An American Land Ethic," in *Ecotactics: The Sierra Club Handbook for Environment Activists*, edited by John G. Mitchell with Constance L. Stallings, pp. 97–105 (New York: Simon and Schuster, 1970).

8. Vine Deloria, Jr., *We Talk, You Listen: New Tribes, New Turf* (New York: Macmillan Company, 1970), pp. 186, 194, 197.

9. Wilbur R. Jacobs, *Dispossessing the American Indian: Indians and Whites on the Colonial Frontier* (New York: Charles Scribner's Sons, 1972), pp. 19–30.

10. William Christie MacLeod, "Conservation Among Primitive Hunting Peoples," *Scientific Monthly* 43 (December 1936):562–566; Frank G. Speck, "Aboriginal Conservators," *Audubon Magazine* (July 1938):258–261.

11. William A. Ritchie, "The Indian and His Environment," *Conservationist* (December–January 1955/56):27; Robert F. Heizer, "Primitive Man as an Ecologic Factor," *Kroeber Anthropological Society Papers*, no. 13 (Fall 1955):1–31.

12. Bernard J. James, "Social-Psychological Dimensions of Ojibwa Acculturation," *American Anthropologist* 63 (August 1961):732–733.

13. John Greenway, "Will the Indians Get Whitey?" *National Review* (March 11, 1969):223–228, 245.

14. W. H. Hutchinson, "The Remaking of the Amerind: A Dissenting Voice Raised Against the Resurrection of the Myth of the Noble Savage," *Westways* (October 1972):18, 20.

15. Clifford C. Presnall, "Wildlife Conservation as Affected by American Indian and Caucasian Concepts," *Journal of Mammalogy* 24 (November 1943):462, 459.

16. John Dunn, *The Oregon Territory, and the British North American Fur Trade; with an Account of the Habits and Customs of the Principal Native Tribes on the Northern Continent* (Philadelphia: G. B. Zieber and Company, 1845), p. 65.

17. Lewis O. Saum, *The Fur Trader and the Indian* (Seattle: University of Washington Press, 1965), p. 166.

18. Dunn, *Oregon Territory*, pp. 65–66.

19. Samuel Hearne, *A Journey from Prince of Wales's Fort in Hudson's Bay to the Northern Ocean, 1769, 1770, 1771, 1772* (1795), edited with an introduction by Richard Glover (Toronto: Macmillan Company of Canada, 1958), pp. 75–76, 25, 26, 42, 48–49, 87, 259.

20. Alanson Buck Skinner, "Notes on the Eastern Cree and Northern Saulteaux," *Anthropological Papers of the American Museum of Natural History* 9, part 1 (New York, 1911):134–135.

21. Udall, *Quiet Crisis*, p. 231.

22. Paul S. Martin, "Prehistoric Overkill," in *Pleistocene Extinctions: The Search for a Cause*, edited by Paul S. Martin and H. E. Wright, Jr., pp. 75–120, Proceedings of the Seventh Congress of the International Association for Quaternary Research, vol. 6 (New Haven: Yale University Press, 1967), p. 111.

23. Ibid., p. 115.

24. Grover S. Krantz, "Human Activities and Megafaunal Extinctions," *American Scientist* 58 (March-April 1970):165.

25. Ibid.

26. See James J. Hester, "The Agency of Man in Animal Extinctions," in *Pleistocene Extinctions*, ed. Martin and Wright, Jr., pp. 169–192.

27. John E. Guilday, "Differential Extinction During Late-Pleisocene and Recent Times," in *Pleistocene Extinctions*, ed. Martin and Wright, Jr., pp. 121–140.

28. Krantz, "Human Activities."

29. Elspeth M. Veale, *The English Fur Trade in the Later Middle Ages* (Oxford: Clarendon Press, 1966); Paul Chrisler Phillips, *The Fur Trade*, 2 vols. (Norman: University of Oklahoma Press, 1961), 1:3–14.

30. Phillips, *Fur Trade*; Harold A. Innis, *The Fur Trade in Canada: An Introduction to Canadian Economic History*, rev. ed. (Toronto: University of Toronto Press, 1970); Sydney Greenbie, *Frontiers and the Fur Trade* (New York: John Day Company, 1929); John Witthoft, "Archaeology as a Key to the Colonial Fur Trade," *Minnesota History* 40 (Winter 1966):203–209; David J. Weber, *The Taos Trappers: The Fur Trade in the Far Southwest, 1540–1846* (Norman: University of Oklahoma Press, 1971); E. E. Rich, *The Fur Trade and the Northwest to 1857* (Toronto: McClelland and Stewart, 1968); Arthur J. Ray, *Indians in the Fur Trade: Their Role as Trappers, Hunters, and Middlemen in the Lands Southwest of Hudson Bay, 1660–1870* (Toronto: University of Toronto Press, 1974).

31. Charles S. Elton, *Voles, Mice and Lemmings: Problems in Population Dynamics* (Oxford: Clarendon Press, 1942).

32. Ernest Thompson Seton, *Lives of Game Animals*, 4 vols. (1928; reprint ed., Boston: Charles T. Branford Company, 1953), 4:447.

33. Lewis Henry Morgan, *The American Beaver and His Works* (1868; reprint ed., New York: Burt Franklin, 1970); Horace T. Martin, *Castorologia, or the History and Traditions of the Canadian Beaver* (Montreal: William Drysdale and Company, 1892); A. Radclyffe Dugmore, *The Romance of the Beaver: Being the History of the Beaver in the Western Hemisphere* (London: William Heinemann, 1913); Vernon Bailey, "Beaver Habits, Beaver Control, and Possibilities in Beaver Farming," United States Department of Agriculture, *Department Bulletin 1078* (Washington, D.C., 1922).

34. Seton, *Lives of Game Animals*, 4:448–449.

35. Ibid., p. 450.

36. S. Newhouse et al., *The Trapper's Guide*, 9th ed., rev. (New York: Forest and Stream Publishing Company, 1894), p. 132.

37. Eleanor Leacock, "The Montagnais 'Hunting Territory' and the Fur Trade," *American Anthropological Association Memoir No. 78*, vol. 56, no. 5, part 2 (October 1954).

38. Calvin Martin, "The Four Lives of a Micmac Copper Pot," *Ethnohistory* 22 (Spring 1975):111–133; Ray, *Indians in Fur Trade*, pp. 195–216; Charles A. Bishop, *The Northern Ojibwa and the Fur Trade: An Historical and Ecological Study* (Toronto: Holt, Rinehart and Winston of Canada, 1974), pp. 12–13, 206–220, 284, 287, 289–296.

39. Ray, *Indians in Fur Trade*, pp. 195–216.

40. Tom McHugh, *The Time of the Buffalo* (New York: Alfred A. Knopf, 1972), p. 17.

41. Ed Park, *The World of the Bison* (Philadelphia and New York: J. B. Lippincott Company, 1969), p. 52.

42. John C. Ewers, *The Horse in Blackfoot Indian Culture, with Comparative Material from Other Western Tribes*, Smithsonian Institution, Bureau of American Ethnology Bulletin 159 (Washington, D.C., 1955); W. W. Newcomb, Jr., "A Re-Examination of the Causes of Plains Warfare," *American Anthropologist* 52 (July-September 1950):317–330.

43. Frank Gilbert Roe, *The Indian and the Horse* (Norman: University of Oklahoma Press, 1955), pp. 192, 339–340, 357–358.

44. Ibid., pp. 192–195.

45. Waldo R. Wedel, "Environment and Native Subsistence Economies in the Central Great Plains," *Smithsonian Miscellaneous Collections* 101 (August 1941); Wedel, "Some Aspects of Human Ecology in the Central Plains," *American Anthropologist* 55 (October 1953):499–514; Wedel, *Prehistoric Man on the Great Plains* (Norman: University of Oklahoma Press, 1961); Floyd Larson, "The Role of the Bison in Maintaining the Short Grass Plains," *Ecology* 21 (April 1940):113–121.

46. Larson, "Role of Bison"; Carl Ortwin Sauer, "Grassland Climax, Fire, and Man," *Journal of Range Management* 3 (1950):16–21; Omer C. Stewart, "Burning and Natural Vegetation in the United States," *Geographical Review* 41 (April 1951):317–320; Henry J. Oosting, *The Study of Plant Communities: An Introduction to Plant Ecology*, 2nd ed. (San Francisco: W. H. Freeman and Company, 1956), pp. 327–334; McHugh, *Time of Buffalo*, p. 223.

47. Omer C. Stewart, "Why the Great Plains Are Treeless," *Colorado Quarterly* 2 (Summer 1953):43.

48. Ibid., pp. 47–48.

49. Waldo R. Wedel, "The Central North American Grassland: Man-Made or Natural?" *Studies in Human Ecology*, Social Science Monographs No. 3, Pan American Union (Washington, D.C., 1957), pp. 39–69; Frederic E. Clements and Ralph W. Chaney, "Environment and Life in the Great Plains," *Carnegie Institution of Washington, Supplementary Publications*, no. 24 (Washington, D.C., 1936):33–34.

50. Charles F. Cooper, "The Ecology of Fire," *Scientific American* 204 (April 1961):150–156, 158, 160; Verna R. Johnston, "The Ecology of Fire," *Audubon* (September 1970):76 ff.; George F. Carter, "Ecology—Geography—Ethnobotany," *Scientific Monthly* 70 (February 1950): 73–80; Hu Maxwell, "The Use and Abuse of Forests by the Virginia Indians," *William and Mary Quarterly*, series 1, 19 (October 1910): 73–103; Gordon M. Day, "The Indian as an Ecological Factor in the Northeastern Forest," *Ecology* 34 (April 1953):329–346; Calvin Martin, "Fire and Forest Structure in the Aboriginal Eastern Forest," *Indian Historian* 6 (Fall 1973):38–42, 54; Henry T. Lewis, *Patterns of Indian Burning in California: Ecology and Ethnohistory*, Ballena Press Anthropological Papers No. 1 (1973).

51. William Christie MacLeod, "Fuel and Early Civilization," *American Anthropologist*, n.s. 27 (April-June 1925):344–346; Robert F. Heizer, "Domestic Fuel in Primitive Society," *Journal of the Royal Anthropological Institute* 93, part 2 (1963):186–194.

52. Melvin R. Gilmore, "Dispersal by Indians a Factor in the Extension of Discontinuous Distribution of Certain Species of Native Plants," *Papers of the Michigan Academy of Science, Arts and Letters* 13, 1930 meeting (1931):89–94; Carter, "Ecology—Geography—Ethnobotany."

53. Tracy I. Storer, "Factors Influencing Wild Life in California: Past and Present," *Ecology* 13 (October 1932):315–327; George W. Hendry and Margaret P. Kelly, "The Plant Content of Adobe Bricks: With a Note on Adobe Brick Making," *California Historical Society* (San Francisco, 1925); Hendry, "The Adobe Brick as a Historical Source: Reporting Further Studies in Adobe Brick Analysis," *Agricultural History* 5 (July 1931):110–127; Lowell, John Bean and Harry W. Lawton, "Some

Explanations for the Rise of Cultural Complexity in Native California with Comments on Proto-Agriculture and Agriculture," pp. v–xlvii in Lewis, *Patterns of Indian Burning in California,* Ballena Press Anthropological Papers No. 1 (1973).

54. Cora Du Bois, *Wintu Ethnography,* University of California Publications in American Archaeology and Ethnology, vol. 36, no. 1 (Berkeley: University of California Press, 1935), pp. 75–76.

55. Maxwell, "Use and Abuse of Forests," p. 86.

56. Frank G. Speck, *Naskapi: The Savage Hunters of the Labrador Peninsula* (Norman: University of Oklahoma Press, 1935), p. 77.

Index

Alcohol: baneful effects on Indian of, 54, 56, 63n*q*, 63–64, 64n*r*, 162; hunt dream induced by, 121; Naskapi use of, 119; spiritual ecstasy and, 153–154

Animal domestication, relative absence in New World, 49

Animal-Indian relationship: communication in, 118–119; conservation as aspect of, 176; "conspiracy of animals" in, 19, 106–109, 129, 148–149; dissolved, 184–185; mutuality of, 18, 114n, 115–117, 176, 186–187; soul-spirit link in, 119–120. *See also* Beaver; Cree; Diseases; Huron; Iroquois; Micmac; Ojibwa; Ritual (hunting)

Axes, 63, 108; steel, 42; stone, 30

Bear (black), 134, 175; ceremonialism concerning, 36–37, 63 n*p*, 80–82, 147; conspiracy of, 107–109; in fur trade, 102n; in myth, 70, 90n; in St. Lawrence-Ottawa River ecosystem, 4; Micmac hunting of, 30, 31; periodicity of, 133n*k*; spiritual powers of, 91, 117–118

Beaver, 6, 32, 33, 56, 69, 101; as domestic animal, 130; ceremonialism concerning, 35–36, 122, 123, 128, 183n; communication with Indian, 62; Cree beliefs concerning, 107, 128, 147; depletion of, 8, 10, 27, 28, 102–104, 105n, 166, 172–175 *passim*; disease in, 135–141 *passim*; ecological effects of, 173–175; human antagonism toward, 106–109, 108n, 146; hunting techniques for, 16–17, 30, 105; in fur trade, 61n*n*, 77, 102n, 105, 132, 151, 164; in myth, 70, 74; Ojibwa beliefs concerning, 74; population characteristics of, 27, 133n*k*, 137, 173; spiritual powers of, 117

Belief system (Indian), 5, 105–106, 126n; Chipewyan, 69–70, 71, 76; Christianity and, 20, 57–61, 64–65, 98, 144–145, 152–153, 156; despiritualization in, 144–149, 151, 154–156; European technology and, 59; fur trade and, 8, 10n, 62–63, 65; hunting and, 33–35, 115–116, 118–119, 122–123, 151; Menomini, 88; Micmac, 33–35; Montagnais-Naskapi, 113–114, 118–119; Ojibwa, 70–74, 93, 124; reaffirmation of, 147; reincarnation of game, 82, 83n; Subarctic Indian, 20–21; Wintu, 183. *See also* Animal-Indian relationship; Conservation of plant life; Conservation of wildlife; Cree; Diseases; Ritual (fishing); Ritual (hunting); Wildlife

Bichronic method, 44–45, 47

Bison. *See* Buffalo

Bow and arrow, 16, 30, 31, 63, 115

Buffalo (bison): disappearance of, 132–134; distribution of, 177; fur trade and, 102n, 173, 176–177; hunting techniques for, 167–172; slaughter of, 3, 165, 167, 177–179, 183–184

Caribou, 4, 5, 30, 32, 95, 104, 118; ceremonialism concerning, 118, 121, 122; disappearance of, 133, 134; epizootic among, 131, 141; hunting techniques for, 16; in fur trade, 173, 175; slaughter of, 83n, 103, 104, 105n, 164–165, 166

Cartier, Jacques: at Chaleur Bay (1534), 8; in Stadacona epidemic, 51

Castoreum, 16–17

Chequamegon, 82–98 *passim*

Chipewyan: geographic position of, 4, 22 (map); in fur trade, 103; slaughter of game, 165

Chisels, 16, 17, 108

Cholera, 99

Christianity. *See* Belief system; Cree; Diseases; Micmac; Missionaries; Ojibwa; Shaman

Ciwetincu (*Chuetenshu*), 123–124, 127, 128

Conservation of plant life, 186

Conservation of wildlife: among Cree, 83n, 126–128; among Micmac, 33, 39; among Ojibwa, 75; among Paleoindians, 183; among Wintu, 183; balance of Nature and, 73–74; effect of fur trade upon, 103, 164, 185; Indian belief in, 16, 83n, 116, 162, 186–187; Indian neglect of, 9, 70na; in hunting, 18, 122, 176; motives for Indian, 17, 18–20, 176. *See also* Animal-Indian relationship; Ecology Movement

Contact population, 43–45

Cree, 103, 123, 135; animal-Indian relationship of, 128; baptism and, 97; bilaterality among, 5; feasting ritual of, 81n; game farming among, 127–128, 176; geographic position of, 3–4, 22 (map); hostility toward wildlife, 106–109, 146; hunting ritual and, 114n, 116–118, 122–124; hunting techniques of, 126n, 125–126; hunting territory system of, 120; mythology of, 70, 71, 88–89; "pet" animals, 120; smallpox among, 100n. *See also* Conservation of plant life; Conservation of wildlife; Shaman

Deer (Virginia), 4, 5, 77, 173, 175

Demography. *See* Population

Diseases: antagonistic wildlife and, 54n, 82, 91–92, 129–130, 144, 146, 148; as sanction, 39, 73, 83, 129–130; Christianity and, 97, 99; climate and, 48–49;

demoralization of Indian by, 53, 152; diet and, 104; ectoparasitism, 137–138; endoparasitism, 137–138; enzootic, 137, 143; epizootic, 131, 136, 137–138, 143–144; Europeans as carriers of, 43, 51, 89, 91, 152; Indian immunity to, 49–50, 144; Indian-land relationship and, 64–65; in prehistoric aborigines, 48–49; Micmac legend concerning, 90; Ojibwa and, 84, 89–90, 92–93; periodicity of, 50; population and, 45–49 *passim*; theme of Jesuit authors, 97–98; treatment of by Indian, 50–51, 92–93, 146; wildlife, 130–144 *passim*; wildlife periodicity and, 134, 134n; zoonoses, 130, 131. *See also* Beaver; Caribou; Cholera; Dysentery; Manitou; Micmac; Midewiwin; Plague; Scarlet fever; Shaman; Smallpox; Tuberculosis; Tularemia; Typhus; Venereal diseases
Dog, 78, 129, 130; as food, 104; ceremonialism concerning, 79, 81; variola and, 133
Dysentery, 53, 54

Ecology (animal): beaver, 173–175; Mistassini knowledge of, 122
Ecology Movement: history of, 157–159; Indian as spiritual leader of, 19, 157, 160–161, 188; Indian "reverence for Nature" and, 166–167
Economic incentive, for Indian fur trade, 8, 9–10, 151–153
Ecosystem: Great Plains, 179, 180; Micmac, 4, 29–32, 35, 61–65; "old" fields in, 182; St. Lawrence-Ottawa River, 4

Ecosystem (change in), 40, 64–65, 154–155; climate as factor, 170–171; fires as factor, 181–182; humans as factor, 171–172, 181; transhumance cycle as factor, 182
Ecotones, 181
Ectoparasitism, 137–138
Endoparasitism, 137–138
Environmental Movement. *See* Ecology Movement
Enzootic, 137, 143
Epidemic. *See* Diseases
Epizootic, 131, 136, 137–138, 143–144
Ethnohistory, methodology of, 6–7

Family hunting territory system, 12, 78, 95n, 120, 175–176
Feast of the Dead (Ojibwa), 85, 86
Fires (cultural), 168–169, 179–180; ecological effects of, 179–182, 185–186; ecological effects of suppression, 181–182
Fish: as food, 4–6, 29–32, 56, 105n; ceremonialism concerning, 37, 118, 122
Fisher, 69, 96, 102n, 173, 175
"Formalist" school of economic anthropology, 11–13
Fox, 70, 91, 102n, 175
Fur trade, 63, 69, 102n; among Ojibwa, 100–105; baneful effects on Indian, 2, 148; *castor gras*, 151; ecological effects of, 173–175; horticultural tribes and, 8, 185; Indian motivation for, 8–10, 10n, 11–13, 148–149, 151–154, 156; Jesuits promote, 101; origins of, 41–42, 172–173. *See also* Animal-Indian relationship; Beaver; Belief system; Buffalo; Hudson's Bay Company; Northwest Company